Sex, Self-Esteem & Sheer Stupidity

Advance Praise

Sex, Self-Esteem & Sheer Stupidity

A brutally honest, witty, insightful, and brave investigation of life, identity, expectations, and redemption. All that and profound love for The Boss. This book is a winner!!
—**Corinne de Klerk,** Human Rights Lawyer, Amsterdam

Tonya Pomerantz is an inspirational, radiant woman who exudes positivity when faced with adversity. She has had her share of obstacles throughout her life, but with her indelible spirit, she has persevered through turbulent times and has transformed into a confident, strong, successful woman. Her wisdom, humour, and expertise are evident in her new book, *Sex, Self-Esteem & Sheer Stupidity*. Her personal stories made me laugh, cry, and feel hope and peace about my struggles. Tonya brilliantly depicts her triumphs, failures, heartbreaks, and vulnerabilities in a relatable manner. She also provides guidance and shares invaluable advice and tips to persevere when life seems unbearable. Many of us can relate to the roller coaster of growing up and making misguided choices due to youth, inexperience, and low self-esteem. *Sex, Self-Esteem & Sheer Stupidity* is a must-read for someone searching for answers and validating their life experiences.
—**Nadia Thornton,** Author of *Don't Look Back: A Coming of Age Story* and *Bundle of Joy*

For any single woman who doubted her self-worth and tried to love the skin she is in and accepted herself as a beautiful and sexual being, this book by Tonya Pomerantz is for you. Reading these pages will open the discussion about female sexuality with your girlfriends,

mom, daughter, and partner. No matter your age, you will relate to the deliciously and artfully detailed subjects in *Sex, Self-Esteem & Sheer Stupidity*.
—**Lynne Parent,** Gatineau

Having known Tonya Pomerantz for several years now through our love of a certain Mr. Springsteen (!), I can honestly say she is a rare commodity in that her words have the power to help you when you are at your most helpless. Having been privileged to read Tonya's words, I know that *Sex, Self-Esteem & Sheer Stupidity* is a must-read for anyone trying to traverse the tricky waters of life. This book is your navigation tool.
—**Dave Thomson,** Scotland
"Everything Bruce Springsteen" group

Any woman who's ever felt alone in the world or "getting it wrong" in relationships and life should read this book. Tonya's experiences, while unique to her, are familiar to us all. The publication of this book is an act of courage that will empower you to connect, accept, and come to love your own sex, self-esteem & sheer stupidity.
—**Breanna Pizzuto,** Registered Psychotherapist
(Qualifying), owner of Talk Tools Training

Sex, Self-Esteem & Sheer Stupidity is a fascinating introspection, and Tonya's experience will be a guide for others to view the concept of success from our inner universe rather than social and economic norms.
—**Ebru Albay,** Immigration Consultant, Ottawa

Tonya is the real deal, and she gets it. She's an amazing woman who connects with readers with her warm and authentic spirit. Tonya shares how her earlier life experiences created her compassion and empathy for career coaching young people with Puddle Jump Coaching. Filled with humour, anguish, aha moments, and advice, Tonya's caring personality creates a deep-dive book about how to find your place in the world and connect with yourself and your community. Genuine and honest, Tonya inspires and empowers me to see that I am, and you are, more than good enough.

—**Dylan Black,** Radio Host and MC

I still remember my very first phone call with Tonya. I was so brittle; I didn't know where I fit in or what I had to offer this world. From that first call, even from 1,093 km away, Tonya was warm, engaging, lovable, and hilarious. She taught me patience and how to love myself. *Sex, Self-Esteem & Sheer Stupidity* encompasses what Tonya is about: heart. It's engaging, lovable, and hilarious, just like she is. I'm thrilled that she finally shared her story with the world. I'm excited that women everywhere now have the same opportunity to know, laugh, and see themselves in her story. Tonya, you are amazing, and I am grateful to call you a dear friend.

—**Julie Leblanc,** Dog Mom, New Brunswick

Tonya's book feels like a warm hug from a best friend who truly hears and understands what it is like to be a woman trying to get through life. It is a companion for all women struggling with their sex, self-esteem, and sheer stupidity.

—**Divya Parekh,** Founder at The DP Coaching/
Consulting Group; Founder and CEO at Beyond
Confidence; Contributing writer at Entrepreneur

Tonya's exquisite and personable character translates beautifully from the real world to print! Her ability to feel depths of emotions with your story is possible as she has endured the same in her world. Hop on and take a journey with her through her self-discovery, learn from her mistakes, and revel in gratitude. We need more loving and empathetic individuals like Tonya in this world. Let there be light! That is what encompasses Tonya's inner glow! One of the most compassionate individuals I have ever come across. The world is a hard place, yet Tonya has remained soft, and through her example – we all strive to shine!
—**Anamika Nandy,** Inquisitive Explorer

"It's rare to come across a genuinely compassionate soul like Tonya. I am constantly in awe of her ability to encourage others to show up as their best and brightest selves. Tonya has written a must-read primer for anyone navigating the tumultuous path of womanhood. I wholeheartedly recommend you add this book to your reading list as it will fertilize your personal growth, courage, and self-compassion."
—**Tatanisha Riggan,** Founder of Usawa Mindfulness

What do the Karate Kid's Mr. Miyagi and Doc from *Back to the Future* and Tonya Pomerantz have in common? All embody a mentor or leader vibe. When I met Tonya Pomerantz, I was a lowly English major at Carleton University, just trying to push through and get a decent grade. Many questions were coming up about "what do you want to do with your life?" "you're an English major; do you want to be a teacher?" The answer to that second question was "hell no." When Tonya met me, she knew she once was where I was in life. She helped me understand myself and see that desk jobs are not for everyone, and it's okay that I'm one of those non-desk jobs people. At that moment, I thought I knew this whole being an adult thing and finding "a real job" ain't for me. However, that was not the truth at all. Eventually, I made this adult working world work for me; it just took a while. And A LOT of emotional breakdowns and setbacks. All those moments allowed me to grow or, as she says, "mature." (What am I, a fine wine?) She allowed me to explore different job vibes and see what worked for me. Tonya soon learned that I had a karate kid in me who had something to offer—a loud offer—to make this world kinder, all while staying true to myself. In that light, she became my Mr. Miyagi, helping hone that loud yet ever so fragile person inside. She was the first person to call me an empath and tell me that I am a "blue" (from this colour book she recommended, which is so helpful). Because I am me and me being me, all I wanted was to help others not go through what I've gone through and still go through.

—**Emilie,** former client, 2011

Sex, Self-Esteem & Sheer Stupidity

Surviving Your 20s and Beyond

Tonya Pomerantz

Spotlight PUBLISHING House

Goodyear, Arizona

First published in the USA in 2022 by Tonya Pomerantz

Note: The author is Canadian, so Canadian spelling is used in this book.

Paperback ISBN: 978-1-958405-37-6
eBook ISBN: 978-1-958405-38-3
Hardcover ISBN: 978-1-958405-39-0

Publisher: Spotlight Publishing House™ in Goodyear, AZ
https://SpotlightPublishingHouse.com
Editor: Lynn Thompson, Living on Purpose Communications
Book Cover: Loreto Cheyne, Lola Design
Interior Design: Marigold2k
Portrait Photographer: Anna Epp, Anna Epp Photography

Springsteen, Bruce. "Born to Run." *Born to Run.* Columbia Records, 1975. Record

Dedication

This book is for everyone who has ever felt alone,
misunderstood, and not good enough.

Contents

Foreword...xv

Preface...xix

Introduction..xxv

Chapter 1 – The University Years...1

Chapter 2 – The Employment Years......................................7

Chapter 3 – The Relationship Years 11

Chapter 4 – The Single Years..19

Chapter 5 – The Counselling Years 23

Chapter 6 – The Hurting Years 27

Chapter 7 – The FML Years...33

Chapter 8 – The Did He Call Years......................................39

Chapter 9 – The English Patient Years..................................43

Chapter 10 – The Two Steps Back Years 47

Chapter 11 – The Secret Garden Years 51

Chapter 12 – The Outside Looking In Years 57

Chapter 13 – The Working Years 61

Chapter 14 – The Chocolate-Strawberry Crepe Years...........65

Chapter 15 – The Bring Yourself Flowers Years 71

Chapter 16 – The Human Touch Years 75

Chapter 17 – The Need to Find a Reason to Believe Years....81

Chapter 18 – The Loser Years..85

Chapter 19 – The Listening Years...89

Chapter 20 – The Searching Years 93

Chapter 21 – The Not-So-Happy-Ending Years 99

Chapter 22 – The Office Years 105

Chapter 23 – The Analyzing Years...111

Chapter 24 – The Finding Myself Years......................................117

Chapter 25 – The Living Alone Years 121

Chapter 26 – The Gratitude Years 125

Chapter 27 – The Decision-Making Years 129

Chapter 28 – The Fairy Tale Years 131

Chapter 29 – The Restless Years 135

Chapter 30 – The Muddy Years...145

Chapter 31 – The Broken Years...149

Chapter 32 – The Moving Years..183

Chapter 33 – The Obsessing Years 187

Chapter 34 – The Puppy Years 195

Chapter 35 – The Troubled Years 201

Chapter 36 – The Reckoning Years 211

Chapter 37 – The Hold Me Tight Years 215

Chapter 38 – The Pandemic Years...239

Chapter 39 – The Sunshine Years..311

Appendix...317

Helpful Resources 319

The Puddle Jumping Philosophy...320

Acknowledgments 323

About the Author..327

Foreword

If sharing is caring, just a glance at the book's title will give the reader a glimpse into how much Tonya cares – and shares. She cares for the community, animals, the world, and our relationships with ourselves.

Although the word sex figures prominently in the bold title, the focus is self-esteem – or lack of it. Tonya's relationship with sex vividly illustrates her lack of inner security and expresses how she feels about herself and the men she met as a younger woman. Sharing her struggles, challenges, and lessons learned along her journey, Tonya will be the first to admit she is – and will always be – a work in progress.

I met Tonya during the sheer stupidity of her 20s. Whether it was just hanging out together with friends or madcap adventures, including last-minute trips to Montreal, we always had each other's back. Many hours were spent driving laps in the college parking lot while working through self-esteem challenges, analyzing the meaning of our latest sexcapades, and solving life's problems together.

Tonya has always been a people person, making her transition to coaching a natural progression. Whether coaching friends or clients or helping newcomers to Canada, Tonya develops a relationship with each person to ensure success. She will do the same with her readers.

A born communicator, Tonya employs the wisdom that age affords us to look back on her challenges navigating the mysteries of sex as a young person, dodging anxieties of life in the 20s and beyond – ultimately revealing the confidence that helped her become the woman she is today. Now a middle-aged woman, she vacillates between wanting to hug and throttle her younger self.

Tonya does not preach when providing insights or sharing experiences. Vulnerability is her superpower, and she shares the intimate details of her past, whether heartbreaking or heartwarming. She draws the reader in and lets them relate to their own experiences, assuring them they are not alone in their thoughts and worries.

As a writer, Tonya is conversational and open, welcoming the reader to sit down with her to enjoy an ice cream treat. She wants to talk about the stuff that matters, and nothing is off the table. Her writing is raw, honest, and authentic. A social justice warrior from an early age, Tonya touches on topics such as gun violence, domestic abuse, climate change, and mental health. You quickly learn she is someone who cares for the marginalized and those who feel they don't measure up – because she spent so much of her life feeling the same way.

This book appeals to all ages as it helps readers understand how past decisions creep in to create their futures. Since 2007, Tonya has built a career coaching young people as they entered the work world, often appearing on local interest TV programs, guesting on radio shows, and co-authoring the book *Unlock Your Future: The 7 Keys to Success.* Founding Puddle Jump Coaching allowed Tonya to help others deal with their anxiety and confusion as they journey through young adulthood. As a career coach, Tonya asks insightful questions and listens attentively to her clients' worries, challenges, and ultimate victories. While working through her self-development, she quickly identified her need to mentor newcomers to Canada, which resulted in her volunteering with the Career Mentorship program at OCISO. More than material goods or financial accomplishments, Tonya is motivated by making people feel welcome and comfortable.

Three mainstays of Tonya's life appear in the book alongside her stories; her love of dogs, her enjoyment of ice cream, and her love of the poetry and song-writing gifts of one denim-clad, bandana-toting, New Jersey-born musical genius. These parts of life continue to provide her with comfort and clarity through life's challenges – as a young woman and beyond.

Bringing her readers together by sharing her stories and experiences, Tonya hopes for this book to help even just one person navigate the challenges of sex, self-esteem, and sheer stupidity that life brings us all. Accompanying Tonya on her journey is like joining her at an ice cream shoppe, where, instead of a single scoop of vanilla, the reader will enjoy a delicious and decadent banana split – with the colourful sprinkles of age and a cherry on top.

—**Steph Coolen**, CPHR-Candidate, HR Manager

Preface

"You ARE good enough."

These are words that many people struggle with all their lives and we so desperately want to believe. Sadly, though, for many of us, we never do.

When we grow up, we often feel we do not measure up. We are too tall, too short, too ugly, too goofy, too smart, not smart enough – our ears are too big, we have braces, we wear a hijab, our hair is too straight, curly, red, blond, dark – we feel marginalized. Like we don't fit in, and we don't count. We are part of the queer community or we don't know where or how we fit in. We are Muslim, Jewish, or any other religion. We are children of new immigrants; our parents don't have much money, we live in a low-income neighbourhood, with parents getting divorced – we feel stupid, we are never enough. I wanted to write this book to tell you that you are not alone. You would be surprised at the number of people who go through their lives feeling this way.

Sometimes you may think everyone else is better than you. That everyone has it easier than you do. Let me tell you, that is just not the truth. To some extent, everyone has these feelings. You don't see the doubts, the questioning, or the fears. Other people are confused, lost, and scared but may not show it. Or you may not see it.

Everyone has their issues and concerns – every one of us. It does not matter how old or young someone is. When you live your whole life thinking you are NOT good enough, this impacts everything in your life.

You make decisions based on a lack of self-esteem; you look for love or attention or approval from other people (sleeping with them, staying in an unhealthy relationship with someone); you don't know yourself (or you don't like yourself). Self-esteem is the foundation of a healthy life.

Back in the '90s, I was a young woman trying to get through my 20s, I started writing.

I kept a journal. I needed to write about everything I was thinking about, obsessed with, that was hurting me. My lack of confidence. My low self-esteem. I continually wondered what it was all about – wanting someone to love, wanting someone to love me.

When I was younger, I always thought I would grow up to be a rich psychologist. I did not want to be rich for the money, but because I wanted to buy acres of land and create a no-kill animal shelter for unwanted dogs and cats (and other animals). I would call it Puppy Haven.

At 23, I had graduated from both university and college. I was lost.

After five years of post-secondary education, I was finally ready to enter the real world. However, my being ready had no bearing on the actual real world. I felt there was no place for me – at least not yet.

Although it was discouraging, I had to keep thinking about the positive. I had my health.

As the summer went by, I waited for a job, any job. I stopped looking for something in my field – communications. I was looking for anything – except serving. I am perhaps the most uncoordinated person in the world. I didn't think anyone would appreciate having their meals dumped on them.

I had read all those books about job hunting and scoured the classified ads in the newspaper every day. The ads were interesting. You can tell a lot about the jobs and the companies that post them. Over the weeks, I learned to read between the lines.

For instance, ads that say "no experience necessary" set off alarm bells. "No experience required." Great – glad I spent so long in school. I should have just saved my money and taken that job. I heard the alarm bell again when I read, "PR, Sales, and Marketing. No experience necessary. Training provided." To the uninitiated, this may sound wonderful. However, to the trained eye and a communications graduate, the translation is "telemarketing or door-to-door sales." Not my idea of public relations!

Some things never change. It took a LONG time for me to figure out that my original desire to be a rich psychologist was a huge clue. Unfortunately, I did not decipher this clue until I was well into my 30s. Consequently, it was a long time for me to drift through life with no sense of purpose or meaning.

My aspiration to help animals has never disappeared. I have always loved animals, and at one point in my life seriously considered starting a dog-walking service – Happy Paws Pet Services. Then I realized that although I loved dogs, I did not like walking in all kinds of weather or the enormous sense of responsibility should anything happen to my canine charges.

Sadly, I ignored significant clues that would have reduced my feelings of meaninglessness. For example, I never paid attention to the importance of relationships in my life and how relevant they would be in my career.

Now I can see that the singularly most significant and longstanding factor was Bruce Springsteen – his music combined with my unbelievable lack of self-esteem. Today, an invisible woman in menopause, I can't believe what I wrote so many years ago. I cringe at having wasted such energy and not cultivating a healthy sense of self.

My memories of feeling ugly, trying to get my parents to quit smoking, having crush after crush on different random boys, and kids bullying me – pepper my life, all the while listening to Springsteen music.

I wish I could look back at my younger years with fond memories. But I can't. When I think of my 20s, I think of sleeping with men to feel better about myself, constantly moving from one apartment to another, and trying desperately to find my way in the world and leaving job after job – never being satisfied or content or happy.

I did not realize what I was searching for until I was well into my 40s. I did not know the impact of health (physical, financial, mental), mindfulness, and gratitude in creating a purposeful life.

For years, education and employment stupefied me. I struggled with choosing a career predicated on my educational choices.

In writing this book for decades, I realized I had mapped everything out like a game of hopscotch; however, that is not how life goes. You can't just compartmentalize everything – this part is mental health, this is finances, and this is employment.

Nope. Life does not work that way.

I have been a prolific poster on Facebook for most of the years since I joined in 2007. I learned I need to share, and FB has given me the opportunity to share my gratitude and appreciation for everything I have in my life. At the end of the chapters in this book, and sometimes randomly, I include FB posts I shared with my FB friends and family to illustrate the path of life I have traveled.

The process of writing this book and my journey have taught me that even though society may think life is linear, it's not. It's messy and challenging, and for a long time, you may go from here to there and there to here and back to there again.

I have discovered that life is not linear – it is a tangled ball of yarn where we must learn to live. This story is about my messy ball of yarn – and how I got to be okay with the messiness.

Tonya Pomerantz

Ottawa, Ontario, Canada

Introduction

My father worked for the foreign service, and my parents started their overseas life in Switzerland; they moved to Belgium, where I was born, then Norway. When the family moved back to Ottawa, Canada, we lived in a non-descript little semi-detached house in the national capital region.

We stayed there until 1977, when we moved to Tanzania. Dar es Salaam was a difficult place to live – we were robbed several times. By the time we left two years later, my parents, two older sisters, and I were all sleeping in our parents' locked bedroom, Dad's machete by his bedside.

A few years later, when I was 15, we moved to Singapore, where we lived without my two older sisters. "The girls," as I called them (18 and 19), had jobs and school commitments. So, only my parents, our family dog, and I moved to Singapore. Leaving them behind destroyed me.

The 26-hour journey was excruciatingly horrible. I was irritable, sad, and terrified of what to expect. Our new home was a stunningly beautiful apartment unit in an equally gorgeous building. Even our new address was pretty – 06-02 Horizon View. I loved how we had a key card for the elevator that took us straight to our floor, to our unit. That was the coolest thing ever. The flat (as they were known, not apartments) was huge. It had four bedrooms, four bathrooms, and a tiny maid suite. There was a fabulous pool view, and by the pool there was a ping pong table, and a barbeque area. I was lucky – my bathroom had a giant cement countertop, a wall-to-wall mirror, and the largest shower I had ever seen.

My bedroom was bigger than my Canadian room, with lots of storage space and big empty walls that would soon become home to my teenage shrine to Bruce Springsteen.

My school friends gave me Springsteen books for my birthday and goodbye gifts. I was well known in our school for my love of him and his music. I still am (known and in love with him).

Walking home listening to my Sony Walkman, songs from his 1980 album *The River* filled my ears and kept me company. His music continues to keep me company throughout my entire life.

It gave me hope as a young woman struggling with self-esteem issues. As young as 16, Bruce's "Drive All Night" was my favourite song. I would listen to it and cry. He writes of driving all night to buy his girlfriend some shoes, taste her tender charms, and sleep in her arms again.

All I wanted was to have someone love me like that.

Bruce's music has always meant everything to me. I would lock myself in my room and listen to his music as loudly as possible. My most prized possessions were my old-school Springsteen tapes. I found refuge and salvation and acceptance and meaning in his lyrics. I never felt alone or stupid or not good enough when I was listening to him.

Music has that effect on us. It can take us back to a special moment or time in our lives and offer much-needed hope. Every generation has its musicians who stand the test of time. First, the Baby Boomers had crooners like Frank Sinatra, Dean Martin, and the whole Rat Pack. Then, along came Elvis, who inspired the trailblazers like The Beatles and the Rolling Stones, and of course, "The Boss," Bruce Springsteen.

Each generation has its musical heroes who make a difference. Think of Lady Gaga, who writes about being "Born This Way." Think of the people who heard her music and finally, maybe for the first time in their lives, felt that someone was listening to them.

I grew up never liking myself or feeling that I fit in. I certainly did not fit in with my family. No one seemed to understand me. I was very emotional – more emotional than anyone in my family.

After our African adventures, we moved back to the national capital region of Canada. Dad worked shift work, the girls and I were in school, and our mother was a stay-at home mom. We always had someone there in the morning to see us off to school, with the radio set to CKBY, and Mom and our dog Bwana (aka Duffy) in the kitchen. We knew when we came home, she would be there for us.

I had little appreciation for this blessing at that point in my life. I had no idea what it took to keep a home running, and I took it for granted that we had dinner and a clean house. I had no idea the number of organizational skills it takes to coordinate a family with three teenage girls. The coaching, cajoling, disciplining, chasing after, trying to keep safe, laughing, guiding, grounding, loving, threatening, soothing, calming, teasing, cooking, cleaning, moving furniture, shopping, driving, sacrificing, hoping, picking up, parent teacher interviews, report cards, moves across the world, listening, going to movies, walking the dog, going grocery shopping, setting tables, doing dishes, doing laundry – the list is endless.

Mom had a successful career as a mother.

Dad was loving and tried hard to understand me. Some of my best memories are watching him shave in the morning. I would be talking with him in the bathroom, and he would scrape some shaving cream off his face and put it on my nose. I would squeal with delight, and it created many wonderful memories that lasted my entire life.

By sharing the highlights of my journey through sex, self-esteem, surviving my 20s and beyond, and what has pulled me through to now, I offer you something to encourage, remind, and inspire you. So, let's start at the very beginning, when I learned the importance of dancing in the dark.

The first time I heard "Dancing in the Dark" from Springsteen's1984 *Born in the USA* album, I fell in love with both the song and the video. He got me. My life was all about crying over a broken heart. Finally, someone understood what I was going through. My mom could not – she was like my sisters, cute and always sought after. My dad tried to understand, but being a teenage girl is complicated – both for the adolescent girl and her dad.

When he wrote about your little world falling apart, I felt it. His lyrics really resonated with me. I did not know it at the time, but I was very anxious. I was constantly worrying about my little world falling apart. Life was not easy. Instead of feeling an ounce of positivity about myself, I languished in ugly. I felt ugly throughout my teen years. I tried to live according to the maxim "beauty is in the eye of the beholder, but character can be seen by all." I tried to assuage my ugliness by positioning myself as a nice girl. Of course, girls with a "nice personality" were most often described as dogs.

One day, during gym class at school in Singapore, a Swedish classmate called me a dog in front of everyone. That just cemented the fact – I was not the only one who thought I was a loser.

When I was 13 years old, I found photos of myself in my mom's closet in a box, waiting for her to put them into an album. I was horrified by those pictures. They were close-ups, and while they did not show anything even remotely inappropriate, in my teenage mind, I was disgusted. I was so ugly – I did not want pictures to exist that reminded me or anyone else of how ugly I was. I ripped them up.

My mother was extremely upset that I went into her closet and destroyed her property, but she never asked me what had motivated me to do that.

Now, as a 50-something-year-old woman, I, too, would be sad and upset if someone destroyed pictures of mine. But I also would have wanted to talk to the person and ask them why they did it. Of course, now being post-menopausal, I can see that my mom was probably perimenopausal and dealing with a young woman going through puberty. That could not have been an easy time for her. I got through my teen years thanks to my father, who injected a dose of logical thinking and rationality into the family.

When I was 15 years old, my father sat me down and had "the talk." Not the sex talk, but rather the drugs talk. I learned to be scared of drugs, and the people who did them. This little talk stayed with me for years. I would meet people and find out they did drugs. On some level, my opinion of them would change. In my estimation, they would suddenly become less intelligent.

This sense of self-righteousness and black-and-white thinking is a hallmark of lacking self-esteem. When you have a healthy sense of self, you can understand that life is a lot of greys – not black and white. When you are self-righteous, you believe you are better than others. And again, healthy self-worth means you can appreciate that everyone is equal, and you are no better or worse than anyone else.

It was not just drugs; everything worried me. I lived in a state of fear and always worried about loss. For example, even though I was 19 when I moved back to Canada, my anxiety about getting into a car accident or not finding a parking spot kept me from getting my driver's licence until I was 24.

As the youngest of three girls, I constantly compared myself to my older sisters. K, the eldest, was cute and smart. S, the middle child, was sociable, fun, and never without a boyfriend. In contrast, I always felt depressed and lacking. I was thin and flat-chested with glasses and braces combined with a poor complexion and low self-esteem. I thought boys would like me if I had a better body. I had wonderful friends throughout my teens and the beginning of my 20s but no boyfriend. Ever.

My sisters often had their boyfriends (and friends of their boyfriends) over. I remember watching them get ready for their respective proms. They were both beautiful young women. On the other hand, I was nothing but a gangly and geeky 15-year-old.

I was the opposite of my sisters in pretty much every way. Where K was buxom, I was flat-chested. Where S was a cheerleader, I was in the drama club.

As I got older, I developed the body I always thought I lacked. Suddenly, I had the long legs, the chest, and the small waist I believed were the answers to all my problems. Wrong. Now men *did* want to have sex with me. But they weren't attracted to me. They didn't know ME; they just saw the big chest, the tiny waist, and the crazy long legs. That was all they wanted. They didn't want to take me to a movie, meet their friends, or date me. No. I was good enough for sex, and that was it.

Somehow, that was okay with me. That was the measure of my self-worth.

Full disclosure: Some parts of this journey include sex talk. You may be uncomfortable and want to put down the book. I get it. I, too, was uneasy at the thought of people reading about what happened to me 30 years ago. Maybe that is why it has taken me all these decades to gather enough courage to publish this book. Either way, I am sharing my journey – the good parts and the parts that may surprise you – because this book is about life. And that's what life is; the fabulous and less-than-fabulous moments. For the record, there is much more emphasis on the excess of sheer stupidity and the shortage of self-esteem than on sex. ☺

The sex part was not the only reason I took 30 years to get this book into the world. Springsteen's music has been so integral in my life that I had to include his lyrics. At first, I believed that I could use the lyrics from his songs if they were fewer than nine words. But then, I learned this is not the case.

You need copyright permission to use any lyrics. So, I put my dream of writing this book on hold. Finally, in 2016, I decided to send some chapters to Springsteen's manager and ask if I could get permission. I did not hear anything back. At that point, I decided to just go for it and included them anyway.

That is, until now. I face that same obstacle again now that the manuscript will soon be published. Being resourceful and determined, however, I figured out a solution. You don't need permission to use a song title. So, now at the beginning of each chapter, I am using the song title where I originally included selected lyrics of significance to me. (A notable exception is Chapter 1, The University Years, where I quote lyrics from "Born to Run" in a university assignment. When you use lyrics in an educational capacity, that is called "fair use," granted without permission.)

His songs mean a lot to me (and other Springsteen fans), but you may not be familiar with them. I hope that when you finish the book (or even as you read it), you are able to listen to his music, read his lyrics, and understand why they became the soundtrack to so many people's lives.

*I am absolutely, completely, entirely,
deeply, magically, forever in love with
Bruce Springsteen and his songwriting genius.
Every day of my life is made that much better
by listening to his music.*

Chapter 1

The University Years

"Born to Run"

As I finished secondary school in Singapore, it was time to choose what university to attend. While many of my friends were debating between Harvard, Yale, or Princeton, I weighed the pros and cons of each Ottawa-based post-secondary institution. Well, not all of them. For some reason, college was never even on the radar. It was a choice between Ottawa U and Carleton University.

The choice was an easy one for me. The campus of Ottawa U in the downtown core of Ottawa has cold, soulless grey buildings that were not particularly welcoming and filled me with anxiety.

Carleton University was in the city's south end, which meant a much longer bus ride. However, the university's pros far outweighed the con of the commute. The verdant campus, filled with many trees and green lawns, was ideally situated between the canal and Hogs Back Falls. It was gorgeous. Hands down, it was a much better fit.

So, I quickly made that decision. Then, almost as quickly, I decided on my program. What was I going to take? I am not a math person; I still remember my grade nine math teacher telling me I would see the light and get it one day. Sadly, I am still in the dark. I still have challenges with lbs vs. kg and spend way too long in the produce department trying to figure out the math. So, what could I take at university? With Accounting, Engineering, and Medicine out of the running, that left me with my strengths – History or English. I knew I would not have too much to show with those subjects, so I moved on to the next possibility – Sociology. I had never studied it before, but the course description appealed to me. I applied, and thankfully, I was accepted. We lived in the suburbs, only 20 minutes away, but it felt like an entirely different country. Apparently, to the postal system, it was. Unfortunately, I found out too late that the week before school officially started, new students were invited to "frosh week" – events and ice-breaking opportunities to meet other students. That invitation never appeared in my mailbox.

I knew no one. I was new to the school, the city, and the country. I was alone. I had no idea what I would do with my Sociology degree. I continued feeling uncertain until I went to the careers department and took the Myers-Briggs Type Indicator test. Then, finally, I could see the light at the end of the university tunnel.

Sociology was my favourite course, thanks in most part to our prof. He was an eccentric instructor who would beseech his class to ask questions – no matter the question. At times, when no one was speaking, he would start to tell us why a dog's lips are black. He got us to laugh and broke the ice. So, thirty years down the road, that is what most sticks with me. Not critical thinking skills, not interpersonal relationships, but why a dog's lips are a particular colour (because of pigmentation; it protects them against sun damage).

For our first assignment, the prof tasked us to take a song and explore the beliefs and values in the lyrics. As a huge Springsteen fan, I knew my choice would be one of his songs. So, it was just a question: "Thunder Road" or "Born to Run"? Back at home, I mulled it over as I sat sideways in the brown chair in the basement. My long legs snaked up the fake wooden panels covering the wall as I weighed the pros and cons of each song. Of course, driving my mother crazy with my legs on the wall was just a bonus for me. 😊

"Born to Run" (B2R) won – it just spoke to me. I found it easy to explore Springsteen's lyrics.

"We gotta get out while we're young
'Cause tramps like us, baby, we were born to run."

"Born to Run" Bruce Springsteen *Born to Run*

His anthem paints a day-to-day portrait of the routine life of the blue-collar workers in a small New Jersey town. In B2R, Springsteen illustrates the dreams and torments of a frustrated generation, the struggle for survival, and the never-ending quest for much-deserved freedom.

The '70s was a decade of disco, pulsating beats, strobe lights, and glittery disco balls. Springsteen injected a hefty dose of raw honesty, integrity, and substance – telling their story through the eyes of a blue-collar worker. The song offers hope in the form of salvation with the wide-open road seen as a source of escape from the dreary existence so painfully led by the younger generation. The sub-culture has its own culture, different from the rest of the country.

Springsteen writes about sweating it out "in the streets of a runaway American dream" and a passionate desire to escape this "death trap" of an existence. The workers in this song are not successful, especially financially. Their world revolves around working under the tyranny of the boss all day and at night, trying (still unsuccessfully) to escape, in the spiritual sense.

In B2R, and many other Springsteen songs, cars play an integral role in the workers' lives. A car, particularly a Chevrolet, is an intrinsic element in the old-fashioned American dream. A car implies one's social position and, in this song, is seen as a source of salvation, hope, and escape. Cars are where all the action takes place and how the youths of this small town manage to leave behind their harsh everyday lives.

The society in this song belongs to the young. The older people have no choices left – they have their jobs, their mortgages, and their families. They can no longer take that "last chance power drive." The younger generation can see the world changing and want to make changes in their hometowns. However, their particular society restricts them, and they have no choice but to leave their town. If they stay, they know they will face the constant drudgery of everyday work, struggling to achieve something yet always wanting to escape.

This song expresses the desire to fulfill the ideals of the American dream while at the same time searching for happiness. To be happy in our society, one has to have a certain amount of personal wealth with which one can purchase the necessary products to live an easier and more comfortable lifestyle.

The young people in this song weren't born to make money, become rich, and fulfill the lofty (and, some would argue, highly unrealistic) ideals of the American dream. Instead, they were born to escape the daily grind and the small-town mentality. They were "born to run."

I felt that same way. I loved that song and proudly presented my hard work to the prof.

One day, several weeks later, I was sitting alone in the crowded theatre. The prof was on the stage, reading a document, walking back and forth. Suddenly, I heard my words coming from the stage. It was MY assignment! I immediately figured he must be reading mine to show everyone what NOT to do. I felt my cheeks turning red, and I slunk deeply into my seat. When he finally finished reading my assignment, he walked over to me. He told me I had a perfect assignment that could be publishable with some fluffing up. He added that when he showed it to a colleague who taught a fourth-year course, that prof said he, too, would have awarded me a perfect mark.

I have always joked that it all went downhill from there! How could I be expected to keep that record going?

At the time, I did not realize my love of Springsteen would be so long-lasting and would get me through the worst times of my life, including my introduction to the real world of work.

Whereas education provides us with academic knowledge and training, employment gives us our salary and identity and can also be our biggest challenge to navigate. Many times, finding a good job that is also a good fit can feel like an unattainable dream for people.

While it may seem impossible to find suitable employment, do what you are meant to do, and work with people you love, it *is* possible. The key to connecting with the right job is understanding what makes you tick and what you find valuable in this world. Once you have identified these essential aspects of yourself, you will have the tools to lay the foundation for a meaningful career.

I did – finally.

For years I have been so very grateful
for the incredible education I received at the
United World College of Southeast Asia (UWCSEA).
Not one day have I taken it for granted.
I am especially grateful that I did not have
to attend high school in Ontario.
What kind of message does the idea of "streaming"

send to our young people? This group is smart enough for university, and this other group is not good or smart enough; those students are only good enough for college. The system is very much broken. Kids should not have to feel they are not smart enough.

I did not do particularly well in university, did not enjoy most of the courses, and hated being one of 300 students. My college experience(s) were vastly different. College gave me the structure, the real-world experience, and the networking that I needed to be able to get a job. Mine was a longer journey than I ever expected, but I am also happier in my career than I ever knew I could be.

Chapter 2

The Employment Years

"Queen of the Supermarket"

My supermarket in question was the first in a series of low-paying jobs in low-brow stores. I was 19 when my retail career began. We had just returned to Ottawa, and, just like all other teenagers, I needed a job. I created what was probably a complete mess of a first resume and took it over to Smiths', a neighbourhood family-run produce store. They offered me a job, to my surprise (but not delight). I was trained on the cash and had to make sure the inventory was fresh. I absolutely hated that job and still sometimes feel sympathy pangs for staff when shopping in other produce stores.

One of the things I hated most about the job was the owner, Rick. One day he told me I should never become an alcoholic because I had an addictive personality. Although not one to argue an adult's opinion, I felt his comment was uncalled for and unappreciated. It was the first of many ridiculous and inappropriate employer behaviours that would follow me through the years.

Sadly, the next place I worked at was even worse. My dad had admonished me and told me to pound the pavement. Pound it I did, and to my father's satisfaction, I found a retail job in a women's clothing store. At the time, I thought I was doing the right thing. Even though my dad was happy and I was making some money, I hated this job as much as the last one.

I am not a shopper and have never been interested in brands and clothes. I asked myself what I was doing there. When I arrived at work, my manager told me to change into the clothes they were selling. Then, when my shift ended, I would change back into my clothes and put the store's clothes back on the hangers. I was disgusted and felt contempt towards the store manager.

My stay there was short – finally, I summoned the courage to confront the manager, tell her what I thought of her work ethic, and leave the store. I was also glad to leave behind the tension and anxiety I had been experiencing the whole time.

Thankfully, I found a job at a different, and slightly higher-bracket department store. My sisters worked there; at last, nepotism worked in my favour.

It was a part-time job during the university school year and full-time during the summer months. From 1990 to about 1994, I worked at the downtown store on Sparks Street. Much more upscale than the other locations, the Sparks Street store was an hour commute from our home – and there were no smartphones, iPods, or mp3 players. So, I was alone with my thoughts on the bus. But of course, not alone, as plenty of people jostled their bags and hit whatever available body part of mine that they could. I hated working at that store. Retail was one of the most boring and annoying jobs I have ever done. I totally hated every moment I worked there. My series of retail job experiences clearly showed me I am not cut out for a career in that industry.

I moved on to the sought-after position of an administrative assistant at a desk job in a car dealership. I could finally sit at a desk rather than stand at a cash register for an entire shift. I felt liberated.

Working at the dealership meant working with a group of bitter, sexist, and unhappy older men; and, of course, the young, smarmy-looking players who would check out female customers looking for a potential hook-up.

After university and in my single years, I would sit at my kitchen table and try to understand what I was doing in life. I was trying to figure out my purpose.

I did not understand the relationship between education, employment, and mental and financial health.

Years later, when I was working as an employment consultant, I shared my feelings of awe with my FB family.

I love my job.
I am blessed to meet the most amazing people –
people I am so proud of
and who continue to inspire me daily.

Chapter 3

The Relationship Years

"Give the Girl a Kiss"

I love it when someone gently holds my face in their hands and tenderly and softly brushes their lips against mine. To echo the lyrics of singer-songwriter Mary Chapin Carpenter, I just wanted "passionate kisses."

I was 19 when I finally kissed a guy. I wanted to kiss someone before that, a full-on French kiss like everyone else had experienced. I had always felt like such a loser, so when I finally did kiss someone (a lifeguard at my sister's pool), and I liked it, I invited him up to the apartment I was housesitting.

We kissed, and thankfully he was respectful and did not try to hurt me in any way. However, when I look back at the risky things I did – like inviting a stranger into an empty apartment – I am grateful no one ever assaulted me or worse.

I have always been an intuitive person, usually following my gut instinct. For example, a few days after inviting the lifeguard upstairs, when I heard a knock on the door, I asked who was there and heard a guy's voice telling me he wanted to use the phone. My gut told me not to open the door to him, and I answered through the closed door, telling him he would have to ask someone else.

Later that week, we heard about someone trying to assault a resident in the building; I was glad I listened to my gut and felt lucky I had not taken a risk.

It was a different story with men I liked (or might like me). I always wanted to feel loved and thought if a guy liked me, that would be good enough for me. If he wanted to be with me, it meant I was good enough. So, I took risks and often didn't listen to my inner voice; but when I did, it paid off. Speaking of listening to my gut, I met the most inappropriate and obnoxious twit of a man on a Friday night while my friends and I were having a great time at our neighbourhood bar. When I was standing by myself, this guy came over and started talking to me. Amongst all the crap he spewed, he *insulted me* – "You've got a hot body, bit of a gut, but a hot body," and sadly, I blamed the gut on the jeans I was wearing. "It's the jeans!!" Then, just when I thought it could not get any worse, we again encountered this jerkoff on our way home. It was classic. He had heard us describe him as a f***ing a**hole, and he still had the nerve (or stupidity) to follow us and beg me to take his number and call him. Right. Like I'm going to do that. You told me you're 33, very single, very horny, and I have a gut. Good luck, buddy.

I just wanted someone to kiss, hug, cuddle, and snuggle – but definitely not that guy.

While starting down the path of customer service jobs from hell, I was also creating my romantic life. I was meeting new people, including The Architect. We met on May 24, 1991 – right before my 21st birthday. Looking back on it, I shake my head at the many red flags I willfully ignored in my quest to be loved.

We met at a local pub, and, as with many young women lacking self-esteem, I teased and flirted, using all sorts of sexual innuendos and language. I realized later I thought I had nothing better to offer – that if I wanted to be liked (to feel like I was good enough), I believed I had to be sexual. (This pattern continued throughout my 20s. Sex was my go-to offer. If I wanted someone to come over or not to leave, I would suggest sex, even though the sting of being left in the middle of the night was always a terrible, empty feeling.)

At the end of the night, he walked me home to my friend's place where I was staying the night, and we made out as we walked. He was a hockey player, so in between kisses, I informed him that although I was okay with some play by the blue line, no one had scored any goals so far. I was impressed with my hockey metaphor. I invited him to come to my house the following night. He accepted.

The next night, The Architect came over to my landlady-less house. She was away, and I was alone in the empty house. In retrospect, it was also devoid of sound judgement and self-respect. I was listening to loud music while waiting for him to show up. When I opened the side door to throw out a bag of garbage, I spotted him crossing the street, walking back to his car.

"Hey!" I shouted to get his attention. He turned around and ran back to the house, and we went inside. Up to that point, I had kissed only one man before. This night was different; he stayed over. We messed around in the living room and then up in my bedroom. He had brought a condom, and we tried to have sex. My body would have none of it, though. NOTHING was getting in there. Ever resourceful, The Architect offered to go down on me. I had no idea what that even was, but hey, I thought, it must mean he likes me, right? He left early the following morning to go to a baseball game. We agreed we would meet up sometime soon. So later that week, in an era way before cell phones, texts, and the internet, we spoke on the telephone, and he asked me out for my birthday. He picked me up in his red, radio-less Nissan Sentra, and we had dinner at a local restaurant by the water. A lovely place – but we hardly talked.

We had absolutely nothing to say.

We went out several times and somehow started "seeing" each other. I was working at the downtown store at the time. We would get together after my shifts, and I usually ended up staying the night at his small condo. In his tiny one-bedroom apartment, The Architect slept in a twin bed. As a tall couple, sleeping together in a little twin bed was an uncomfortable challenge. So instead, we would often sleep in the living room, alternating between falling asleep on the floor or his mishmash couch-like piece of furniture.

One night in June, I left my virginity and self-respect on his living room floor.

It was so vital for me to be in a relationship with someone, I accepted this type of behaviour. Deep down, it hurt, but I settled because I felt no one else would ever love me.

When you settle for something or someone, you are not living your truthful, authentic life. Instead, you are living in a state of fraud.

When we find that we are not being truthful with ourselves, we are living in that same state. Regardless of our intentions, we may find ourselves living in fraud. When we are not honest about things (life, feelings, relationships, work), we create conflict. This conflict can be with others, but most often it is within us.

Once you accept responsibility for your actions and figure out a way to live with truth and honesty, you will reduce the conflict. The first step is acknowledging and accepting reality. Even though you may not like to experience negative feelings, it is essential to recognize certain truths when you want to move on and create action and momentum in your life.

Living in truth is living in the present moment. This revelation was huge for me and this concept constantly challenges me. But just because

I discovered this new awareness did not mean everything magically changed. It did not. It was and continues to be a work in progress.

**Think of your own life.
Are you living in a state of truth or a world of fraud?**

Even then, I knew I was settling but desperately feared being alone.

I was so insecure about my looks. I had no idea it would take a few more decades until I could feel remotely good about myself. I understand that not everyone feels this same sense of inadequacy. For women who believe they are just as good-looking as models, I say, good for them.

But it seemed that it was not only me who felt (or feels) this way. I watched a documentary about girls as young as 14 getting nose jobs and liposuction. I was flabbergasted. For years, I had agonized over my nose and blamed every not-so-successful romantic venture on it since it is neither tiny nor cute. A veritable force to be reckoned with – my nose is a part of me, and while I don't love it, I have come to accept it. More importantly, I knew I had to accept myself with all my flaws and more attractive attributes. The thing to do is accentuate the positive and eliminate the negative. I had learned this strategy – so it was a question of applying the knowledge and trying to forget about all the other women in the world.

**Try to be the best YOU can be and forget
about comparing yourself to everyone else.
It causes more grief and harm than you can imagine.**

I wished I had listened to my 26-year-old self instead of spending years lamenting my looks. I seemed to have had the vision but severely lacked the follow-through.

When I was in my 20s, there were times that I considered doing something drastic. The voice inside my head was on a loop – "if only your nose were smaller." My complexion had mostly cleared up, but nothing would change the size and shape of my nose – except surgery, which was not appealing to me.

I was constantly judging myself – and always felt lacking; all the time.

At some point or another, we are all in a state of judgment. We even judge ourselves for being too judgmental.

In fact, criticism and judgement are in the same family. Criticism measures something against a set of competencies or theories, like an assessment. Most people don't enjoy criticism, but some find they take everything personally. Often, these people have low self-esteem.

When you realize that criticism is the practice of judging, it can make you think about how much you judge yourself and how you communicate with yourself.

"Why did you say that to him?" "That was stupid of you." "She must think you are an idiot."

You can help by paying attention to the words you are using. Just recognizing and knowing the difference that positive language makes can help you move away from that negative state. You can also breathe – getting some oxygen to your brain can help to let go of the judgment.

After experiencing an unhappy relationship for four years, I thought I had it figured out.

It took me a long time, but I finally realized that instead of being in an unhappy relationship, I wanted the opportunity to meet more people and learn about living life on my own.

It takes a strong person to live life on her own, to go out and meet people and go through everything by herself. It is much easier to have someone there, to lean on someone. To make that someone the focus of your life. I used to believe when you are part of a relationship there would always be someone to kiss or hug.

Such youthful innocence and naiveté! In hindsight, I realized being in a relationship did not mean there would always be someone there. That person might be upset with me, not be in the mood, or living in another city because they could not find a job in the same town. It is selfish and naïve to think otherwise. Although you think people in relationships are happy, that is not necessarily the case. I was not happy with The Architect; I was never happy with him. I had a rough four years with him. Yes, there were some good times, but that handful of good times do not balance all the truly damaging experiences that were the basis of the relationship.

I decided to take a better approach to the whole thing, and I learned a lot about being part of a relationship:

- try to be nice all the time or at least as much as possible
- have a smile and be pleasant
- be independent; don't make anyone drive you anywhere
- if he is abusive in any way – leave
- if he does not keep his promises – to call when he says he will or do whatever – leave
- treat him with the same respect that I want him to treat me
- be thoughtful, and don't get angry with him for forgetting something
- communicate!!!!!!!!!!!!!!!!!!!
- date him – don't just start living with him

- learn to see if we get along together – if we have compatibility – if not, leave!!!

It would be a couple of more years before I would have another boyfriend. When I did, I tried to be a good girlfriend. But unfortunately, once again, we started living together early in the relationship. Finally, I decided not to live with another man until we had been together for at least two years.

Marriage is definitely not the romantic notion we see in movies and on TV. It is extremely hard work and very challenging. Love itself is not enough.

Chapter 4

The Single Years

"Tunnel of Love"

I spent my 20s searching – for a relationship, for a purpose, but mostly for myself. But during that time, I just didn't get it. I lived and reacted to each day as it came.

Of course, it did not help that my mother forced me to move out of their house. Well, forced was how I perceived it. In retrospect, I could see my mother had a legitimate complaint. She resented me using her house as a hotel. And if I had any self-esteem at that time, I would have listened to my mom's thoughts respectfully and used my critical thinking skills to assess the situation honestly.

Instead of simply responding to that situation, I reacted. Instead of thinking logically about my options, I acted impulsively. I was so desperate to be loved by The Architect that even though I had identified that we were not compatible early in the relationship, I didn't pay attention. Instead, I started bulldozing my way into his life. I had no other place to live; he HAD to ask me to live with him. At least that's how I presented it to him.

It all came down to the fact I didn't believe I was good enough on my own. When The Architect introduced me to his parents as his "friend," I should have walked away. When he refused to buy a double bed because he did not want his parents to know that he was in a relationship, I should have walked away.

Instead, I told him he should sell his one-bedroom condo and buy a house. I struck a deal with him. If I could get the condo sold, he would buy a house. He probably believed I couldn't do that. But I called his bluff and found a great real estate agent who sold the condo. He kept his end of the bargain and bought a house in the suburbs.

It was a lovely house but horrible for someone with no driver's license or car. The city bus system was (and is still) brutal, and The Architect resented me asking him for drives because it cost him money for gas. I quickly recognized he was exceptionally thrifty – cheap with his money and his affections. I should have walked away.

When I told him we were not compatible, and his response was "compatible, schmatible," I should have walked away. But I could not bear the thought of never being loved, and I did not trust or believe in myself. Our relationship was so bad that, because he rarely gave me gifts, one day, I bought a piece of lingerie and asked him to give it to me as a gift. I should have walked away.

But I didn't. Instead, I just stayed and became sadder each day. I should have walked away when he never kissed me while we were having sex. But I did not. I waited, thinking he would change, and even bulldozed my way into an engagement. I believed that getting married was the next natural step in the relationship, no matter how messed up it was for us.

When he refused to go to a jewellery store to look at engagement rings, I bought one myself. That's right; I paid for my own engagement ring. One night in September 1994, a friend and I were in our room teasing The Architect about having the ring and asking when he would give it to me. Without missing a beat, he got up, opened his sock drawer, and grabbed the ring box. He threw it at me and told me to shut up. I should have walked away.

But I didn't. I continued living with him and attending Sunday dinners with his family even though I hated going. I should have taken that as a red flag and walked away.

But I did not. I stayed. One of our last exchanges was about a table. While I was struggling to assemble it in the kitchen, The Architect was in the living room, laughing at me.

Finally, I just let it out. "What the hell is wrong with you? Can't you see that I need help? Instead of helping me, you're sitting there laughing at me. You are such an unbelievable asshole."

Shortly after that, I broke up with him. It was the 15th of March 1995. I had an appointment to get my hair cut and spent the whole time lamenting the death of our relationship. I arrived home only to be confronted by an angry Architect.

"You left your pack of gum lying around. The dog found it and made a mess. I left it for you to clean up."

That was the last straw. I initiated the break-up talk. But sadly, I did not even want to break up necessarily. I suggested I move out into an apartment and date him. Have him court me; pick me up, and go on actual dates. But that did not work for him. "No," he said. "You either stay here, or it's over."

After way too long, it was over. I walked away.

Finally, after four years, I was living my truth. No matter how painful or challenging I would find the future, at least I knew I was being honest with myself.

*The most splendid future will always depend
upon the necessity to release the past.*
~Unknown

Chapter 5

The Counselling Years

"Lion's Den"

I started counselling to help me get over my breakup with The Architect. The counsellor tasked me with writing a letter telling him my feelings and how our relationship had affected me (and warned me never to send it to him).

Look, you loser,

I hate you and the pain you caused me. I hate you for not loving me. I hate you for what you brought out in me. I have so much love in my heart. I always have. But you did not appreciate anything I gave you. You could only understand material things. But I could not offer you anything like that. I only had a lousy little retail job. You were the architect. You cheap bastard. You had no idea of what a great person I am. You simply did not care, and you let me go. You let me leave and get on with my life. And I am so happy I did because you stifled me beyond belief. And because of you, I thought all men were like you. But they are not.

Some are romantic and thoughtful and kind and sweet and passionate. But you are none of these things. You never made a fire in the fireplace. And what the hell was with not kissing me????? I told you the only thing

I wanted to do was sit on the sofa and make out with you. And you just laughed at me. You had no clue what you were doing to me. You still have no idea what you did. And men are not all like you. You are just a huge jerk who had no idea of how wonderful a person I am. I am so happy I left you and got on with my life. But I hate the fact you are still part of my mine. I want everything back from you. You are so cheap. With your money, with your emotions, with your affection. I don't think you have any of those things, except for money. I know you have money. You never resisted showing that to me. You always could point out that you have money, but when I wanted to do something, like drive to Montreal, you would always throw such big fits and make up all these ridiculous excuses not to go. Not in the winter; it's dangerous to drive. Well, then, we'll take the bus. No, if I am going to Montreal, I want to drive. We'll go in the spring. Yeah, right. Spring never arrived.

I hate the way you made me feel about myself. I hate the way you always turned on the blower thing in the front seat of the car even though and maybe just because you knew it irritated my contact lenses. I cannot even come up with words strong enough to tell you what I think of you. Because I think so little of you right now and always will that I am just trying to get all the hate out of my heart; I know there is space for someone else because I deserve to have someone wonderful in my life.

Strong words that, at the time, made me feel better. But somehow, the passage of time made the hurt go away. Many years later, I bumped into The Architect and his daughter at a cancer fundraising event. By that point, I felt no bitterness or hatred – not even pity. I felt nothing, and that felt good.

Looking at the letter now, I realized the writing was an outpouring of anger directed at me. I chose to stay with someone for four years because I was scared no one else would ever love me.

I did not value my feelings about the relationship. If I had, I would probably have listened to myself and the clues and left the relationship much earlier.

In retrospect, I can see there was nothing wrong with The Architect. He was a logical, kind man who loved dogs.

Unfortunately, he was just not the right man for me.

Think about your life for a moment.

- **What are you settling for because you are scared?**
- **Have you ever written a message, text, note, email, or even an old-fashioned snail mail letter – that you did not send?**
- **Was the letter addressed to someone else yet meant for you?**

**Give yourself space to consider your
options, feelings, and priorities.**

Over the years, I learned the value of being honest with myself, even when I was feeling bad. Like when I was taking my coaching training and felt that familiar feeling of not being good enough.

Wow.
Filled with self-doubt right now.
*Feeling like the world doesn't need another
coach. Feeling overwhelmed.*
Feeling stupid.
Feeling scared.
Feeling alone.

Chapter 6

The Hurting Years

"Living Proof"

It was just the beginning of the year, but I was already so hurt I wanted to swear off dating, thinking about, or dwelling on men. It was the 23rd of February. The month was almost over. And as always, every day was a learning experience. Even on those days when I didn't do anything of much significance, I learned something.

I had taken Friday off to spend some time away from work. A day off other than a Saturday or Sunday. I really needed it. I felt the change. I became more energized and felt ready to continue through the last stretch of winter.

A friend had bought me an excellent book about men, women, and love. It helped me a lot by reminding me I am normal. Before, it felt like I was always wrong and that I was in a losing game with men. And that I would never (ever) figure out the rules. But now, I had developed a game plan for myself that had nothing to do with men.

I decided I was not ready have a relationship with a man. I would not be man-oriented for an entire year. I had stopped thinking about and dwelling on men, including focusing on why I was not involved with someone and why I was alone. Because I enjoyed being alone, I felt it was much better than being with someone unsuitable for me.

On some level, I felt lucky because I was with myself, and I didn't need to share myself with anyone.

Nevertheless, I was constantly struggling between being ready for a relationship and being single – or rather, being happy as a single woman. I was only happy about being single when a man liked me because it meant I must be good enough.

Good enough.

Some people spend their whole lives never feeling good enough.

It's like wearing a very tight-fitting T-shirt (or tank top) underneath your clothes all of the time. On the back are the words, "I am not good enough."

You could have the most amazing life. Attend the best schools, graduate with fantastic grades, and have an incredible job. You could share your life with the most awesome partner. You could have fabulous children.

You may live in the most beautiful house and own a garage full of expensive cars and other toys.

You may have the most fashionable wardrobe, take super vacations, and enjoy eating at only the finest restaurants.

But guess what?

You could have all those things, but if you wear your "I'm not good enough" T-shirt, nothing (and I mean nothing) will make you truly happy.

You always feel that you are lacking or not good enough.

The cool thing is that you CAN figure out a way to remove that T-shirt and replace it with one with the words, "I AM good enough."

Granted, even when you have replaced the T-shirt, there still will be times in your life when you will automatically reach for the one that says you are not good enough. For example, when you are tired, stressed, or anxious – when you are not living in the moment.

The "not good enough" T-shirt is comfortable for you. It's like that oversized sweatshirt or robe that you wrap around yourself to create your comfort zone.

But life begins outside of your comfort zone.

So, I am asking you:
What are you wearing?
What do you choose to put on each day?
Who is dressing you?

No one else can make you wear that "I'm not good enough" T-shirt. That is all you. But sometimes, we can feel like someone is making us feel that way when they are in a bad mood or feeling insecure about themselves.

Years before Oprah popularized the phrase "an attitude of gratitude," I was practicing gratitude. I was always thankful for everything I had.

My eldest sister wrote me a letter when I was 11, noting that she always appreciated my ability to say "I love you" to people.

Keeping a gratitude journal is a key component of living a life of gratitude. Every Sunday, I write my gratitude lists, which include tiny things. Things like getting a pull-through parking space at the grocery store or getting a parking spot at work, going out for lunch with a friend, or being happy because I had my umbrella in the car when it started to rain. Gratitude is not necessarily about the big things in life – it's about appreciating what you have rather than focusing on what you are missing.

A few years ago, the book *The Secret* became very popular. The idea was that you focus on what you want to attract into your life, and by the power of attraction, you would manifest what you want.

This idea does NOT mean if you want a mega yacht, you need to think about it and say how much you want one. It does not work that way.

It means you must focus on what you have rather than dwelling on what you don't have. When you live in a state of abundance, you attract things into your life.

When you live in a state of lack, you may not realize you are choosing to focus on what you feel you are missing. Sadly, most people seem to think that they NEED stuff.

We don't need stuff. We need self. Self-esteem. Self-awareness. Self-efficacy. Self-regulation.

This concept of self-regulation is a great way to begin the conversation about mindfulness.

Mindfulness is essentially considered the ability to be fully present. It is living in the now, not dwelling on the past or worrying about the future, which produces anxiety.

But for so many of us including me, it is not a simple thing to do, and we can slide into worrying.

When you are in your 20s, if you are worried, you are likely concerned about the immediate future, such as the person you like not responding to your text or what you should do after you finish university or college. Sometimes it's about needing to save money so you can take a trip.

When I was in my 20s, I would worry about death. I would always worry about dying. I was so scared of dying in many ways (cancer, Parkinson's, Alzheimer's, AIDS, car accident, heart disease). Then I realized that I could only conceivably die one way. Believe it or not, that took a lot of weight off my mind.

When I realized death could only come because of only ONE reason, life became somewhat less frightening.

That did not change the fact that when I was living alone, I would always check behind the shower curtain when I got home, or that when I was dog-sitting in someone else's house, I would sleep with the lights on because I was terrified someone was going to break in and attack me.

It did not change the fact that I would always worry about driving with someone in my car just in case they were injured or worse, in an accident.

Or that when I wake up in the morning, I don't worry about my husband having had a heart attack, a stroke, or Alzheimer's like his father. Or having an aortic dissection like his mother.

I will always say, "I love you" when I say goodbye to my family (in person or over the phone). After leaving any family gathering, I will be the person waving until I can't see them anymore.

So many things that seem easy for others are not so simple for me.

I am grateful to my friend E in Virginia who introduced me to a meditation program with Deepak Chopra and Oprah. I found the exercises to be effective at calming and centering me. I even found myself designing my own meditation program.

Thankfully, I found Calm, a meditation app that offers me ten minutes of Daily Calm. For ten minutes, I sit with my eyes closed and my body still. My monkey mind, however, is less still. It swirls and thinks and obsesses quite a bit.

But then I remember to breathe.

Breathing is a foundational element in living a more mindful life. I practice various breathing techniques that bring me back to the present and help prevent my obsessive thoughts from taking over.

So, this morning there was an incident on our drive to the dog park.

A driver in a pickup truck came barreling out of a residential parking area and cut us off completely.

I felt my reptilian brain reacting to the situation, and I consciously told myself to breathe deeply. When I did, I was able to let those thoughts go.

Yay, mindfulness – it works.

Chapter 7

The FML Years

"Human Touch"

Growing up, I couldn't even handle looking at myself in the mirror. Finally, one day in my 20s, I discovered a way. I told myself my eyes were full of love. I needed to be convinced there was some goodness inside me.

I could never appreciate the reflection looking back at me. I thought of how wonderful it would be to look into the mirror and absolutely adore that person.

Even though we had broken up, I still spent a lot of time thinking about my relationship with The Architect, and what was going to happen in the future. I told my sister I had been thinking lately of getting a nose job. Would men find me attractive with a smaller, more delicate nose? I guess this thinking is the same for some small-breasted women. I consider these body modifications to be a way of fitting into social constructs more easily, to blend in. I don't want to blend.

I remembered making pancakes the first time after I broke up with The Architect. It turns out I was not as bad at cooking as I thought. Perhaps because whatever food I tried to cook for The Architect was never right, never good enough. "No, that is not the way to cut carrots." "No, that is not enough sugar in the spaghetti sauce." "No, you don't do it like that." Okay, then. I decided to stop. And I did.

I kept obsessing about being alone for the rest of my life and never meeting anyone – ever. I just didn't get it. I was not sure how things ever progressed to anything beyond a friendship. I wondered if I was even *friends* with a man.

I was too hostile to men. When we met, I didn't trust them – it was an instant mistrust. I tried to understand where all this hostility originated. My parents have a loving and long-standing relationship, but neither my sisters nor I had met anyone we would like to marry. Correction. We had all met guys we were going to marry, but then sanity settled in. Thank God. If The Architect and I had stayed together, we would have broken up at his suggestion. I knew he was not happy and who could blame him? I was a dependent, annoying, and petulant girlfriend. I clearly remember standing in the living room in the middle of the night (still in the condo), telling him how I just needed him to be tender. I just needed to be loved. And my needs never changed. He never loved me the way I needed, and I still stuck around. I know I would not have stayed with him if he had been abusive. I certainly would not have thought about marrying him. But I stayed because I did not see that I could be happy in my life. I could not have been more wrong.

Over the next two years, I grew a lot. I developed and learned more about myself and what makes me tick. I found I did love myself, warts, and all. And I still thought the right man (if there was such a thing for me) would be the luckiest man in the world. I have an enormous capacity to love. I was like a dog. I wanted to be loved and nothing else. I knew the man just had to realize that loving me includes doing and saying certain things. It means bringing me flowers because he knows I love them. It means taking good care of me when I am sick and always being considerate. Do what you say you are going to do. Keep your word. Don't lie, and don't ever cheat. If you ever feel you are not in love with me, break up with me. Have the balls to do something, and I will have the balls to do the same thing.

Even though I was unsure about everything else to do with relationships, I was sure I would know what to do if I was no longer in love with someone. But unfortunately, I was wrong about that, like so many other things I tried to believe back then.

I could not trust other people – or myself.

I would not allow myself to be involved with someone just because I believed it was better than being single. I learned that being in an unhappy relationship felt like one of the worst things in the world. I was trying to leave behind my hostility and bitterness towards men. I was trying to learn to trust them and be nicer to them. And I liked those I felt didn't threaten me. Maybe I just feared the unknown. I feared one of them hurting me again. But I knew I had to give them the benefit of the doubt. Just because I had been hurt a lot before does not mean it would happen again.

In hindsight, I recognize extremist thinking and the mistaken belief that I had figured things out. Perhaps instead of spending so much time dwelling on relationships, I could have developed some self-awareness and learned to recognize these patterns in my life.

I was lost and alone. I felt like I was the only single person in the world.

As a single person growing older, I felt my destiny was to be alone forever. Couples were omnipresent; everywhere I looked, their apparent happiness confronted me, and I felt even lonelier.

I knew I had a lot to offer that special someone. I wanted to be there for them, to provide them with that haven in a heartless world. Whenever I watched a hockey game on TV, I always wanted to be the one at home offering love and support for a losing team member. I wanted to be there, to help, listen, console, share and give. Sometimes I wanted someone in my life so badly my heart ached. I was so lonely.

From my perspective, it always looked like everyone in a couple was happy. I didn't see any conflicts or arguments often part of a relationship. I couldn't see any doubts, aggravation, or mistrust that may be present. I wasn't aware of any internal conflicts that might be tearing one of them apart. I only saw a façade of contentment.

However, one thing was definite: I was alone, and they were together. And as Bruce Springsteen wrote, *"when you're alone, you're alone."*

I felt that same sense of loneliness at university. I struggled throughout it and disliked the whole auditorium style of teaching. I felt nameless and insignificant. I hated writing research papers (and still do) and always wondered why my professors didn't just read the books themselves. Why bother to get my take on it?

But the thing is, I never really knew I was struggling. I didn't know myself enough to understand the feelings I was experiencing were so detrimental to my well-being.

I didn't know the importance of understanding myself. Even though I had bookshelves full of self-help advice, I didn't know how to get to know myself.

When getting to know yourself, it's important to figure out who you are. You can do this by understanding your values.

- **Think of the most important things in your life. What can't you live without? What are *you* all about? What is life all about for *you*?**

- List your top five values. I bet one of two things will happen. Either you won't have any ideas about what to write, or you won't be able to stop at just five.

Now, look at what you wrote.

- Are you living in alignment with your values? If you value a healthy diet but eat a lot of junk food and drink alcohol, are you living in alignment with your values? If you value helping people but spend your days doing nothing to help anyone, are you living by your values?
- Think about times in your life when you have been unhappy. Think about what was happening during those times.

Chances are you were not living by your values, which caused (and causes) your inner conflict.

People have often asked me how I can be so positive with my posts on Facebook. The answer is because I get it. I have identified my values and the need to live according to them. I know what success means to me, and because it means happiness and gratitude, I believe I am living a successful life. And this knowledge fills me with gratitude.

Chapter 8

The Did He Call Years

"All or Nothing at All"

When I met someone new, my friends would immediately ask, "Did he call?" It's strange how one day you don't even know someone exists, and when you meet this person, the biggest question in life becomes, "Is he going to call?"

Nowadays, of course, calling has evolved into texting, and if the guy DOES text, the next question has become, "Will he continue to text me back?"

So, as with the old-fashioned phone tag, the chase is still the same. The analysis has not changed. If he does not text you back immediately, why not? It must mean he doesn't like you. But is this true? Is it not possible that other things are happening in his life? We take things so personally, like everything is about us.

At the end of 1996, I met New Guy (also known as Dentist Boy or DB, as he was in dental school). As a lover of food and sweet things, it seemed fitting I met someone in the specialty dessert café, Oh So Good in the Byward Market. The desserts were delicious, and the servers were relatively friendly as we closed down the place.

I had decided I was NOT playing games anymore. I gave DB a day to call me. He did not, and I resigned myself that it was over. Or was it?

In the spirit of technology and romantic love, I received an email from a good friend at work telling me to call DB. Stop playing this game. Call him.

I took this advice and left a message. I wondered if he would call but figured he would not. While enjoying our desserts, he had mentioned going to a movie, but I knew people (especially men) could change their minds. I learned this from a man's previous lunch invitation that he hastily offered and quickly withdrew.

DB did call, and even then, I questioned his motive. Would he still be interested in going to a movie? He was, and we met up a little while later, enjoyed an evening of getting to know each other more, and then watched a tragically beautiful love story. He had enough sensitivity to appreciate the movie by describing it as touching. He also had enough of a sense of humour to crack a hilarious joke after the movie that broke the ice and shifted the mood away from tears and sadness.

Again, it was his idea to go out and talk afterwards. But I realized he could have suggested it because it was a safe option since he knew it was late and not feasible. I know; stop analyzing the situation.

But back to my original premise. I led a happy and contented life, working and hanging out with friends. Then, I suddenly met a man who was not a jerk – a significant accomplishment. And even better, I met Not a Jerk Guy in Not a Bar! Yay! Score one for me! Finally, I met someone outside of the unreal and discouraging world of bars.

Okay, so here we go again. The age-old "Is he going to call?" question.

But he did not call again. So, in my twisted mind, he was not interested in me. This conclusion was probably a typical *female* thought process because, on the flip side, men often attribute female disinterest as a problem with something else, not with them.

Later in life, I would watch the movie *He is Just Not That Into You* and cry as I realized how many times I had chosen to feel so badly about myself in my 20s. I took everything so personally and let so much hurt me.

I didn't want to wear blinders and get all obsessed over anyone again. I always said I wanted to be friends with someone before I entered a sexual relationship with him. And I also felt very strongly that I would like someone to get to know *me* before they got to know my body. I didn't like the idea of just sleeping with someone or getting close to them physically and again, not hearing from them.

Back to the DB issue. I wanted things to go slowly, but at the same time, I wanted to know if he was interested. I wanted to be friends first. I did get the feeling like he may be interested in being more than friends. He had a silly sense of humour and loved Star Trek. No one was willing to see the latest Star Trek movie with him, and I thought it would be fun to suggest I would see it with him, but that would mean seeing another movie with me. I liked him – as much as I knew of him. He seemed outgoing and fun and very smart. And most importantly, not a jerk. I did not know how I could discern that, but it seemed I could; I wanted to believe he was not a jerk.

Until he told me how much he liked golden showers. (Just in case you do not know, a golden shower is a sexual act involving someone urinating on their partner. Nowadays, this guy could have been into things like truffle butter or something equally unappealing to me).

And yet – I still wanted him to call. There was no middle ground with me – like the Springsteen song, I wanted it all or nothing at all. As I grew older, I learned life is not black and white (that belief was due to my lack of self-esteem). I needed to grow more comfortable living in the nuances, the grey part of life.

In my 20s, I learned physical intimacy does not mean someone liked me or even wanted to spend time with me. Like the Mauler. He was a friend of a friend, and it was a semi-blind date. Before the internet, people could not google their potential dates. They had to rely on the old-fashioned way of getting to know them. We met for dinner and drinks at a restaurant close to my apartment. I was never a big drinker, so it did not take long for me to get a little tipsy. He walked me back to my apartment and came in – for whatever reason. I trusted him as he was a friend of a friend. The trust disappeared when he reached for my shirt and started lifting it over my head.

Thankfully, when I told him to stop, he did, and left. But that was a real wake-up call for me. After that, I never invited anyone else up to my place again.

I look back at the conflicts I felt about men and sex and wish I had known the importance of living according to my values. I started living a more mindful life the moment I learned that.

A little note to 18-year-old Tonya: You will be so happy in your life. It will take A LOT of time, and you will go through A LOT of challenges and sadness, but you will be so happy. All the important things to you – health, love, family, friendships, a satisfying career where you are making a difference in people's lives, and living authentically will lead you into the life you always imagined. And after many struggles, you will learn the reason for your happiness – you are living a life in congruence with your values.

Chapter 9

The English Patient Years

"When You're Alone"

On my date with the New Guy, we watched the movie *The English Patient*. Based on the novel by Michael Ondaatje, the film won nine Academy Awards, including Best Picture in 1997. I was very moved by it when I first saw it in 1996.

Never once had I felt what I experienced when I watched that movie, a film so rich in passion and love.

I came out of the film wanting one thing – to share such a passion with a man. I thought I would never have the luck (or whatever it takes) to have this with anyone. "I can still taste you." "The heart is an organ of fire." These are two of my favourite lines from the film. I wanted someone to say those things to me. I wanted to find my Count. My ownership. My love.

It was so hard sometimes to think of living without ever experiencing that feeling.

It was really hard living with such loneliness.

I cried.

Not with sadness, but with an ache that I would never feel that passion. That burning desire for another person and the feeling that person wants me.

I wanted this experience so badly.

I had an abundance of love and lust in my heart. The whole point is to meet someone in life that you feel madly in lust for and like tremendously at the same time. I wanted that intensity. That desire. That passionate need. I trembled at the thought of sharing the look that K and the Count shared. It was possible to recreate it on the big screen, so why couldn't *I* have it? It was the one thing I wanted more than anything in life. Who needs a car or a big house? I longed for the day someone would bring me flowers simply because he was thinking of me and knew I loved flowers – and bring me ice cream, too. Someone who wants to please me, love me, and who values that I feel the same way for him. And who enjoys gifts and treats, and appreciates how I show affection to him.

I knew I was not beautiful on the outside. That my nose is big and that my hair is not the greatest. But I knew I was a worthy person. I had so much to give the right person. And I was sure such a man does exist who could receive and reciprocate. I debated the merits of the friendship-first argument versus the chemistry from the second two people meet. Sometimes I believed in a loving relationship based on the friendship between the two participants. But then, at other times, I longed for the instant attraction, that spark that ignites passion between two people.

I still wanted to have someone look at me for the first time and immediately want me. But usually, when that happened, the wanting disappeared after getting their fill of my body. And it was not like I had the most incredible body in the world. I was not in good shape at all. Not toned in the least – flabby arms and a bit of a gut (to quote the most recent remark in the procession of men I encountered in my 20s). I was so tired of men only wanting something sexual. I had been through this letdown. I didn't need to repeat the same mistakes.

Spoiler alert – I found the special guy in 1997 when I started working at the graphics company. I found the man who looked at me like he believed he was looking at the most beautiful woman in the world. I found a man who was romantic, thoughtful, kind, loving, sensitive, and everything I ever wanted in my life.

I found him, but my lack of self-esteem almost destroyed my marriage and continued to act as a catalyst for making poor decisions.

When fear of losing something (a partner, house, job) motivates you, it can be challenging to make well-informed decisions.

A quote (from the TV show, *The Office*) resonates with me:

> **Fear plays an interesting role in our lives.**
> **How dare we let it motivate us?**
> **How dare we let it into our decision-making,**
> **into our livelihoods, into our relationships?**
> **~ Robert California**

As I grew and developed, I started realizing I was not the only person with a relationship with fear.

Thank you so much, everyone. I so appreciate your encouraging words. It is amazing how much one can change and feel secure when living an authentic life. And even if there are moments in the day that I feel dumb or do something or say something

that I regret, it does not change me. There is a sense of security within myself. And the more I listen to Springsteen and Obama, the more I understand how prioritizing a personal sense of security within ourselves is integral when creating a secure, loving, and compassionate society. Then one is not motivated by fear and hate but inspired by love, respect, and gratitude. ♥

Chapter 10

The Two Steps Back Years

"One Step Up"

I have always liked the New Year and the chance for new beginnings. In 1996, I took the opportunity to look inward.

New Year's Eve was upon us once again. And once more, I debated the pros and cons of making traditional New Year's resolutions.

My list:

1. Do a breast self-exam each month
2. Develop a nicer and less harsh attitude towards men
3. Try to become less judgmental of others, especially before I get to know them
4. Be more adventurous, more flexible
5. Become more active – continue to walk back and forth from work
6. Try and eat healthier – make sure to eat vegetables at least twice a week
7. Figure out a solution for my job – what makes me most happy in the world

8.   And probably the foundation of everything else, develop a healthier attitude towards myself

It seemed like I was getting it – and then other times, I would struggle so much with the voices in my mind telling me how horrible and ugly I was. I didn't understand that number 9 was the most important factor – and it was the basis of creating all those other things.

I was demonstrating a sense of self-awareness but was not listening to the different clues around me, like paying attention to what makes me the happiest in the world.

The first step in your journey is to create a sense of awareness. You can:

- **Write in a journal. You do not have to keep a diary or write a novel. Simply keeping a list of what happened to you during the day will help.**

- **Think about the qualities and character traits that are important to you. Do you see them in yourself? Do you want to see them in yourself?**

Reflect on what kind of people you admire; this will help you figure out the qualities and traits you wish to emulate.

- **Start to notice patterns in your life. If you are not happy in the present moment, are you focusing on the past or what you want to happen in the future?**

Being able to step back and recognize a habit can be immensely helpful. When you can identify your patterns, you will be able to change your behaviour.

- **Write down your goals. And remember, they don't have to be business or work-related. You can have personal goals – lose weight, eat healthily, travel to Europe (or wherever), or do whatever you would like to accomplish.**

- **Use your values to create your goals. Decide what is important to you, and then focus on how you want to live your values.**

For instance, let's say you want to start living more healthily. You can create your self-development plan by writing down:

1) Lose five pounds by the end of three months. Make SMART (Specific, Measurable, Attainable, Relevant, in a Timeframe) goals.
2) You can ask yourself – is this goal specific? Yes, indeed. It is clear and concrete. It is not airy-fairy. You are committing to losing five pounds, and that is five pounds.

Is it measurable? Yes, you can measure this. You will be able to tell if you lose one, two, or more pounds. Is it attainable? Yes, five pounds in three months is entirely achievable. You can do it in a healthy way. Is it relevant? Yes, it is. If your goal is to live a healthier life, losing five pounds fits in perfectly with that overall goal.

And three months – that's in a timeline. But it is important *not* to keep pushing the deadline – to say that three months will start in a couple of months. No. You must begin when you commit, knowing it will be three months from that moment.

Your self-development plan will promote self-awareness and provide you with needed structure. You will be able to create the goal, objective, strategy, and tactics you will need to implement. As well, you will understand the need to reflect on the plan and how it is progressing.

The joy of creating goals is that you can modify them. For example, if you notice that you are not meeting your plan of writing a page every day, focus on why you started to keep a journal in the first place. Through your journal writing, notice patterns emerging in your life. Notice what you DO, and do NOT do.

I did not get to that point where I created a self-development plan. Even though I recognized something was not feeling right in my life, I did not know what to do or how to fix it.

Embarking on another year – some of my thoughts – I will create the life I want to live. I am going to be mindful and appreciate the moments. I will continue filling up with gratitude for everything I have. When things don't go as I thought they would, I will take a step back and regroup. I want to use my critical thinking skills and think before I respond instead of react. I am going to develop my goals, and I am going to support young people to become the people they want to be.

Chapter 11

The Secret Garden Years

"Secret Garden"

I was 26 and living in a one-bedroom apartment in the downtown core. My middle sister lived in the same building, so I felt a sense of security. Even so, I felt very alone and confused and sad.

I was not sure if I was ready for a sexual relationship. I wanted the cuddling and the intimacy but was not sure if I was ready for the whole physical thing. But, as I had promised myself time and time again, I would not jump into anything until I was ready for it.

I knew the only way I would be ready for something was by being honest with myself and remembering that yes, the best things in life are indeed worth waiting for. I would not have sex with anyone until I could trust him, including his post-sexual intentions. I did not want to be physical with someone only to have him say, "See you later," or even worse, to ghost me.

I thought about the other men I had been involved with and knew I was unprepared to deal with the after-effects of a sexual night (or day) or whatever. I had shared a level of intimacy with Kingston Mike for two reasons. First, I had physically wanted to have sex. At least I made myself believe that. And second, because I thought I trusted him. I assumed we would continue seeing each other in some fashion or another. Not necessarily the typical way, but in some long-distance kind of thing. No big deal, but certainly some commitment. And I am not saying I was interested in marriage. Nothing could have been further from the truth. Rather, I was concentrating on the idea of not being dumped after sharing a night with a man. I didn't think this was too much to ask.

I just wanted someone to kiss me, touch me and want me.

This desire is natural, and I should not have been ashamed of it. I didn't want a man to maul me. Once is enough for that treatment. I had no interest in being touched in inappropriate ways or places.

Even if things didn't pan out with Dentist Boy, I was not interested in doing anything with anyone if I didn't find them attractive. I thought this was a good decision, and if DB was not attracted to me, that was okay, too.

At this point, I was working at a printing company, and one of my clients sent me a stuffed teddy bear I called Poppy. I was delighted.

Poppy was great, but I really wanted to have a dog. I wanted to share my life with a dog. I had no desire to have a child. All through my life, everyone always told me that I would change my mind.

I believe parenthood, especially motherhood, is the most important job a person can have. And I was not prepared to meet this halfway. I had no interest in that. But the bottom line is that I could not even entertain the idea of a child or children since I did not even trust a man enough to date him or have sex with him. So, forget children for a very long time – if ever.

I was growing older. I would soon be 30 and on some level felt I was only getting better. And Poppy Bear was sitting on my lap, just enjoying hanging out with me as I created my list of reasons that I wanted a man to love me for:

- My enthusiasm
- My love of dogs (and animals)
- My ability to type fast
- My thoughtfulness
- My love of Bruce Springsteen
- My love of the CD series – *Sounds of the 70s*
- My rambling stories that sound good in my head but tend not to make sense when I say them out loud
- My healthy appetite
- The fact that I like to stay up late at night
- The fact that regardless of how late I stay up at night, I can always get up for work the next morning
- My sense of humour
- My kindness to other people
- My ability to do laundry so well
- The fact I do a good job cleaning my apartment
- I can cook (even though I don't enjoy it much)
- My liking to go out and have a good time
- My liking to stay home and just hang
- My not drinking that much
- I enjoy meeting people
- I like going to movies and then discussing them
- I enjoy doing some new things (gaining flexibility)
- My personality – interested in other people, my ability to get along with pretty much anyone and get to know people
- My apartment and my sofa

My sofa was important to me. When I was with The Architect, we looked for a sofa to replace his battered old makeshift bachelor mess. We were in the furniture store, and I fell in love with an overstuffed, sea foam green sofa with big cushions for the back. The brightly coloured cushions made me happy. He liked the style of the sofa but hated the colour of the cushions, so he refused to buy that one, instead choosing one with much more muted colours for the cushions.

(Years after we broke up, when I was moving into a one-bedroom apartment, the first thing I bought was that sea foam green couch with brightly coloured cushions.)

Once again, the clues were there, but once again, I was not listening. Many years later, I would see Oprah Winfrey live and recognize myself in her words.

Oprah spoke of how we hear a whisper but ignore it. Then, we hear a shout. But again, because we are so good at ignoring things, we ignore that, too. Finally, it is like an entire brick wall collapsed on us. This catastrophe does not have to happen – it happens when we ignore that initial whisper.

Think about your own life.

- **Do you hear the whisper?**
- **Are you ignoring the clues all around you?**

Sometimes the clues are about a job or career. Other times, they are about our relationships (with partners, parents, colleagues, and friends).

We can make positive changes in our lives when we pay attention to the clues that are all around (and inside) us – something I didn't do for a long time. But when I did, I shared my gratitude with my friends on FB.

I am so overwhelmed by the stories that people share with me. I am insanely grateful for having figured out what I am meant to do and be while on my journey through life. Listen to the clues. The answers are right there – you will see them when you pay attention. I am so happy I did – and continue to notice them.

Chapter 12

The Outside Looking In Years

"Outside Looking In"

I was single, and all my friends were in relationships. I was alone. Very alone. My friends all believed I hated men. Somehow, I didn't think I exactly hated them. It's a strong word. I would probably go with mistrust or even harbour-resentment-towards. Hate is much too strong. It requires way too much energy.

I kept vacillating between wanting to be part of a relationship and remaining single. I told myself I loved being single. But I also loved the idea of being in a happy and satisfying relationship. Sadly, I could use none of these adjectives to describe my previous situation with The Architect.

People always say, "It happens when you are not looking for it." Okay. But I didn't know exactly WHAT I was not looking for – I mean, I knew what I wanted in a man (and what I wanted a man to want me for) but I was so confused. It was all part of the journey I was on. I was trying to figure things out for myself, but it was scary.

It occurred to me I could have died, and my death would have no impact on anyone. I didn't have a partner. My parents were not in the country (they were somewhere down in the States), and my job had no real importance in the grand scheme of things. I mean, it certainly did have importance for me. And I guess, in a roundabout way, there was some impact since my colleagues and I (and the whole printing industry) provided people with the documentation necessary for upgrading or developing computer skills. And because of our work, these people could have better jobs or find well-paying employment, put food on the table and clothe their families and themselves. So, I suppose, when I did my job properly, I did have an impact on people.

What I did know for sure was how much I wanted a dog. I REALLY WANTED A DOG. I love them. I knew where I wanted to live, and I knew I wanted a dog. I wanted a dog in my life more than I wanted a man. Dogs are unconditionally loving, sweet, kind, just fantastic. I knew I would adopt a rescue dog who needed a good home. I wanted to live in a house with a dog and a washer and dryer to do laundry whenever I wanted. I hoped I was not dreaming too much.

Wanting a dog got me into a lot of trouble. Still dogless a few years later, I toyed with the idea of adopting a kitten from a neighbour down the hall. Or rather, I wanted to adopt three little kittens that the neighbour needed to rehome. As I was not working at the time, it was probably a good thing I came to my senses and realized I truly wanted a dog, and although I love cats, I knew I would be settling for them.

I could not say the same for my relationships, where I had always settled. I realized way too late in my life that by settling I was undervaluing my sense of self.

If you are considering getting a dog,
please adopt one from a rescue organization.
You will never find a better friend!

Chapter 13

The Working Years

"Factory"

After I graduated from the PR program at the local community college, I found a job at a technology firm. I was the marketing assistant and joined a team of fun, young co-workers. My boss was the notable exception. We never got along, and I always felt bullied by him. It was so horrible I had to go on stress leave. I chose to take that time to find another job and recuperate from the trauma of being bullied.

I had a great relationship with our print salesman, M. He suggested the printing company was looking for a customer service representative. I told him I didn't know anything about printing. "That's okay," he said. "You just need to be good with people."

In January 1996, I started working with M. At that point, I had moved to a bachelor apartment in downtown Ottawa. I didn't have a lot of stuff; a futon (my bed and sofa) and a little futon chair. A cute table and chairs were perfect in the surprisingly large kitchen, and my wafer-thin dresser fit nicely into the walk-in closet.

I loved that place. It was conveniently located. I could walk to work, and it was a quiet building. I even had a wide balcony, the same size as the other larger units.

To me, the best part of the apartment was that my oldest sister lived in the same building. I loved that.

But as much as I loved the apartment, I was not happy at work. I was almost 30 years old. I thought I deserved a higher wage than I was making currently. I had no idea what the other customer service people were making, but they were both parts of a double-income couple. If they were earning about $30,000 each, they were bringing in roughly $60,000 together. That is entirely reasonable. But on a single salary, I could not live on what I was making.

I knew I would never be able to buy a house, car, or anything with that salary. I had to make a change, but I was scared. I had received a raise in September, but I was still not earning nearly enough and could not continue like that much longer. Something had to give. So, I decided I needed to change things.

Something DID give. I moved to a one-bedroom unit in my other sister's building. I told myself I would save some money and get better value for the rent. That was the beginning of the running. I wanted to believe I was moving towards something better, but I was really running away from myself.

The running affected both my homes and my jobs. I left the printing company in 1997. Thankfully it was of my own volition; they did not fire me. My supervisor (also a friend) had given me the heads up – unless I changed my attitude, they would let me go. I did not have a positive attitude at all. I was sick of working hard just to make the sales reps more money and increase the company's revenue but not my own.

Even though I used my single status as justification for making more money (I needed a job that paid more), it was my inherent worth I needed to acknowledge.

At least I identified I wanted to find another (better-paying) job. But that was it; I never seemed to do anything with that knowledge. I knew I needed a new job, but I did not do anything for a long time.

What about you?

- Is there anything you would like to change about yourself?

- Is there anything that would make you feel lighter if you stopped doing it?

We need to own our goals. If you say you want to lose weight, but do nothing positive to change your weight, then maybe you are committed to something else. Essentially, you are committed to staying the same way. Like I was, even though I knew I needed to find something new.

It is important to create realistic timelines when you want to reach your goals. So, instead of saying, "I want to find a job in the next two weeks," you need to look at the timeframe realistically. Is it likely that you will find a job in such a short timeframe? Probably not. If you set that unrealistic goal, you may not reach it, and you will feel worse than ever.

Never underestimate the difficulty of changing your thoughts and feelings. You have been thinking and feeling this way for a long time, and it is not a simple (or fast) endeavour to change. Just because you want to change does not mean that it will be easy, so prepare yourself. As the saying goes about getting out of bed – "it's simple but not easy."

It takes some time to recognize the negative behaviours and thought processes and replace them with positive and healthy ones. Reward yourself when you make these shifts in perspective – even tiny ones.

What about distractions – aka real life? What happens when real life gets in the way? For example, when your child tells you right before bedtime that they have a bake sale in the morning? Or when you need to put in some overtime at work? Or maybe you need to take your car to the mechanic? Real-life details can impact your ability to make a change in your life.

Maintaining changes can be challenging, but you can create a sense of inner accountability. Understanding that it is going to be challenging is half the battle.

When I was younger, my goals in life were to get my driver's license and see Bruce Springsteen in concert. I drive every day, and every day I am thankful that I have had the honour of seeing Springsteen in concert not just once but multiple times. And at the end of each epic (in the truest meaning of the word) show, he would invariably (and very accurately) exclaim, "You've just seen the heart-stopping, pants-dropping, house-rocking, earth-shaking, booty-quaking, Viagra-taking, love-making Le-gen-dary E - Street - Band!" And I cannot wait for the next time!!!! Note – at the time of publishing, I have seen Springsteen in concert eight times (and always hoping and waiting for the next time).

Chapter 14

The Chocolate-Strawberry Crepe Years

"Sad Eyes"

Men always intimidated me. Guys could say mean things, like calling me a dog or, as one guy called me in high school, Beeker. Guys could hurt me, and that was scary. But it was a different story for the men who dated my friends. I knew them and I loved them very much, and I never felt threatened by them.

They didn't share a lot of physical similarities, but they were all clean-cut, and most were non-smokers. It made me think that women (or at least my friends and me) have less exacting standards than men. It doesn't matter to us if he is a requisite height, if his eyes are blue, not brown, or if he is putting on a few pounds. These things are just not significant. If you don't have a solid character, you don't have a leg to stand on.

No matter how attractive the outside, what counts is on the inside.

My male friend R and I were talking about relationships the other day. He asked me if women really valued the inside. I thought about it for a second and replied, "Women of substance do." I will be the first to admit some women are just as bad as the male jerks out there. Just because you have a vagina and estrogen doesn't make you a good person. Some people (both women and men) are so vapid and vacuous that it makes you wonder how they even function in society. They rely on their looks and don't bother developing a warm and positive personality.

My friends were all good and kind people with equally good and kind men. They gave me hope.

One similarity between these boyfriends was that they all had a group of good friends. They may not have been the life of the party, but they were all positive, energetic, and outgoing people. They had a solid network of friends that enriched their lives.

Their friends were more than people they saw at a hockey game once a week (like what The Architect did); they planned activities together and spent quality time with each other.

I noticed these relationships did not revolve around food, unlike female friendships. It feels like every relationship I have with women is based on food. When dessert is involved, that is about the closest friendship possible. Two women talking over dessert is the most intimate experience. You both know you should forgo dessert, or at least, settle for the fruit plate. Screw the fruit plate. Let me dig into a few chocolate-strawberry-and-banana crepes covered with mounds of whipped cream and drizzled with Nutella. That's a relationship! ☺

It seemed healthy relationships were the priority for a lot of these men. Each of them had a healthy and positive relationship with their mom. I knew how difficult that could be. I sometimes had a pretty volatile relationship with mine, but I always have had respect for her and love her dearly. These guys had a good feeling for their moms too. They appreciated their taking the time to raise them and give them everything they did. They were not afraid of hugging them or saying, "I love you."

I knew what it was like to live with someone who did not have that type of relationship with his mom. When The Architect and I broke up, I was the one who had to call his mom and tell her the relationship was over. When I told her that part of it was because he was so distant and unaffectionate, she told me that it was how he was raised. They did not give hugs in their household, and when their son turned 12, he just turned off. For a while, he stopped talking to his parents, especially her. She told me that when she would ask him how school was, he would just say, "Fine," and leave the room. It must have been a challenging relationship with a child like that.

I learned that when parents raise their son with love and affection in his childhood, as a man, he is more likely to show affection for people in his life – in this case, that could have been me.

I discovered an off-shoot of a healthy relationship with mom is a supportive relationship with your partner. The men involved with my friends were not whipped, but supportive. If a friend wanted to pursue acting as a full-time gig, her boyfriend fully backed that decision. And not just in words. He would do what he could to provide her with the necessities of life so she could continue with her passion. That's the kind of relationship I wanted.

One of my friends hated her job of six years with the kind of hate that made her so sick she could barely get out of bed in the morning and had a never-ending headache. It was the kind of hate so powerful that she willed herself to be hit by a bus or struck by lightning. She needed to quit. Her boyfriend stood behind her decision to leave first and then find another job. He would pay for everything until she got back on her feet. Again, more encouragement.

Being a good partner is showing up when needed. For example, when my friend's parents moved away, it emotionally destroyed her. At the same time, she was busy and exhausted, so her boyfriend volunteered to stay in the city to keep her company instead of going to the cottage as planned. "I am your partner. You need me, and I am here for you," he told her. That is what I wanted – someone by my side when I truly needed him.

These men were thoughtful. They did kind things for their partners. For example, when a friend's boyfriend visited her place for the first time and noticed her burnt-out light bulb in the hallway, the next night, when he came over for dinner, he brought a bottle of wine and a light bulb. He replaced her burnt-out bulb. That's sweet.

Flowers are also a good thing. I have always loved flowers. And even though no one had actually ever given me any, they show that a person is thinking about you. I like that. I spent four years with someone who never once said I was pretty or looked great (with prompting from me, he would grudgingly agree that I looked nice). He only said something once about me when we were talking on the phone early in our relationship. He told me that he liked my breasts. But he didn't call them breasts; he referred to them as guns and hooters. Hello. That should have given me a huge clue. It did not.

We did not have a healthy relationship. Even my mother later told me that she knew it was wrong when she saw us together the second time. It was powerful stuff to hear. My mother saw it clearly. I, too, knew it was not right between us. After that, I never wanted to spend another second with someone when it was not right.

Please take my word for it. If you know in the first month of getting to know someone that you are incompatible – leave. It's worth it and better than dragging yourself down.

A lot of women believe they are nothing without a man. They settle for someone who is "just okay" for them rather than being alone. They choose to stay with abusive partners because they think they cannot manage life alone. I passionately believe that girls should be taught early on in their lives that they are empowered beings in their own right and don't need to be with a man to be considered valued members of society.

In my 30s, I wanted to develop a program to be implemented in elementary and secondary schools around the country. I want to see young girls growing up confident and strong, with loads of self-esteem. I want them to see themselves being effective in their community. And I want them to be able to recognize abusive behaviour very early on in a relationship. Because at that point, girls and women can safely leave the situation before they invest more time or energy and without further abuse from their partners. I have no idea what it is like to be in an abusive relationship. Some people may question my ability to empathize. But I can – very much so. A man (or a woman) does not have to be physically abusive to hurt you. Emotional abuse can be just as painful and traumatic.

I always believed an empowerment program like this would be helpful in creating self-esteem in people. All children need skills and support to be able to develop self-confidence. They need to know they are loved even when they make mistakes. Dr. Sue Johnson writes about "secure attachment" in her books *Hold Me Tight* and *Love Sense*. Both books could revolutionize the world and change the reality of relationships with others, ourselves, and marriage.

Speak to people with love and compassion, and you have the ability to create change in them. ~ Matt Valentine

Chapter 15

The Bring Yourself Flowers Years

"Pretty Flamingo"

Twice in my life, I was called pretty. I know exactly the first time anyone ever used that word to describe me – a friend of a friend, and I remembered that feeling for a long time.

I sometimes wondered if I was too ugly ever to have a boyfriend. Partner. Lover. Companion. Someone to love me. I wondered if that was why I came home alone every night. That no one wanted to spend time with me, make love to me, or care about me.

Then I thought, no, I cannot be that ugly. I must have some attractive qualities. Maybe I had just not spotted them yet. I felt ugly. I felt hideous, like a monster. Like that was how other people thought of me. I knew people like and are attracted to those who are confident with high self-esteem. I always tried to have that confidence, and I did in some ways. For example, I knew I was a great worker and felt confident in my abilities at work. But then, I would step in front of the mirror and be reminded of my appearance. Ugly. And I thought others must have thought of me that way as well. It was that constant battle between those two forces within me. The goodness says, "Yes, I am a beautiful person, and people love me." And this second feeling says, "You are the ugliest person on this planet." That is pretty heavy stuff and I tried to keep that second force in check. I tried to quell those thoughts and ideas. But it wasn't easy. I wondered if I was the only person to think that way, or did others sometimes have those thoughts? I wanted to wake up in the morning – at least one time in my life – and feel gorgeous like Cindy Crawford or Elle MacPherson. But I knew the whole irony in this. Those women do not wake up gorgeous. I was sure I would be just as beautiful if I had the legions of staff working for me – doing my hair, wardrobe, and makeup and paying me to stay in shape. But my problem seemed to be with the other more average women I encountered in my life.

I compared myself to everyone, and I always came up short. My big nose, my oily skin – I joked that I had more oil in my body than most Middle Eastern nations. I hated that, and I hated my body, thinking I had the oddest-shaped body: long skinny legs and big boobs.

I was sure that if someone did not know me and heard me described, one would be shocked to see the real me. If I wanted to, I could have described myself as tall, with blonde hair, blue eyes, a great figure, and long legs. But for me, I had a huge nose. I would often wonder if I should do anything about that situation. Should I get a nose job? What would getting a nose job do for my life? What if I hated that nose more than I hated this one? What if something went wrong and I died? Could I imagine being so vain that I would die for a nicer nose?

I wondered if I acted like I was attractive for just one day, would things be different? Would men look at me differently? I was annoyed with the way that men seemed to leer at me. It felt like they were just interested in sex with me, and that was it. I would have loved for a man to want to woo me and to like me enough to do something nice for me. To be thoughtful. But I didn't think that was going to happen. They always say you should do these things for yourself, but how silly do you feel buying flowers and taking yourself out for dinner? But it would eliminate a couple of problems – who was paying for dinner and whether you would call yourself the next day. 😊

I did just that when I was living in my bachelor apartment. I bought a beautiful bouquet, set the table nicely, and cooked a delicious meal. It was lovely, and although I may not have remembered what I made, I remembered the experience for a very long time afterward. I also remembered feeling valued and worthy during that special dinner. **Treating yourself with the same love and appreciation that you would treat a partner is an absolute gift.**

When I was not working, I was hanging out and wondering what I wanted to do with my life. The biggest thing I had to worry about was always making sure I had enough money in the bank for the rent to clear. I knew that in the grand scheme of things, I was lucky. But I was missing something. I was hungry for something, though I didn't know what. A friend and I went out together, and we discussed this situation. I told her about my employer always bringing up the idea of me working for him in the UK or Australia. Of course, I would go there. How could I pass up an opportunity like that? But the whole issue was – did this opportunity exist? Or was he saying that to appease me and to make me stay with the company even though I was getting bored with it, and I would have liked some more challenges? It was time to look at other options, but what did I have to offer an employer? No one would pay me to be nice and enjoy their company. Well, at least not legally.

After much discussion, my middle sister and I decided to move in together. We had both been thinking about it for nearly a year. We knew we would sacrifice our privacy, but we felt it was better than to continue to live separately.

Many people don't think about the finality of their own death. Instead, they may go through their lives, rarely imagining that their life will end one day. I do not go through life this way. I realize my life is a fragile gift, and one day it will end. That is why I say, "I love you" so often and do my best not to take a moment for granted. 🩶

Chapter 16

The Human Touch Years

"Human Touch"

I spent my entire 20s just wanting to be loved. Springsteen's "Human Touch" was exactly what I was longing for. Once again, he got it; he got me. I felt so alone but tried desperately to be both single and happy. Finally, in 1997, I thought I had a handle on my feelings.

I had discovered many benefits of remaining single in a world that sometimes resembles one long high school dance, and I had to express my feelings.

Being single is not just a status. It is a way of life. If you cultivate this lifestyle over a long enough period, you may even prefer to cling to the single life when presented with an opportunity to become one of Them.

Because regardless of what self-help books and therapists might say, it is a case of us against them: Us – single, free, liberated, VS. Them – cloying, sharing a life, having to be considerate. I was the only person I had to consider in my life. Well, myself and the company I worked for as they paid my salary.

This lack of responsibility and commitment was so freeing. You are supposed to grow up at some point in life, but when there is only yourself to think about, why bother? It is up to you if you don't want to eat your veggies for an entire year. No one is sitting there prodding. No one cares. No one cared if I ate my veggies or not – except my parents. No matter how old I got or how far away I was, they would always suggest perhaps I could eat more. Or at least better. They attributed my vegetable-less lifestyle for any reason for melancholy or negativity in my life. (Note that my vegetable-less-ness was more often an economic necessity than a choice.)

It took many years, but I finally discovered the importance of eating well. When I was 30, I noticed my metabolism wasn't the same anymore. Gone were the days I could eat pie, cake, and ice cream for breakfast. Back in the day, I could (and did) eat whatever I liked and never worried about gaining a pound. Suddenly what felt like it was overnight, I was forced to change my eating habits.

I also discovered my veggie-less lifestyle was not the cause of the negative things in life. Rather something more insidious was at the root – my lack of self-esteem.

There were many great things about being (and) staying single. Remaining single for some people can be quite challenging as they go through life on their own, without a partner. For me, it became easier each day as I cherished my independence and freedom even more. I had plenty of friends involved with people, and it seemed they lost their sense of self and identity as they started to see themselves as an extension of their partner.

I found this behaviour extremely destructive and could not understand how it was possible. Or rather, I should say that I could not possibly understand the idea of losing my identity at this point in my life and development. I was a single woman in a world of couples.

I didn't deny that it could get lonely sometimes. When I started feeling sad about going through life solo, I just thought about the crappy things about being in a relationship and noticed what other people were going through with their "better halves."

I loved coming home to an empty apartment (even if I was anxious). No one was there to tell me to cook dinner, or to tell me I was sleeping too much, or I should get up and do this or that. If I wanted to do laundry at 1:00 am, I could. It was up to me. If I got the urge for a Ben and Jerry's Chocolate Chip Cookie Dough ice cream treat, there was no one else to get it for me. Finally, I was as self-sufficient as I had always wanted. My friends were the best things in my life, but I noticed they would tend to become cloistered in their relationships. When you are in a couple, you may lose your friends because you choose that one person over everyone else. But when you are single, that never happens.

Of course, dogs were another fantastic part of my life. Some people may feel the same way. Some people don't want to have dogs like I did not want to have children. Sometimes, I would feel less than a natural woman because I didn't have that biological clock ticking inside. Even if I did have one, I certainly couldn't hear it. Which was a good thing because that would have meant even more pressure to date and find the right man. It would have been unbearable.

I did not grow up around younger children. Our family was very insular, with just my parents and sisters, and we lived far away from our extended family and their children.

I loved being single, but I wondered if I was saying that to convince myself it was true. I wanted to meet a nice guy, not just some jerk in a bar.

I quickly discovered unless you were a supermodel, you likely can't randomly start chatting up that cute guy you see. I had read those articles in Cosmo. "How Not to Stay Single." "The Most Interesting

Places to Meet Men." Not a word of a lie, one of the recommendations was to go to sites of natural disasters. And it listed them! Fires, tornadoes, hurricanes, floods. Curiously, it did not go so far as to suggest what you should do once you arrive at your destroyed destination. Something tells me it was not to volunteer your time to help people in need, but rather to scope out the guy who just lost everything, "Hey, Cute Guy, who just lost your house and everything you have, wanna grab a coffee sometime?"

I thought maybe I could meet a nice guy at a party I went to, but I was not in a good mood. Everyone seemed to be smoking cigars, and although I knew it was anti-social, I went into a bedroom and hung out with their cat; I had to get away from everyone.

There I was, just sitting with the cat, and then a bunch of people joined me. We hung out in the bedroom for a little while and then ventured back into the living room. Thankfully, the cigar smoking appeared to have abated, and the living room was bearable again.

While in the bedroom, I learned one couple was in a huge fight and that another friend's boyfriend was angry and punched a hole in her closet door. All I could ask was, "Why?" Why would anyone stay in a situation where they were unhappy? Perhaps this question was unfair to ask. I mean, I had stayed in a relationship for four years, knowing I was not happy. I stayed with The Architect for various reasons; the biggest goal in my life was to make sure I never repeated those same mistakes again.

Once again, I loved living alone. I felt blessed and honoured to be able to live alone without relying on anyone – male or female. I loved the privacy. I loved being able to walk around naked. Or looking like crap on the weekend and just drifting from bed to sofa and back to bed again. I loved not putting up with anyone else's taste in music or cooking. I can't say it enough. I loved it. I believe that without the years with The Architect, I would not have been in the same spot. I was thankful for everything.

Even though this was true, I was constantly conflicted. I wanted to be happy in my single life. In theory, I could appreciate all the great things about being single, but I was lonely.

I thought of essential factors in a relationship:

1) A compatible sense of humour
2) A compatible lifestyle: I am not a good fit for someone who is that physically active
3) Enjoying spending time with each other: a partner who is a friend and we have fun together

It occurred to me that some partners really do enjoy spending time with each other. The Architect and I did not have that feeling. We never did anything together; as noted, we were not compatible. It took a great deal of strength to admit that to myself. I would have liked to believe because of the way we met (we just started talking to each other at a downtown pub) that we were meant to be together. I laboured under that misconception for our entire relationship.

I was determined to pay more attention to men's actions. For instance, if someone did not call me for a long time (if ever), that meant he was not interested. I was not willing to sit back and wait. I had waited and played those games before, and I was not going to do it again.

I often like to say that since I am the archetype of Gemini and a woman (a frighteningly indecisive combination), I cannot make up my mind.

The conflict was there all the time. Would he call me or not? I analyzed the hell out of everything. Looking back, I wonder why everything was so important.

When I reflected on my journey, I noticed my lack of confidence and self-esteem impacted me in the most peculiar ways. For instance, I ate an unhealthy diet. Although it was delicious and easy, dessert for breakfast did not give me the energy and the nutrition I needed to be healthy.

Believe it or not, keeping your room (or your space) tidy is also an effective way to honour yourself. Think about it for a minute. Where do you feel calmer – when you are in a messy place or in a clean home?

Many people spend their childhood in a constant state of war with their parents. "Clean up your room" is the parental battle cry, with big garbage bags and the threat of grounding the weapons of choice.

Then you grow up and move out on your own. Suddenly there is no one there to threaten, coax, or cajole you into cleaning up. It is your stuff and your place. When you get over this novelty, you start to understand there is no one to clean up after you or motivate you. It is all up to you.

When you take that step and clean up, you instantly feel better about your surroundings. Even if everything goes wrong, like during the opening song of _Friends_, it hasn't been your day, your month, or even your year, you will feel better in a clean environment.

Try it for yourself.

Clean your space, clear your mind.
~ Unknown

Chapter 17

The Need to Find a Reason to Believe Years

"Reason to Believe"

In my 20s, I was not only lonely and desperate for a reason to believe. I needed a sense of purpose and meaning. At that time, I had no idea what made me tick. I had no level of self-awareness. I felt conflicted and very lost.

When I was almost 27 years old, I still didn't know what I wanted to be when I grew up. I hadn't found out what makes me happy. At least what would make me happy and pay me.

I was thinking about moving to Europe to find work. But I wasn't sure. Sometimes I really liked living in Ottawa and felt extremely comfortable, so I would miss my friends and family if I left. Other times I thought I didn't have the roots or commitments that most people have, so why not? It was the perfect time to live abroad. I would get a lovely little flat somewhere in London and a dog. I would also use the time to travel to France, Belgium, and other places. Why not?? I could do it.

Wrong. I learned quickly I did not have dual citizenship, so I had to say goodbye to that dream.

It would be a long time before I was able to visit Europe again, but it was spectacular and completely worth the wait when I did.

Much less quickly, I learned another foundational element in a purposeful life is mindfulness.

Some people think that word is overused, while others believe mindfulness is the key to living a satisfying life – that and yoga. I always have to remind myself that mindfulness is living in the moment, not worrying about the future or dwelling in the past. While it's a simple idea, it is one of the most challenging things to do (or be).

I spend most of my time persuading myself to live in the moment. But it's tough. My automatic thought pattern is one of loss.

When you are a child, you only have a few things to worry about (or at least you should only have a few things to worry about). You go to school, you do your homework, and continue this routine for as many years as you can handle being in school. Some people love school and eventually get their Ph.D., while others want to leave school as soon as possible and get on with the real world.

At least, that is how it used to be.

Now, children are holding global marches and protesting the adults who can't look after their world and are running it to the ground. The children are fighting for their future and the future of this planet.

They are fighting for gun control because they don't want to lose any more lives due to the inaction and inability of political systems to do something. No wonder there is an epidemic of anxiety in Gen Y and

Gen Z. Who could be calm and live in the moment when they don't know if they even have that moment?

As I grew older, I discovered that "adulting," as they call it, is scary. That's when you have a mortgage or rent (and your parents aren't paying it), bills, a budget (if you were lucky to have any financial literacy education), kids to raise (if you have them), and parents getting older who eventually pass on.

I believe we do pass on to something, but we don't know what quite yet. I heard an empowering quote the other day:

> *"We are not human beings having a spiritual experience. We are spiritual beings having a human experience."*
> *~ Pierre Teilhard de Chardin*

We watch hormones attack our bodies – excess belly fat not there a few years ago; middle-age acne, thinner skin on our faces, breasts surrendering to gravity, varicose veins appearing out of nowhere one day. Bloating is more common, period completely out of whack, incessant hunger, more emotional than ever (is that even possible?), and hair starting to thin and fall out, and short-term memory fading as you worry about getting older and losing your health.

This time of life, this perimenopause (and later menopause), is simply ridiculous.

But (and it is a significant "but"), I am no longer the unconfident, insecure, and lost young woman I was for so very long.

There are some positive things about growing older. Looking after your financial health allows you to transition into retirement with ease and security. It gives you the freedom to take vacations, buy what you would like, and be able to look after your family.

Without a sense of financial security, you may worry about the basic needs and wants of life – food, lodging, and transportation. Economic insecurity will increase your stress level, potentially decrease your sense of happiness, and ultimately negatively affect your sense of self. Although I have struggled with living mindfully, I have always been my authentic self, which has never changed. That is why it always hurt so much when I had no one to love or love me in return. I realized much later that there was always one person I loved, who I knew loved me back. 😊

First of all, I am so grateful for my journey and for reaching this point. I struggled for so long to truly love myself (including all the ridiculousness and things I don't like about myself), but it is when you love yourself that you can you truly love others and be happy – or feel joy. I never understood that love yourself thing. It sounded weird and strange. But as I have gone through my life, I have come to understand that loving yourself comes from living your authentic life, and you have to KNOW who you are to BE who you are. And I am someone who tells a woman that I like her hijab, that someone does a great job in their role of CSR in charge of returns at Walmart, asks someone about their tattoo, and then engages them in a conversation about what it means to them. I am someone who will stop and ask about a dog, talks to dogs (and other animals), feels things so very deeply, cries when watching a sad (or sometimes happy) video, and loves connecting with people. I spent so much time of my life hating myself and thinking I was not good enough. I am so happy to be spending the rest of my life loving my life, who I am, and who I am yet to become.

Chapter 18

The Loser Years

"Hungry Heart"

After a couple of years of living in my noisy apartment, I was near the end of my printing company job. I still felt incredibly alone, sad, and lost. When Springsteen sang about how no one wants to be alone in "Hungry Heart," he was singing about me. I had almost given up. I had lost hope of ever being involved in a loving, caring relationship, and I had no idea what I wanted to do. I had no idea of what would make me happy.

I could not play a musical instrument – or sing. I am not athletic. I don't enjoy swishing down the slopes or blading in the park. I questioned the quality of my writing. I write for myself as catharsis rather than for anyone else.

Even just watching TV, I questioned everything. With the remote control in hand, I surfed through the channels. Then, it happened.

This immense feeling of inadequacy flooded through me. I measured everyone else's happiness and compared it to mine – that person must be happier. She is involved with someone; she is in a relationship. I wasn't. I was a loser. I looked at people with wedding rings, and it was like when I was trying to get my driver's license; I could not even watch car commercials on TV. It felt like everyone was in a massive conspiracy. I was a loser because I could not drive. There was no way I'd ever get to buy this car because I would never get my licence – because I was a loser. And now, that is how I felt when I saw a wedding ring on someone's finger. I was a loser because I was not in a relationship. I would always be a loser because no one would ever want me. I was pathetic and I would be alone for the rest of my life. I was such a LOSER!

That voice was pretty tough to ignore. I sighed and tried again to figure out what I was good at, and once again, I came up with nothing. I was not a good cook. I couldn't keep plants alive, let alone an actual living creature. Maybe I needed someone or something in my life. Another weekend faded to black. We were moving towards spring, to my sister's birthday and then to mine. Where would I be at that point? Would I be in the same job, doing the same thing, watching the same shows on TV, sleeping alone in the same bed? The answer to those questions was a resounding yes. In the spring, I *was* doing the same thing (customer service) but for a different company. I was living with my sister in our three-bedroom townhouse, but it was the same bed, and I was still alone.

I had heard about the idea of energy but never understood the concept of vibration and frequency. I thought it sounded a little weird, a little out there.

While getting your head around this concept can be challenging, there is value in it. Some values (pride, anger, desire, fear, grief, apathy, guilt, and shame) have a corresponding emotion and energy level much lower than healthy values and emotions. For instance, we value joy, bliss, abundance, and love at higher levels than the corresponding negative ones.

Ultimately that means the more positive you are, the more positive energy you are contributing to the universe – and the more positive energy comes back to you. Gratitude can make energy shift. Sometimes it is tough to summon positive energy when feeling broken or defeated. But that is the exact time that you need to! You need to dig deep inside yourself and find that strength and courage to get through the next few minutes. Then you can handle the next few minutes after that. And sometimes, that is all we can muster.

Seriously, in this world with so much hatred, we need to surround ourselves (both virtually and in person) with people (and furry companions) who fill us with love and positive energy.

Chapter 19

The Listening Years

"Leap of Faith"

In my 20s, I wasn't just mourning the dearth of romance in my life; I was also obsessed with trying to figure out my career. Then, finally, I knew I had to make my leap of faith.

I wished I had grown up wanting to be something. A lawyer, a doctor, or anything. Something that gives you motivation and identity. When you don't know what you want, it gets harder the older you get. I was almost 30 years old, and I still didn't know what I wanted to do. I had a B.A. in Sociology-Anthropology, a diploma in Public Relations, and a year of marketing experience with almost a year and a half of customer service experience. What next? I had no idea.

I went through times when I wanted to have a house, a dog, and yes, even a partner. But other days, I thought I just wanted to travel and experience life. I wanted to travel and see the world. I wanted to see that people the world over share things in common, regardless of their ethnic origins and mother tongues – to experience love and kindness and know everyone is here on earth for the same reason. I wanted to find out that reason. I wanted to discover what makes people tick – what made me tick. I had so much to learn about life, and I was ready to get out and do it. Not to climb mountains or ski hills or ride or glide or bungee jump; I just wanted to get out and do and see and live. I didn't know what was stopping me – or what I might have been running away from. I had a contented life in Ottawa, was happy in my apartment, and wonderful friends. But I wanted to be out there. I wanted to welcome people and have fun and make them feel comfortable. Finally, I knew what I wanted, but I still had no idea how to get there.

I had always thought life would be easy once I graduated from school. I bought into what our society tells us. At first, I thought graduating from secondary school would be excellent. My friends said that university would be fun and that "there would be men standing in line for me." That is a direct quote from a school friend of mine in Singapore. As it happens, neither part of that sentence came to fruition. University was okay, but not the best for me. I made some friends but not many. After university came college, where I made some close friends, had a good time, and graduated with honours. Then I moved on to a couple of jobs over the summer, followed by the tech firm.

Life began again for me when I started working at the printing company. I was comfortable there and felt at home. People liked me, and I thought they would miss me if I left. But I was trying to figure out what I wanted to do. I had public relations knowledge, but sadly, I had not practiced it for a little while. The most fun I had at the tech company was hosting the Users' Conference. I had a blast. Organizing it was fun, and I had a fantastic time hosting it. Meeting everyone and having people come to me when something was wrong or they needed something was great. I loved it. Sigh. I still felt lost.

It took a long time, but I eventually started listening to the clues around me. And once I did that, I never looked back. Like many young people before and after me, I believed a university education was the answer. And why wouldn't I? Growing up, I often heard the familiar mantra – "Get an education, girl."

Other young people hear their parents say that they should not get into trades. Instead, many parents suggest (and steer their children towards) getting a 9 to 5 job with a pension and benefits.

I left school and became mired in "customer service jobs from hell." I had no idea what I could do until I was 34, when I found my place in the world. The Career Assessment Questionnaire from Charity Village was one of the most life-changing tools for me.

https://charityvillage.com/career-assessment-questionnaire-2/

What about you?

- **Have you found your place in the world?**
- **Are you listening to the clues in your life?**

Many years later, I shared a big Aha moment on FB.

I was never meant to be an "anything." My purpose was to be other than a physician, a musician, a mathematician, or anything else. My purpose is to support others to reach those goals, to help them figure out how to contribute their skills and

strengths to enhance the world and make it
a better place. I am not a writer; I write.
I am not a counsellor; hopefully I give good counsel.
I am not a teacher; I teach. I am not sad that I am
not an "anything." I am celebrating that I have
figured out my place and purpose in the world.

Chapter 20

The Searching Years

"Two Hearts"

Springsteen's 1980 album *The River* was full of songs that I could relate to; I could feel. Especially the desire to keep searching for that special person. Before I left the printing company, I was confused about love and spent a lot of time thinking about M, my former co-worker at the printing company. I thought I liked him, but I was unsure.

Did I really like him, or was it just because we were friends? It was difficult to figure out. I didn't know. We had a lot in common, and I knew we wanted the same things from a partner. We wouldn't have been rushing anything – we had known each other for three years, so it would have been taking things slow for me. But I knew what I wanted from someone. I had my written list. I also knew what was non-negotiable.

Regardless of *my* feelings, I was not what he wanted. He wanted someone gorgeous, warm, appreciative, sweet, and thoughtful. He wanted the all-in-one package. I thought it was asking for too much.

I didn't understand it. Sometimes when I thought I was hideous, I remembered the guys who had been with me. I was not *that* hideous. I thought I was attractive, albeit not cookie cutter.

It was weird. I was very well-liked by all my friends' partners. It seemed they all respected me. That was refreshing; I just had to meet someone who liked me for me and wanted to have a relationship with me.

I was proud of myself regarding my job. I had not been happy with the situation, so instead of just bitching, I chose to do something about it. With my amazing luck (as a woman, I am too modest to admit my skills got me the job), I got a great job. I would make more money in six months at my new job than at the printing company.

I knew I would miss my team at the printing shop. It had been a great two years. I was sad to leave, but I knew it was the right thing to do.

I kept asking myself if I liked M. Did I even want to like him? Why didn't I like him? He had everything I wanted from someone, so why wouldn't I like him? Finally, I remembered – because he did not like me.

I was finishing up my stint at the print shop and always had time to offer support and words of encouragement to others – even to M, who had once asked me if I was a lesbian because I was always single. If he meant it as an insult, it most definitely was not. But his whole attitude should have been a big clue too. Remember, I was very good at ignoring clues.

It was the 23rd of September, Springsteen's birthday.

I was still trying to figure out my feelings about M. It would have been his second wedding anniversary. It was a tough day for him. I told him I would have loved to be with someone like him, and one day he would find someone who would love him the way he needs to be loved. I knew he was hurting, and reminded him he was getting stronger by getting through this time. I suggested that he should not immediately rush into a new relationship.

At the time, I did not realize that being single was a much better option than going from one unhealthy relationship to another. I was so worried about being alone forever that I did not understand that being alone at the time was a healthier alternative.

As the single person in my group of friends, my love life (or lack thereof) was often the subject of conversation within the group.

A friend came up with a theory. She thought I was getting closer to reaching my eventual goal of meeting a wonderful man because I knew what I wanted from someone – to be sensitive, kind, thoughtful, generous, friendly, and not too flirtatious with other women.

I was not sure if that described M, but I was sure I did not want to be his rebound woman. There is the sexual rebound, and there is the actual transition woman. His main problem was his desire to commit too soon and easily. Get a grip. Stay single. Just because you are single does not mean you have to have sex with every woman in sight. It is about figuring out what you want, what you like, and what makes you happy.

I was spending way too much time thinking about M.

I knew he was not right for me. He was single and kept getting involved with woman after woman. He was always searching for The One. He always believed something better was around the corner. But he never felt he was good enough. Ah yes, the lack of self-esteem. Another clue!

It was my last week at the print shop. It was hard to believe that I was leaving, especially while the whole M thing was freaking me out.

The weird thing was that he really liked me. He had told a client about me. He described me as highly intelligent, a thinker, a profound philosopher, and great company. But I wanted someone to actually *like* me. Not many men had taken the time to get to know me. Why was it so hard to find a guy who liked me and wanted a relationship? Why was this combo so difficult to find? Was it because I just didn't attract the right men? I mean, there was Gut Guy and all the rest.

I could not be satisfied with M liking me as a friend. Why was I so motivated to do something about it? I was attracted to him more because of his personality. Guys always seem to think that all women are attracted to them. But they don't understand what makes someone attractive. A sense of humour is a person's most attractive asset. I could see right through someone's looks. It is all about substance, and I wanted someone who had some!

I wanted to be pursued. So, I decided I would be more aloof and distant with M; if it was meant to happen, it would. I cringe at how much time I wasted thinking (and writing) about him.

Once again, I was right. When I spent too much time wrapped up in whether M liked me, I was not being true to myself. I was not valuing what I thought, wanted, or deserved. Sadly, this lack of appreciation continued through the next phase of my life.

Later that month, I had an intriguing weekend. I met this guy, A, at a local bar. He was really nice – a short, small man, so I felt like an Amazon woman compared to him! He was down-to-earth and quite sweet. He held my drink when I went to the bathroom. And at the end of the evening (when all we did was talk), he asked if I wanted to come back to his place for a drink. "No, thank you," I said. He also asked for my number. I gave it to him, but I was sure he would not call. More importantly, I didn't care if he did. I had an enjoyable time there. His friend had made my night when he came up to me and said, "You are a good-looking woman. You should expect to be hit on." It was unusual for me to hear those words.

I spent a lot of time thinking about M and his martial situation. Divorce is horrible. All of a sudden, your whole life is turned upside down. Everything you used to take for granted is new. Something as simple as getting up in the morning without your partner can be hard. Even if there was no love in the relationship, you could still miss the whole routine. You look around, and you are distinctly alone. It was different for me. I loved that. I thoroughly enjoyed waking up alone and going to bed alone. I adored sleeping by myself with no one to get in the way. And I loved the creaky noise my bed made in the morning when I first dragged myself out of it.

I thought I had the M situation figured out. I was wrong.

M and I kind of got together. It was ridiculous. He said he would call before he came over so that I knew when to expect him. I walked down to the supermarket, liquor store, and beer store. I bought some wine (red and white) and then bought him a 12-pack of Canadian. I lugged it all the way home (what a sight!) and then got ready.

What in the world was I doing? I did not have a car, M did. I did all that walking and shopping just so that he would see how good I was. That I was good enough.

Dinner was at a local steakhouse. We split a bottle of wine over dinner. We had fun chatting and then went back to my place.

We had sex. It was fast and furious, and it hurt tremendously. It was more painful than losing my virginity. It had been a year since I had had sex, and the unlubricated condom made it extremely uncomfortable. Afterwards, I told him that he could not just sleep with me and expect me to forget it happened.

M left around 3:00 am. I always hated it when a man left in the middle of the night. But somehow, I let that happen – I thought I was not worth staying with for the whole night.

At 51, those memories have faded. That is the joy of getting older – you forget the crazy things that happened to you when you were younger. It does not matter if they were big deals then; give it a few years and you won't remember them anymore.

Years later at the end of each calendar year, I started to write a review of the year that was ending. I found it a really helpful exercise to look at what happened and focus on what I wanted to happen in the future. I realized that all of these days were the hyphen on my tombstone; the days between the day I was born and the day I will die.

I want to take a moment and celebrate the beauty of the world. Thinking about the friend whose mom rang the bell after completing her last round of chemo, the friend whose children graduated, the friend whose dad just celebrated a special birthday with family, or the dogs and cats rescued or found and reunited with their owners. Celebrating the everyday little things in life makes our time on earth so special. My question today – are you happy with your hyphen?

Chapter 21

The Not-So-Happy-Ending Years

"Mary Lou"

I don't know how he did it, but it felt like many of Springsteen's songs were written for me. For example, in "Mary Lou", he warns her that she will end up with a broken heart if she is determined to find a happy ending. I too wanted so much to have that happy ending and felt determined that it would happen one day. I spent hours and hours mulling over each phone call or lack of phone call, always searching for the fairy tale that does not exist. I believed my happiness depended on someone loving me. I never believed in myself.

Think about it for a moment. You will likely make poor decisions when you don't believe in yourself. You are likely to settle for things (a job, a partner, your life). You end up feeling resentful. You could end up depressed, even with thoughts of suicide. You don't live your authentic life because you don't know who you are, and you may feel you don't deserve to be happy; you react, rather

than respond. You operate from a state of insecurity – you never believe you are good enough.

I thought about my track record with men. When DB and I were "together," I knew he would not be calling. I knew it was the end. At least I had learned that I didn't have to become physically intimate with someone for them not to call me again. I was quite used to this. I just did not want to be part of any of these mind games.

And yet, I was confused about the situation. Had I really liked DB? Had I been interested in getting to know him? As usual, even after time had passed, I was still analyzing what had happened.

Because really, I had been playing the "why did he not call?" game, but I could not think of any good reason – short of disinterest. But this goes back to the night we met and after – why did he act like that? Was I just a joke or something completely meaningless to him? I questioned all of it, but *I was not questioning myself* for the first time in my life. This lack of response from him had nothing to do with me. It was all about him and his inability to behave in an appropriate and socially acceptable way. I found it entirely inappropriate that he should act one way that night and suddenly become indifferent, and even rude by specifically not calling me.

He was acting immature (although a professional man and almost in his 30s) and still could not pick up the phone and make a call – if he had any sense, he would call me sometime during the day when he knew I would not be available. Then he could leave any message he wanted on my machine without having to talk to me. A coward's way out, but still better than not acknowledging someone's existence. Trust me, a lot better.

I had no idea I was describing the phenomenon of "ghosting," not returning someone's call or, as in the show *Friends*, "cutting someone out." I just chalked it up to me being unlovable and unattractive.

But if that was the biggest problem in my life, I was pretty blessed. Because worrying about whether or not a guy will call has got to be the biggest waste of energy and time. And still, I seemed to have that experience time and time again. I was so tired of it all and those stupid games people play.

I had not given up hope altogether. I still believed in love (if not for a lifetime, at least for a short time, like a year). Even though I felt it was possible two people could hook up and have a great partnership, I didn't believe it could happen to me. I was not sure who I would be happy with, apart from myself. I was extremely happy just hanging out in my place and going out with my friends. Apart from the obvious sexual aspects of a relationship, I was not lacking anything. I adored living alone and living my solo lifestyle. The only thing I asked of people (including my good friends and potential romantic interests) was that they have the good manners of returning my phone calls. I was diligent at making sure I returned mine. But, if someone does not have respect for others and cannot return a phone call, well, screw them. Forget that. Life is too short for people who don't return calls.

Life is also too short to spend analyzing whether some random guy you just met is going to call. At times, I seemed to understand things and listed them in the Top 10 Good Things that Happened to Me on January 9, 1997.

- I spoke to The Architect and then later his girlfriend. Hopefully got things sorted out between them. She called me because she was worried about him cheating on her. I told her that all the time that we were together, cheating was never anything I had to worry about – he is a faithful man.

- I looked nice in my green suit – I am still slim enough to wear it.

- I got postcards from Mom and Dad

- I got a nice reference letter from an American client

- I had a lovely walk at lunch time

- I had a tomazzo bagel and a bagel dog – now know what I think about them

- My friend J got a job interview – good for her!!!!!

- I wore my new pants yesterday. Love them!

- I will be going out tomorrow night with friends from work, maybe

- Getting enough self-confidence that I don't take rejection personally anymore

I hoped things would get better in the relationship department. I knew everything I would go through in my life was to get me to a certain point. Until I went through what I needed to go through, I would not be able to grow. I would continue to remain at that place.

I had been thinking about careers and what I wanted to do with my life. I knew multi-culturalism was important to me, as are interactions with different people. I enjoy talking to people and making them feel comfortable. I like learning new things and can be extremely extroverted at times. I was just not sure what type of career I should have been focusing on with those skills and traits. I was not sure if PR was what interested me. I certainly didn't regret the years I took it in school. If not for that program, I knew I would not be where I was.

I loved my life and was thankful for it. I knew things would work out for the best in any case. I was completely confident about that. Or at least I wanted to be.

Being able to write and express my feelings was helpful, and it had always helped me gain clarity. Not enough to make well-informed decisions, but enough to get me through the day.

A lot of people spend their 20s feeling lost, alone and confused, precisely because it *is* that time of life. Some people (women especially) try to hold on to their youth and are afraid of growing up.

It is a time of conflict between the little girl you were and the woman you are chronologically becoming. Growing up is scary.

A wonderful Saturday night – wearing my onesie, enjoying a yummy (and healthy) dinner – listening to the music I remember from my adolescence and childhood. Remembering times spent with my parents in Singapore –listening to Billy Joel's "The Bridge" and remembering growing up and listening to Simon and Garfunkel's "Bridge over Troubled Water." So grateful for a life filled with love. From the beginning to now, regardless of what is happening – the good and the bad times – love is ever present. Xoxo

Chapter 22

The Office Years

"Tougher than the Rest"

My friends knew I was searching for my place in the world, and on August 23, 1997, two called to tell me about a job they saw advertised in the paper. It sounded absolutely perfect for me – customer service oriented, yada, yada, yada – I applied and got an interview.

Cool. The only resume I had sent out, and I got a positive response. But I had no idea what the company did. It sounded like it dealt with graphic designers or something like that. So, after I applied, I got busy researching on the internet (a new thing back in 1997).

A woman named Julie had scheduled the interview, so I figured it would be with her. I wore my long forest green skirt with the slit up the side, the matching forest green jacket, and my silk sleeveless tank top. I felt fabulous. I arrived early (following etiquette) and waited for her to call me in. "Your interview will be with L S, the manager, and L P, the customer service manager," Julie informed me.

WHAT???!!!!! I panicked internally. I was not prepared for a man to interview me, now TWO men – ARGH! I could not handle it. I thought quickly. Should I back out and just run for it? I pondered the situation, and then Julie interrupted my mounting panic to say they were ready to see me. OH NO.

"Great." She took me to the empty boardroom, and I sat down with the slit in my skirt showing off a lot of my night-shade stockinged leg.

In walked this tall thin guy who introduced himself as L P – glasses, short brownish hair, and khaki style pants with a long-sleeved green and white plaid button-down shirt.

The interview started in earnest when L S showed up. He began by offering me a cup of coffee. I told him I don't drink coffee. He offered tea. I told him I don't drink tea. He appeared surprised and asked me what my vices were. "Easy," I said. "Ice cream."

That broke the tension, and we were off! We discussed all sorts of customer service situations and my reasons for wanting to leave my last job.

I remember L P bringing up his wife in conversation. I didn't know what that meant, but it confirmed that he was married, and I had already noticed the ring on his finger. That was fine with me. I had my problem situation with a man anyway, and I didn't think about it again.

That is, not until I went to see the two Ls again to sign my contract after work on September 19. I wore my black skirt, green silk button-down tank top, and the black ribbed jacket that made me look like a spy. I never thought I was sexy or attractive, so I did not think twice about dressing that way. I never thought anybody would ever like me. So, it did not matter what I wore. I wore what I liked and what made me feel good.

L P walked me to the door and shook my hand. He looked into my eyes and told me I had been first for both of them on their lists. This news made me feel good and happy about my decision to finally leave the printing company.

Time moved along, and I started working with L P on October 6, 1997. I had to work until 5:30 pm every night, and often it was just the two of us left at the end of the day. From the moment we met, I felt a connection between us. But I never thought he felt it too.

Our working relationship turned into something much more special. We quickly became friends. We joked we were the most normal of everyone who worked in customer service (except for our co-worker who had transferred into our department). I remember hating what I was doing; I had no idea paper was so math-based – which I hated, and I was horrible at it. My cubicle was right across from his office, and I remember turning around, and we would laugh and laugh together. It was the best thing about working there.

Later that fall, while I was living downtown, a bunch of us went out for dinner with the sales rep from a mill. She was a bubbly little blonde; our co-workers talked with her the whole night. That left L and me to sit there and talk. We had each other laughing and having fun. I knew I was feeling something for him because I would think about him when I was not at work.

We continued along in our work relationship. One day, we were sitting together having lunch in the kitchen, and I told L it would be fun if we got together one night after work for a drink. At this point, I meant it just as a friend, and I think I even mentioned bringing his wife. He joked about it and suggested he would leave her at home. I laughed and didn't think much more of the situation.

But then I started to feel something more for him. I felt guilty for even feeling those things. I tried to ignore the feelings, but I could not help it.

I suddenly found myself talking about L all the time, even speaking *like* him. I met his wife. The first time I met her was when he drove me to the bus station. His reaction was strange when he saw her. He panicked and freaked out, jumping out of the car. "Oh my GOD!!! There's my wife!" he exclaimed. I told him to relax; he was just giving me a ride. It was no big deal. I did not understand at the time why he reacted this way. When he introduced us, she did not seem to notice or care; we said we would see each other the next day at the company Christmas party.

As the only single girl at the Christmas party, I caused quite a stir with my black semi-backless dress with the slit up the side. I felt awesome that night and at ease when I saw L there. I thought, *oh, this is what he looks like when he is dressed up.* And then, *oh – there's his wife.* She wore a blue dress and looked very nice. When L and I started talking and joking, it felt like even his wife could not miss the chemistry between us. We did not do anything or talk about anything inappropriate. As usual, we argued about the music of Bruce Springsteen.

Later I discovered that L had paid attention to what I was wearing, and he noticed what I did and how I looked. Life went on. We continued to have a great relationship at work. Then, he went to the Dominican for his holidays (with his lovely wife, of course). I was jealous and knew I felt something genuine for him by then and did not want to admit this to myself or anyone else. I was sad; I felt stupid and did not want to continue having this feeling, so I just tried to forget about it.

Like that would ever work! I tried desperately to ignore my feelings towards him.

I noticed at the Christmas party the way he seemed to love his wife. I wanted someone to love me like that and look at me the way he looked at her, and I imagined how I would feel having my arm around him as she had. L and I always had a fun time just talking and laughing together. We spent most of the time at work laughing and joking together. It was like we had known each other forever. We had an easy relationship and rapport together. While trying to suppress my inappropriate feelings for my supervisor, I still had sex with other guys. Or almost.

I almost had sex with a friend's former classmate. And it is not like I was interested in him. In fact, for the first time, I finally understood you don't have to love someone to have sex with them. You don't have to like them very much; you can both give in to the passion and then go your separate ways. I knew I did not want to have sex or a relationship with that guy. I was beyond proud of myself for not having sex with him. I respected my boundaries, and I felt good about that. Although I thought I was proud of myself, I was just trying to make myself feel better. At the same time, I was impressed by finally realizing I could have sex without loving him. At least, I thought it was possible. I was wrong. Maybe other people could have sex without loving someone, but I definitely could not. Once again, I started paying attention to that clue later in my life.

Found this quote, and love it –
"Sex is the consolation you have
when you can't have love."
~ Gabriel García Márquez

Chapter 23

The Analyzing Years

"Dollhouse"

In 1997 I was still living in my one-bedroom apartment. Without a car, the downtown location was perfect. But that was about the only perfect part of my life. Once again, Springsteen seemed to be writing about me, to me, in his songs. When I listened to "Dollhouse," I felt he could definitely see the sadness on my face.

I was tired of the whole "I'll call you" thing from men. Uh, no – you won't be calling. Don't even mention that you will call me. It is not going to happen. The phone will not ring, and it will not be you on the other end. It will sit in silence on the almost-decade-old, slowly falling apart rattan shelf my parents bought for me in Asia. My answering machine will not have to pick up any messages, and my call display will not have to work because there will be no phone calls. Not true – my friends were calling to ask me, "Did he call?" No. He did not call. The phone has not rung since you called me three days ago. ☹

I sat in my nearly-silent apartment, save for the always-on TV or radio. I listened to our local country music station. I avoided that station for the longest time because it reminded me of growing up and listening to the country music my mother favoured. I hated it. In my teen years, I opted for more classic rock stations. However, since the end of 1995, I had chosen country. I felt like I had lived or was living every country song written.

I wondered where I would be for the rest of my life. I wanted to find a place to live where I could do my laundry when I wanted to and feel safe. That's always been very important to me. I loved living downtown. I still didn't have a car, so it was wonderful to have the accessibility of a prime location. I could walk pretty much anywhere I needed to go. I had the mobility I did not have when I lived with The Architect and Clancy, our black lab mix. If I had known it would have been that hard to leave her, I am not sure if I would have been as quick to leave the relationship and the house. It was a lovely house. Three (plus one) bedrooms, three bathrooms, a big living room, a great kitchen, a big deck, a good-sized yard and not a bad location (except for those who took the bus. For us it was brutal). I had felt isolated from my friends and family, though. Even just visiting someone was an entire day on the bus. Staying out late was impractical. It simply could not happen.

I really loved that house. I loved the fireplace, even though The Architect never once made a fire in it. I had never lived in anything bigger or more beautiful.

I was single and liked it. But I would have loved to have the opportunity to have sex with someone again. I wanted to have a partner. A wild, fun, passionate, considerate, thoughtful, sensual, and romantic partner – someone who showed up with flowers *and* a vase. Someone who wanted to make intense, crazy, and wild love. Someone who wanted to cherish, enjoy, and love every part of me. That's all I wanted. And I wanted someone who wanted to take a bath with me, to snuggle and to lie beside me. Someone who wanted to bring me ice cream and eat it with me. Someone who wanted us to feed each other strawberries dipped in chocolate. Someone who wanted to put whipped cream, honey, ice cream, chocolate sauce, all over my body and eat it from me. Someone who wanted me to do that to him. Someone who wanted to shower me with kisses – deep and long and hard. Someone who wanted to enjoy me at all hours of the day or night. Someone to wake up with and someone to sleep with me. I was learning a lot from my experiences with men. Dentist Boy taught me that I was not interested in being with someone who just wanted to have sex with me. (And it was not even regular vanilla sex – I was *not* into his ideas of orgies and golden showers).

I had friends who had nothing but good sexual encounters with men. Very different from my encounters – there was The Lifeguard who turned out to be an Engineering student at Carleton, B from RMC in Kingston, and D who was dating someone. R – the first guy after the end of my relationship with The Architect. We had bad sex on my futon in my apartment.
My friend C was next. We met at college, and I had always had a huge crush on him. However, I was always in the "friend zone." I listened to his romantic conquests and wanted him to want me. One day he suggested that we should keep our engines running between relationships. (Translation – I am horny enough to have sex but you are not good enough to be my girlfriend). A horrible idea.

Twenty years later, we bumped into each other at a networking event. By then, C was married and the father of three daughters. He apologized for being such a dick (his word) back then. Even after all that time, I was happy to hear the apology.

Then there was S; we were pseudo co-workers and one night we spoke on the phone for nine hours. Seriously? That was longer than some of my relationships! He came over late one night and we fooled around. Never heard from him again, which was fine with me.

A glutton for punishment, I somehow ended up having sex with R again. While we were attempting to have sex in the morning, I must have said something to make his (barely there) erection soft. Suddenly, there he was – limp inside of me. Where did the condom go? "Don't worry," he said, pulling out his flaccid penis. The missing condom was still inside me. I pulled it out and promptly booked an AIDS test which thankfully came back negative.

Now I had a new situation with this new guy I had met.

Amazing was the best way to describe my weekend. Starting on Friday night getting a drive home, and then going to the Heart and Crown and meeting N. He was 34 and becoming an officer in the Navy.

He had called me on Sunday. Finally, a man I was interested in thought enough of me to pick up the phone and call me. No one had ever done that before. I was completely flabbergasted.

I did not sleep with him, although we could have. I am sure it would have been fantastic because he touched me in a way I had only dreamed about and seemed completely intrigued by my body. I felt safe and comfortable with him. He was a good kisser and he wanted to go down on me. That's right – he *wanted* to – but I said no, and he respected my feelings. He was a nice guy.

It was wonderful being with him, but still, I didn't know what would happen.

I was still thinking about the whole relationship thing that I could not figure out. I had no idea how friendships turned into *relationships*. The entire topic scared the hell out of me. I had no clue how things worked. I didn't know what I wanted.

Okay, so I DID know what I wanted. I wanted someone to love me. I just did not know at the time that *I* needed to be that person.

Fast forward to many years later: I finally found a house that truly feels like home. My husband and I have lived here for almost 18 years. It is far from perfect; the entryway and the stairs look like someone just moved in. The painted walls remain outdated, and there are bits and pieces of drywall showing, but the love that exists in this house – our home – is what makes it beautiful.

We often enjoy roaring fires in the gorgeous fireplace my talented partner designed and built himself.

One of those nights – **Love Actually** *is playing, the fireplace is going, my colourful star lights are on, I finished a delicious mug of hot chocolate, and our puppy is on his green chair. Listening to some songs that I love – starting with "Songbird" by Fleetwood Mac. It feels perfect.*

Chapter 24

The Finding Myself Years

"Better Days"

For many years I felt lost, alone, and very confused. I wrote in my journal as a way of working through those feelings. I always hoped to find some answers; I was waiting for my better days.

We all have the right to live happy lives, but I had seen many people like me searching, trying to find ourselves. Growing up, I watched the TV program *That '70s Show*, and they would be talking about finding themselves. I used to think they were full of crap.

Then I grew up.

And suddenly, there I was, too, trying desperately to find myself, find my passion in life, and make a difference in people's lives. I felt torn in so many different directions. I wanted to be happy, but I thought the only way I could be happy was if I had the right job.

I asked myself – what the hell could I do?

I started making lists – one of my most favourite activities. I thought about what I most enjoy and am good at, and realized that expressing myself, sharing, and writing were all things I thoroughly enjoyed and could do.

We only have one life (as far as we know) on this Earth. It is up to us to live it. No one else can live it for us; the worst feeling in the world is to know you are wasting your potential.

I knew how that felt. I had this horrible feeling in my stomach, thinking that life was passing me by, wondering, how many of us feel this way? We figure we'll be "happy when" we pay off that loan, get married, have children, finish school, go back to school, move to a new house, pay off the mortgage, buy the dream car, meet the person to live with forever. I used to dream about being happy once I won the lottery. I discovered I was wasting my time because the lottery ticket dream is not a real one. I wanted to dream about something that I could make happen.

So, I started reading. I read and read. I spent about four months immersing myself in self-help books. I wanted to learn; I was ready to grow and change. But I knew I could not do this without research.

I needed to go and do something I love. That was the opposite of wasting my life.

Although I started thinking about happiness in 1998, for the next 17 years, I kept ignoring the clues that were revealing themselves to me.

Without knowing it, I was full of compassion for people who were going through pain in their lives. For most of my life, I believed everyone has empathy for other people. However, it took me a long time to understand that empathy is a gift.

*I wonder what it must feel like not to feel things
so deeply, not to cry when a song takes you
right back to 1987, hanging out by the lockers
at my high school in Singapore. I will never know.
As the tears mix with my anti-aging night cream to
sting my eyes, I carry my emotions with pride.
I am emotional, sensitive, and deeply empathetic –
especially for that sad and alone 17-year-old girl
listening ad nausea to her* **Tunnel of Love** *tape.*

Chapter 25

The Living Alone Years

"Cover Me"

When I was younger, even though I had no idea about empathy, I had it and wrote about it.

So, you're single. It may have happened suddenly, or you may have had plenty of warning. Either way, your heart feels like it is breaking.

It feels like the world is ending, and you'll never be happy again. You remember all of those wonderful memories. Or you make up some wonderful memories because you know the relationship was not really all that happy anyway.

Eventually, you will feel better, but until you do, here are some tips to weather the storm.

1) **Ignore everyone, especially those people who have opinions about your life and feel the need to share them with you. That is just rude.**

2) **Get busy. Keep busy doing things at work. It will help you concentrate on something other than the demise of your relationship. If you aren't working, volunteer. Get out there. Get outside yourself.**

3) **Move on. Yeah, sure, much easier said than done.**

4) **Read. Read. Read and read. When you finish reading those books, read more.**

Reading helped me get through my breakup period.

Being single is not a death sentence. But so many people think it is. One of my newly single friends constantly heard, "Oh, you don't have a boyfriend yet? I don't know how you do it."

How you do it? It's not like she was climbing Mount Everest or battling cancer. It's living alone. And it's fun!

It *is* fun; even though we believe that to spend our entire lives being alone is a fate worse than death. Only if we are married do we mean something in the world; if we are single, we have nothing to contribute.

I became something of an expert at being single. I could go out anytime, walk down the street and bump into many acquaintances. It was comfortable. It was easy.

Then I moved out of the downtown core. It was an interesting transition. I used to live in the same apartment building as my sister. It was my idea to share a townhouse. She would cook, and I would eat – a living situation made in heaven – or so I thought.

We moved in at the end of January. Things were okay initially, but over the summer, things started falling apart when I told her I was thinking about getting a car. I had been a bus rider for more than ten years. I did not think I could ever afford a car.

I realized most people who are driving cars cannot afford it either. So why couldn't I get a loan and make car payments just like the rest of the car owners?

Living with my sister did not work out. We didn't see eye to eye (an understatement) on anything, and our lifestyle habits were not compatible. Once again, I would be leaving and finding something new.

As a 52-year-old woman, I recognize our relationship has changed significantly. I think it would be fair to say that about every relationship I have with my family. I am not the same person I was, and living an authentic life aligned with my values made the difference.

The gift of family is unbelievably meaningful.
I am so incredibly grateful for my mom, dad, sisters,
extended family (and friends who are family),
community, and canine and human soulmates –
and our good health and ability to enjoy
every moment of life.

Chapter 26

The Gratitude Years

"Happy"

Even though I never wanted to have a family of my own, both my immediate and extended family mean everything to me.

I always had a great connection with both of my aunts. One told me I needed to figure out the most important thing I wanted from a relationship. After reflection, I realized I wanted to be cherished. I had spent my entire younger life not being cherished by anyone in a relationship, and I had never cherished myself.

After a conversation with this aunt, I thought I had figured things out. I told her about P, my nice, patient, and kind co-worker. She suggested I make a list of the most important qualities in a man, and when someone has three of these qualities, I should choose him.

Choose him? That made me laugh. As if it was that easy. Relationships were the least of my worries but were all I could think about all the time.

I thought about her suggestion and pondered the pros and cons of each aspect of a man. Finally, I decided he must be thoughtful and cherish and respect me (all three) because he would not be the right person for me if he did not cherish me.

I wanted so much to be with someone again – who was romantic, gentle, and kind.

P was the nicest guy ever. One day, he asked me what was wrong, and instead of just settling with my "nothing" response, he asked again, but stopped asking when I told him I was not in the mood to talk. Then, a few hours later, he checked with me again.

While driving to a co-worker's place for a party, he was patient and calm about the whole thing instead of getting mad or pissed off about not knowing where we were going. He was completely unlike The Architect, who would quickly lose patience when he was lost or when things did not work out the way he thought they would.

When he knew I needed a ride (or might have needed one), he called, picked me up, and took me where I needed to go. Then, at the end of the night, he drove me home.

P drove me anywhere I needed to go, like to my hairdresser's and then to my aunt and uncle's place. He always did that without any questions. Even if he was tired and had had a long day, he would always go out of his way for me.

P was sweet, kind, and funny. He was also good with money. Although the Architect went out of his way to make me feel stupid about money, P patiently helped me improve my financial skills.

He was a wonderful, platonic friend. I wanted a happy relationship where someone had respect for me, cherished me, and was thoughtful. That was all. Everything else I could obtain for myself, and I did.

I didn't want things to go too fast in a relationship. I wanted to just have fun with someone who enhanced my life, not someone who made me feel bad about myself. I was tired of that feeling.

I didn't know what else. I just knew I was happy living my life. I had a wonderful apartment that made me very happy and had a terrific group of friends that always made everything better. I was lucky, and I *felt* lucky!

As usual, I seemed to have an insight into something that would have made a big difference in my life.

Gratitude.

Years later Oprah spoke about "an attitude of gratitude." I never really caught on to that, which is interesting because, unbeknownst to me, that was how I was already living my life.

I learned how to acknowledge someone. Instead of saying, "Hey, great shoes," I acknowledged something about their personality, like telling them how thoughtful they are, or how I respect their ability to raise their children while going to school, or how they inspire me to be a better person. Some more things I've learned to share with you:

A compliment is nice; acknowledgment is valuable. Learn to say thank you; it makes all the difference in every relationship (business, professional, romantic, friendships). Try it and notice what happens.

A sense of gratitude leads to higher energy, enthusiasm, and optimism. Being aware and grateful for what you have will change your life.

When you have gratitude in your life, you are operating from a state of abundance. You already have things. The opposite of abundance is lack – like you are missing something. When you focus on lack, you send out a message of desperation.

I always seemed to understand the idea of gratitude but did not truly understand just how significant this attitude would be in my life. Some people keep a gratitude journal, while others post positive thoughts and messages on their social media platforms (like Facebook, Instagram, and Twitter).

Start paying attention to what other people are saying and doing, and you may be able to see how you want to show up.

Finally, in my 50s, I feel like I am living my dream. I share my life with my husband in a happy and healthy relationship, and we enjoy our wonderful canine. And I live in a house with a washer and dryer.

I can identify strongly with the It Gets Better Project *because I have lived it. If I could go back in time and tell the 16, 18, 20, 25, 30, and 35-year-old me that I would be so incredibly blessed in life, I probably wouldn't have believed it. Every heartache, unrequited crush, and tears I shed were all worth it. A lifetime will not be long enough to spend with my best friend.*

Chapter 27

The Decision-Making Years

"With Every Wish"

As my self-awareness developed, I could look back at my life and consider the pivotal moments I wrote about but never realized were so important. How did Springsteen know that even when things look like they are working out, something dangerous is hiding under the surface?

Like toxic decision-making.

Our lives are entirely dependent on decisions. Do I sleep in or get up now? Do I take that way home or choose another route? Do I call my partner to say I will be late?

Why then do some decisions we make end up costing us so much? So much money, heartache, time, and energy go into the consequences of decisions we make. If only we could put that energy into making good decisions. Positive choices enhance our lives instead of putting us light years behind where we feel we should be at this point in our lives. Just about 35, I never expected to be where I was; I got there through a series of toxic decisions I made throughout my life.

People often ask themselves, "Why did I make that decision?" or the proverbial "What was I thinking?" about their wardrobes or hairstyles.

While these decisions about temporary situations can easily remedy themselves, it is not so easy to change your life, your marriage, or your career. When you make decisions based on a lack of self-esteem or knowledge, you are almost assuredly doomed to regret them, keeping in mind there are always exceptions to this rule.

We go through life and keep making all sorts of decisions. We may question ourselves in "What if?" land. For example, "What if I had chosen something else?" "What if I had stayed in that class?" "What if I did not drop out of school?" "What if I had not married that person?" "What if I did not have children?"

When I was in my late 40s, I performed an autopsy of the decisions I had made in my life.

Those pivotal moments in life – my interview on the radio led to my teaching gigs with CEGEP's continuing ed department, which shone a new and extraordinary light on my passion for helping people see what a difference they can make to the world. That insight led to my Adult Learning course and discovering how my career history and love of career development dovetail so nicely with adult learning facilitation. My previous experiences with CVE, Calian, the Community Employment Resource Centre (CERC), March of Dimes, and Puddle Jump Coaching flow beautifully into each other. I continue to experience and appreciate the joy of life in all its forms.

Chapter 28

The Fairy Tale Years

"I Wanna Marry You"

1998 was another crazy year for me. In December of 1997, I was dog-sitting for a close friend when our mutual friend J phoned to speak to her. He told me he had broken up with his girlfriend and he was single. I bravely suggested he could give me a call if he wanted to hang out sometime.

One day about six months later, he called me at work to ask me out for dinner and a movie. I was stunned; I had liked him for a while, but our mutual friend had warned me about him. It took some time, but I eventually figured out that it was because that friend had a crush on him.

We went to dinner at a steak restaurant where we talked about dating, marriage, children, and my boss. Afterwards, we went to see *There's Something About Mary.* Suddenly, we were dating.

He was a big guy and loved animals, especially dogs. I started staying over nights and driving with him to visit his parents. The summer was fun and full of getting to know each other. It was amazing. For the Labour Day weekend, we visited his family in Toronto, and during the six-hour trip back to Ottawa, started planning our wedding. I was happier than I could have imagined.

It was the most fulfilling and contented time of my life. We decided we wanted to get married one week after starting to see each other. And the pieces just kept falling into place. I was delighted to marry such a wonderful man. Even though I had written all about not getting married, I just knew J was the right man for me. He had what I had always wanted in a partner and more.

A month went by. Friday, October 9, 1998, was a terrible day for me. Twice that day, my boss summoned me to his office. The second time, I was scared I was losing my job.

Suddenly, J walked into the office, dressed as a giant teddy bear! He was carrying a bouquet of two dozen roses – all red except for one lone yellow one, symbolizing friendship. On the yellow rose was a beautiful diamond engagement ring that had belonged to his grandmother. He took off his teddy bear head, placed it on the desk, and got down on one knee. It was everything I had wanted a proposal to be (although having my boss in the same room was a tad awkward until I motioned for him to leave). We planned our wedding; I loved planning. We visited different venues and settled on booking a lovely restaurant. I found a gorgeous dress (wedding dress #2 for engagement #2).

I was beyond happy. Or so I thought. Or so I desperately wanted to be; I did not write for a long time.

Although I thought J was in love with me, I later understood in fact he was in love with the *idea* of me. He wanted a wife, a dog, a house. I fit the bill.

The girls at work were happy for me, and I started obsessing over the wedding. I bought copious amounts of magazines and focused solely on wedding planning. I took it very seriously; dedicating hours to find the right venue, dress, and music.

One day in April of 1999, I got a phone call from my boss, L. He had the day off and asked me out for a coffee.

We got together, and, as usual, spent the time laughing together. We got along fabulously, sharing a sharp sense of humour and a strong emotional connection. We could talk about everything – nothing was off limits. I would tell L about my relationship with J, and he would talk about his marriage.

We continued to see each other every day at work. We ate our lunches together, driving to a grassy spot where lunches became picnics.

At work, we kept each other sane. He would keep his door open so we could chat and laugh together.

He noticed that when I was excited about something, I would wiggle around and do what he dubbed "my happy dance." When I took a day off, I left an army of gummy bear soldiers on his desk to enjoy in my absence. After he told me he loved Fudgeeo cookies, I bought him a package to keep in his desk just in case he got hungry. Unwittingly, we were falling in love with each other.

Love is like the sun coming out of the
clouds and warming your soul.
~ Author Unknown

Chapter 29

The Restless Years

"Cautious Man"

1999 was supposed to be the year J and I got married. When we celebrated New Year's Eve in a bar in downtown Ottawa and watched the ball drop at midnight in Time's Square, we looked at each other and said, "This is going to be our year."

It *was* our year – to break up and go our separate ways.

We had started seeing a counsellor that spring and summer. I had been going for counselling for a few years, and we both thought getting some proactive couple's counselling would be wise. J's parents had divorced, and he was scared his marriage would end the same way.

We talked about children. Neither of us wanted to have kids. I did not want to have any because I did not want my child to feel ugly like I did, and I thought that if I got pregnant and lost my figure, I would have absolutely nothing going for me. J was terrified of repeating his parents' mistakes.

In late spring we went to a high school reunion where a friend's husband danced with me in a very sexually inappropriate way. I was extremely uncomfortable with this experience and told J. The next time friends asked us to an event I knew that guy would be attending, I politely declined with J's blessing, and he would go on his own. When I told him that I would be bored at home without him, he suggested that I call L and his wife to see if they were busy.

They weren't. L's wife was not there that night. L and I talked on the phone and made plans to go out to Chapters, the local big box bookstore. Like we always did, we had a lot of fun just goofing around. Spending time together was always fun; once, we were at the National Gallery for a work event, laughing so much, someone asked if we were on our honeymoon. Although I loved having fun with him, I felt horrible. I wrote about what was happening in our lives so that I would hopefully feel better. I never did.

I wanted to write about everything – to get it all out my system and into the computer. As if that would make me feel better.

It didn't.

Soon after, he left his wife; then, we got together.

A few months later, L, my manager – and boyfriend – was going through a divorce. He was separated from his wife and finalizing their divorce. He lived two apartment buildings away from me, and I knew he was unhappy.

He left his house, tools, and lifestyle when he chose to leave his wife. He was miserable living in the one-bedroom apartment.

I started obsessing about him thinking he had made a mistake and would be returning to his wife; I convinced myself the same reasons that made him leave his marriage in the first place were still there.

Besides, I figured his wife had undoubtedly moved on in some way. They say women are more likely than men to get on with their lives. I knew she had a strong network of support from friends and family. He did not. He had me. I was the friend, the confidante, the girlfriend, and worst of all, the co-worker. I needed to find another job. Regardless of everything else, I needed to get out of our common workplace. He felt trapped because of his debt obligations. He thought he needed to keep his job because it afforded him to pay off his debts. If all went according to plan, he would be debt-free in five years. I knew it may have sounded like a long time, but not when you compare it to the opportunity cost of living with someone you know is not the right person for you.

Look out for yourself in life. No one will make you happy; that is up to you. And if making yourself happy means hurting someone you care for deeply (like he did), that is a choice you must make. No one can make this choice for you, and you must live with the consequences.

I bought a book about divorce and spent all night reading it and highlighting many passages to give to him.

I hoped he would read it, and it would help him a bit. I wanted him to feel the pain so he could move past it. I had no idea know what divorce felt like – I could only imagine. The rejection and the pain you feel must be unbearable. It must be like the rug has been swept pulled out from under your feet, and you are just lost. You have lost your friend, companion, lover, and security. This must be brutal. And this goes for both him and his ex-wife. He had lost everything too, but the difference is that he chose to do it. I don't believe he had known how painful it would be. I was delusional, convinced we both genuinely believed we were soul mates. I tried telling myself our relationship was not just a physical thing. No, I told myself, this was pure friendship, mixed with mutual attraction, desire, and passion.

It was wonderful. Only it was now up to me to stick around and be there when he got through the pain he was feeling. It hurt me because there was nothing that I could do to make him feel better. It was something he needed to do for himself when he was ready. I didn't know what to do. I wanted to be with L, and I hoped we could still be together and at the same time, get through the divorce and the dissolution of his marriage. I thought about his wife every day.

Maybe he had not been ready for marriage. Maybe he had been content just living with his girlfriend, and perhaps when he was ready, he would have done it on his time and terms. I knew he did what most people would have done by marrying her. Then he did what most people would not have done. He dared to do something about his life because he was not happy. Surely, a person has the right to live a happy life.

Looking back at it I recognized I had done the same thing with The Architect. We had lived together for a couple of years, and then I figured getting married was the next logical step. He was a few years older than me, and we had been dating for a few years, so why not?

I had trapped him into asking me to marry him. I should not have pushed him. But I knew that somehow it had worked out for the best. I realized getting married was not the right thing to do and left the relationship. It hurt, but I knew I was doing the right thing. Finally, I came to my senses. I learned a lot from that relationship. Mostly I learned life is too short to spend time with someone when we are not happy with each other. Someone who truly loved me (in the way that I needed) and wanted to be with me would not treat me like he did. I was finally paying attention to the pattern.

In retrospect, I recognize the relationship with The Architect was pathetic. I had desperately wanted to be loved and feel attractive, and I saw this possibility in him. I thought we could have worked at it even if we weren't compatible. No. You cannot just work at it when you are two entirely different people. Then, after I broke up with The

Architect, I met a guy at a party at the end of April and fooled around that night. Later the next month, I slept with him. Afterwards, I made the mistake of telling him that he was only the second man I had slept with – put that on the list of things you should never say to someone. It was awkward and uncomfortable, but I did feel attractive. Someone finally wanted me, and that made me feel good.

This feeling was short-lived, as I quickly discovered he wanted nothing more to do with me. I asked him to lunch. I believed I wanted to be involved with him. When he did not return my phone calls, I felt hurt and stupid, yet sadly, I did not learn my lesson that time.

No, it took a few more guys, and I never once set out to have a one-night stand. Instead, whenever I got involved with someone, I believed we could have a relationship. Now that I had embarked on the latest one, I felt more lost than ever. L was visiting his mom and family in Toronto. I hoped he was having a good time. All I could think of was his mother and relatives telling him he had made a mistake and he should go back to his wife. It hurt me so much because we could usually talk about things and work it out together. But that weekend, he would not be back until Sunday – two more nights.

I didn't know what was going to happen when he got back. I felt helpless.

He came home on Sunday night. The time I had spent alone, mulling and obsessing, had been horrible.

I had worked myself up into such frenzy; it was unreal. My stomach was tossing and turning. I felt like throwing up. Chugging Pepto Bismol, on Sunday evening I called him to see if he was there. The voice mail came on. My first reaction – oh, he is there, but he does not want to answer the phone. I was resolute. He had decided, and he was avoiding me. I was terrified at the idea of him being over at her place. I needed to relax. I would take a walk.

I tried to walk, but it turned out that I just walked right past his apartment building (I mean, it was right THERE). Whenever I heard a car, I looked to see if it was him. Of course, it never was. So, I walked to the end of the road and started to walk back home. On the way, I decided to go to his place and knock on the door. I knew I would have no trouble getting into the apartment because they almost always have the front door open. I knew I could not buzz him from downstairs because he would not pick up if he was trying to avoid talking to me on the phone. I took the elevator up to his floor. I was full of anticipation and fear. It was terrible. Sweat was pouring down my back. I am sure that I lost some weight during that obsessive period.

I knocked on the door. I took a deep breath. My mind was swirling. If L was there and had not answered the phone, I figured he was going to break up with me and needed the time to figure out a way to do it. If he was not there, he was over at her place. Or he was still on the road, and my God, what if something happened to him and he was lying in a ditch somewhere on the side of the highway, dying, covered with blood?

I knocked on the door again. I put my ear against it to hear if the TV was going (because it was always on if he was home). I could not hear anything and was ready to turn and walk down the hall. Suddenly I heard the sound of the chain inside, and the door opened. He was there, looking like he had just woken up. How long had he been there? Was he there and just avoiding my call? Why had he not called me?

He had arrived about half an hour before. He was tired and had not even unpacked.

I looked at him and asked him he still wanted to be with me. I hoped the answer was yes. It was. He was a little freaked out because I was obviously agitated.

I was so relieved. We hugged tightly.

His family time had been fun. The only thing anyone ever said regarding his "situation" was an aunt who asked him if he was divorced yet or still going through it. He told her he was still going through it.

He enjoyed himself and he still loved me. Cool. Yet I didn't think he was ready to jump into a situation with me. I had brought the divorce book with me and gave it to him. Stupidly, I told myself he appreciated the gesture and would read it. I showed him all the similarities – the leaving, the depression, all of that. I thought it would help him to see that other people had been able to get through it and make a happy life.

Although everything was fine between us, while he was away, I concluded that even though we had decided to move in together in the fall, it would be a better idea to wait. He had to mourn the loss of his marriage, and only after he had would he be able to join me in this relationship fully. He agreed with my idea. I was willing to stay in my apartment with the most annoying upstairs neighbours. Even though I knew it was the best idea, it freaked me out that I had come to that conclusion on my own. I was growing up. I didn't think it would ever happen to me, but it seemed like it was happening on its own. At least that was what I liked to think, but then I would go and do something stupid and knew I was still a kid.

The same day I felt a sense of maturing, I saw my old boyfriend, J. It was just lovely to see him. We sat in his van and talked for more than an hour. My co-workers had seen me in there, and I was sure someone would think I was back with him. Nothing could have been further from the truth. Even if I wanted to get back together, J had told me before that we would never be an item again. I understood and agreed. It was the healthiest way to go. Another one of my theories, completely unsubstantiated, is that when people break up, they are not meant to get back together. After all, you broke up for a reason, right?

My co-workers suggested that I should write a book. I felt that if I did, I would write a book because I wanted other people (more than likely women) to understand that their thoughts and feelings in life are okay. And that they are not alone.

I especially wanted to speak to normal women of the world.

Real women are not supermodels, but in my 20s and even into my 30s, I was constantly comparing myself to those women who appeared impossibly beautiful, which did nothing to help increase my self-esteem. Until my late 20s, I didn't think anyone could find me attractive. Sure, I had dated a few guys, but it was never a positive experience. Then, at one point, I had three guys who were interested in me simultaneously. That was a first! It was exciting and allowed me to be choosy about them.

When I look back at that, I am flabbergasted; I spent the next decade comparing myself to others – and always coming up short. My hair was never good enough, I was not making enough money, people were living in better apartments, had cars, and I didn't. Some people had dogs; others liked camping – the list was endless.

I developed an entirely different perspective due to the coaching program I took in 2011.

Some things I am grateful for, in random order:

1) *my marriage; I am incredibly blessed.*
2) *my health and that of my family and friends.*
3) *my beloved canine companion.*
4) *my fulfilling and unbelievably satisfying job.*

5)   *my house may not be perfect or finished, yet we fill it with more love than I ever thought possible.*
6)   *the fall (I love this time of year).*
7)   *my spiritual community.*
8)   *my support system from near and far, and*
9)   *my life.*

Chapter 30

The Muddy Years

"The Big Muddy"

Sigh.

When I was single, I waited for the phone to ring. Like to hear the phone ringing was the be-all and end-all of my existence. Why did I let a phone call determine who I am? I clung to the hope L would call me. Why? What difference would it make in my life? Was I so self-absorbed that I couldn't see he had his own life? Was I so self-centered that everything was about me? What if he was tired, sleeping, or out somewhere? Why should he have to speak to me at night? He saw me every day and listened to me complain about my lack of self-improvement.

I wanted to just come home to a home, not have to drive up five levels of a parking garage and then walk down five levels of stairs.

I could see I was developing some self-awareness, a fundamental component in establishing self-esteem. I knew even then I did not want to live in an apartment – I wanted a house that would feel like a home.

Later I learned that love, respect, and mutual support turn bricks and mortar of a house into a home. Looking back, I see the problem was who I was, not where I lived. I was maturing just a little bit.

During our relationship, I was desperate to be loved. I analyzed everything. I wanted L to want to marry me or live with me or something. Then I would be good enough. Then I would be happy.

L came over for dinner one night and brought me a beautiful bouquet. The card said, "The flowers are to take care of the day; I'll take care of the night." I loved them! They were gorgeous. The week before, I had told him that I wanted flowers. He listened to me, and I thought that was romantic. It meant so much to me.

A friend told me she thought that sooner or later, L would move in with me. That was news to me! He was not talking about moving in with me. I was confused about the idea of living together. At times I thought if someone loved me enough to live with me, they should want to marry me. Other times, I figured, what the hell does a marriage matter anyway? The divorce rate was off the charts.

I did not realize it for the longest time that I was running away. I always thought that something better awaited me, and I would be happier in a different home. I had no idea that until I was happier within myself, I would never be satisfied – regardless of where I was living.

Wow.

***What an unbelievable day – and now, I am listening to Springsteen and President Barack Obama talking on the podcast* Renegades: Born in the USA.**

As I was listening to it, I thought of that same feeling
of not fitting in like when I was growing up.
I felt that way for a very long time and became
part of the drama club. I don't know if all the
drama kids felt like that, but I certainly did.
It was a place for me to be someone else, not Tonya with all
my anxieties and issues, for a few minutes. I was Sid Sawyer
(the brother of Tom Sawyer), or Rose Hoffman in Studs
Terkel's Working *as part of the* Life, Liberty and the Pursuit
of Happiness *production at UWCSEA. I never realized*
that I was always just trying to run away from myself.
Hmm – I think as I was writing that, it was a bit of an Ah
ha! moment. That feeling of not being good enough and
running away continued into my 20s and 30s – likely why
I kept moving so often. Finally, I figured out that all my
issues and anxieties make me who I am, someone to help
people feel hope, motivated, and ready to reach their goals.

Chapter 31

The Broken Years

"This Depression"

In the summer of 2001, L and I broke up. To be clear, I broke up with him. I knew it was not working, and I knew he needed his own space.

I was depressed. I had lost ten pounds and was miserable. L was no longer my manager; he had joined the sales team.

I went to my doctor who gave me a note to be off work for three months. I was planning to take this time to visit a friend in New Brunswick and try to find a new job when I got back home.

My employer had a different plan for me. One afternoon I was ambushed by my new manager, who was letting me go. The company knew it was a wrongful dismissal and forced me to sign an agreement saying I was not allowed to speak to our clients, and they would continue to pay me (and include benefits) for six months. As well, they told me that if I found a new job, I would have to tell them and then I would only get half of what they owed me.

So, there I was. No boyfriend and no job. Writing is what kept me sane.

I thought I would have turned into a complete wreck by now. But surprisingly, I am doing better than I thought.

I am sure that L is not doing as well as I am. I know I did the right thing. As painful as it was and still is, I am confident I am choosing the right option. I knew the holding pattern was not doing me any good, but I did not know it was hurting him too.

Today I woke up and felt okay. At night before I go to sleep, I just read my book and fall asleep with the light on, which I love. When I was going out with L, we always just went to bed and turned off the light. We never listened to music, and I love having music or talking to put me to sleep.

Guess I slept okay. I cannot remember waking up or anything And I think this is all because I am doing the right thing. I made the right move. I feel mature. Maybe I am actually growing up.

Sigh. I am sure he is going to come around. But will I want him back? I am getting on with things. The main thing is that we don't have contact with each other and regardless of my feelings about the situation, I am going to have to be okay with it.

I am hungry but really don't feel like eating. I know he is doing the same thing. I feel sorry for him because I am special, and a hard act to follow!

That is a little confidence showing through. Good.

After I received notice my rent was going up, I found a new place to live.

Picked up the lease for the new apartment. Really looking forward to moving at the end of the year. I cannot believe how excited I am to be moving.

I still did not realize that I was running away from myself and my life. I thought if I moved to the second floor of the triplex, everything would be better. I was – as with most times in my 20s and 30s – wrong.

Up to that point in my life, breaking up with L was the most difficult and painful thing I had ever experienced. Certainly, I had experienced loss to some degree (all my grandparents had passed away as well as a beloved former teacher who died suddenly and unexpectedly.) But I had never felt this kind of pain that gnawed at my soul. Each day was a huge challenge to get through. I had no job to take my mind off my own personal issues. I was drowning in sorrow and could not see a way out.

I needed to write to get through each moment.

Day 3

Well, I survived another night. Stayed up quite late. Went to bed with Conan O'Brien on the TV.

I am moving into a nicer and bigger place and have great things to look forward to. See, I am in a happy place. He is not. And as much as I would like to help him, I cannot. He must get to the happy place on his own. And if he never reaches it, well, that is a sad life.

I still love him. I always will. How can I not? We are made for each other. If it is meant to be that we are together, we will be together. If not, well, we won't. There is nothing more I can do about it. Just step back and get on with life.

And I am doing just that.

Day 3 still

I need to start living my life over again. But I am not ready to meet anyone new and get involved with anyone. How screwed up would that relationship be?

Because I am not taking him back. This is the end of the relationship. If he does call back, he should be prepared to be rejected. I feel sick, but at the same time, I must understand this is the end. I don't like it, but I must accept it. I am angry and hurt and feel SO very betrayed by him.

And he still has my vacuum cleaner I lent him. I would like to get it back (it cost $200.00), so I may have to ask a mutual colleague to help me get it back.

It seems that every time I think I am doing okay with this, I start thinking about things. I want October, November, and December to go by so quickly. I want them to go just as fast as the summer did. I am so full of anger and resentment towards him. I don't understand. If that's how I feel, why am I having to try this hard to get over him?

I am so sad. I am just crying. I don't understand how someone who loves me and knows we are perfect for each other can make me feel this way. I am so sad and lonely.

Day three felt like forever. It was one of those days that I was just grateful – and so happy – to see end.

I was still living alone in my high-rise apartment. I had nothing to do all day but immerse myself in my toxic feelings. Thankfully, it was in the pre-Facebook era; if I did not go out of my way to see him, our paths would not cross. Even though we still lived within a 30-second walk, I could not believe how we never saw one another.

He would go off to work, and I would spend the day crying, writing, and figuring out ways to get my vacuum cleaner.

When I read that now, I just roll my eyes. If I could say anything to that young woman, I would let her know if she was honest with herself, she would realize she just wanted to be able to see him again. The vacuum cleaner was just a silly excuse, and deep down, she knew that.

I did not know that L was going through his pain and simply needed to process it in a different way. I also did not know helping someone else was the best way to get out of my pain.

The breakup broke my heart. I felt empty inside, and writing got me through that time – writing was cathartic, day by day, hour by hour, and even minute by minute.

Day 4

Okay. I made it through another night. So far, so good. I felt sad this morning but last night, I thought about it. I am just going to continue thinking he will figure things out and decide to have a relationship with me. That way, I can get through the next few months. If it turns out that in the next few months (or whenever) he does not come back to me, I will have at least gotten through the worst time.

If we can get through the next few months without speaking to each other, I know it will eventually be okay. Remember, that which does not kill us makes us stronger. I feel stronger than before.

I want him back, but I want him on my terms, the terms of a proper, decent relationship.

I am sad and lonely. I still love him, but it is getting easier. I hope he is healing.

Day 5

I finished reading the book Starting Over. *I think I am doing okay, especially considering I think that we started ending things in June. But I know that he feels conflicted because he did not grieve his marriage ending.*

Now is the time for him to do just that. He is single and can get counselling and get in touch with his feelings.

Grieving will not be easy for him. I must understand this may take a year, but I don't want it to. I want him to come around in three months. I want us to get together and start over together.

I must accept this situation. I know that I need to have an open heart to be able to get on with my life and move on to another relationship. I would love to have a relationship with L; a healthy, giving, loving relationship, when he is ready. I don't know if he will ever be ready, so I don't want to get my hopes up.

We are soulmates. We are perfect for each other.

Sadly, the realistic part of me knows I will be alone. I will get on with my life. I will not distrust men, but at the same time, I will not be rushing into anything. I have learned the essence of a relationship is not about sex. I am not going to be having sex with anyone. I don't want to share myself with anyone that way right now.

I want L. I cannot help it. I love him so much it hurts. He must be so conflicted right now. He needs to grieve his marriage to be able to move on. It sounds so easy, but I know it is the most difficult thing to do.

I don't want to imagine my life without him. And I hope he is feeling the same way. He loves me very much. It has been a very painful breakup because we both want to be together. The bottom line is we want to be together, and he is doing what he needs to for that to happen. I love him.

One week and counting...

My family and I celebrated Thanksgiving today. We had a good time, and as always, enjoyed a delicious turkey dinner.

Again, I am very sad. Last night I spoke to J (my lovely ex-fiancé). I told him about what happened with L and me. He was great. He really helped me. He told me he and I would not have stayed together because he really was not committed to the relationship. He had a major problem with commitment due to his family situation and his upbringing. He thinks it was excellent that we got counselling together before the wedding. I agree.

He worked on things and was single for a long time. And then he found the woman he wants to marry, and they want to have children together. I was so happy to hear this news! He is just the type of guy who should be a dad. And it sounds like he is in a much better place emotionally now.

I hope that L gets help. There are some things I need and will insist on if we do get together again (or regardless, in my next relationship):

1) *Be romantic with me – don't just appreciate my romantic overtures, please occasionally be romantic yourself.*
2) *Enjoy spending time with me. If you cannot just hang out with me, it is not going to work.*
3) *Introduce me to your family – as your girlfriend. Be happy I am this person in your life.*
4) *Keep pictures of me and us around your place.*
5) *Cook dinner for me occasionally, and yes, breakfast too!*
6) *Be creative – don't just leave that up to me.*
7) *You must have a wacky, dry, crazy sense of humour.*
8) *You MUST love dogs. You MUST be able to deal with me stopping to speak to any dog, at any time. I will ask about the dog, its name, and maybe its history. The cuter the dog, the more information I will want to find out. Do not roll your eyes and think I am strange or weird.*
9) *Understand my happy dance. When I am happy, I tend to wiggle around. It has been a LONG time since I have done my happy dance.*

I truly think that we will be back together. I have faith. Regardless of what happens, I will be stronger for getting through this terrible time.

One week and one day

Got through another brutal day. I find the best way to get through things is to talk to people. I don't have to talk about L necessarily, I just need to talk. To listen to someone else. To hear their voice. Not just the voices on TV.

Really? This surprised me – the writing does not indicate that I wanted to listen to anyone; I wanted to talk about how much pain I was in, and how L caused it. If I had stepped outside of myself (even for one moment) and thought about how L felt (not just my warped perception of his feelings), I would have been thinking about someone else – not just myself.

I have learned so much in the past. I know that I should have done things differently, but I can't live my life with should-haves. That is not going to help me at all.

If he wanted to leave me, he would have done that a long time ago. We are crazy about each other.

We live so close to each other that it is unbelievable that we have not seen each other even in passing. I think that this is good because it means that we are taking time away from each other. Obviously, this is what is meant to be. Otherwise, we likely would have bumped into each other.

If it means we are over, I must adjust to that. This time is the make-or-break for us. We have finished seeing each other, but this does not necessarily mean we have finished loving each other. Because we have not. I am sure he is just as sad and lonely as I am. I am not the only one who has lost a best friend.

Still Tuesday – Still broken-hearted

Still love him. Feel better right now, but still missing him. I love him so much, and I want him to be happy. Fortunately, or unfortunately,

I want him to choose to be happy with me. I really cannot see him deciding to live with me in the next few months. That is one thing that I have learned – don't be in a rush. Don't rush into things. If you want to move in with me and start living together, that means you love me enough to want to live with me, but do you love me enough to marry me? But why does marriage mean so much to me? Sometimes I just want that fairy tale wedding, but maybe I don't know what I want. I just want a happy relationship with someone who respects and loves me. And who wants to and can commit to me. I don't think that is too much to ask of someone.

Wednesday. Halfway through the week.

Wow. Clearly, I loved L, or at least I believed what I felt was love. When I look back, I realize there were elements of honesty and truth in my thoughts, but most of the time was spent wallowing in my pain. By choosing to focus solely on myself, I caused my pain and suffering. Even though I said I hoped L was getting better, I could never admit it was not only him who needed fixing.

I was so busy figuring out what I wanted but did not take responsibility and acknowledge a relationship is made up of two people – it's not just about blaming one person.

Reading this over so many years later, I feel sorry for that young person. She was lamenting so deeply; it is no wonder that things could not work out. Or rather, it is no wonder things worked out the way they did.

I had a counselling session today. I am learning I am my own person, and that I am nice to be around.

It was not particularly pleasant for anyone to be around someone so obsessed and moping around. Looking back, I am disappointed and embarrassed by my obsession. Every word I wrote was about L. I wrote about strategies of how to see him again and then of how messed up he was. I was all over the map. One foot in, one foot out – and the rest of me was just completely screwed up.

I hope L knows I am still waiting for him. I love him so much it is crazy. I want to wait around, but I don't want to.

I love L and I don't want to lose him. But I must take a risk. I cried during counselling. She thinks I am private and don't share my grief with people. I told her the truth. That I have cried at least once every day since the whole thing happened. I just want time to go by as quickly as possible. But then, if I wish for things to pass by quickly, I will miss out on the good times that are available to me right now.

Oh girl! A glimmer of hope and sanity and then more obsessive thoughts.

I am just so sad. I love L so much.

I am trying to deal with things, but everything just seems to be about loving him.

I am thinking back over the past little while. And I am going to try to concentrate on the times that he pissed me off and I did not feel good. But then I start to think about how good I felt sometimes and then that's all I can think of. I hate this. I want to be able to grieve the relationship, but I want to just be able to get through the near future. I just want to be able to survive. I do not want to meet anyone or go out with anyone right now. Even as a friend. Because I would just be talking about L and how much I love him. And then I would be comparing everything that L does or would do with what the guy is doing.

I don't want to date anyone. Ever. But I don't want to be alone. But I don't want to be with anyone else. I just want him. We have the same sense of humour. We have the same philosophies. We share the same values. We share so much together. I love him so much. I don't like feeling this way. I just wish someone would give me an answer. Tell me what to do. Because I don't know. I don't know if I should wait. Which essentially, I am doing because I am not ready to move on and date anyone else. But then I don't know what he is going to do. I love thinking happy thoughts about L and me. He is my soul mate.

If only I could go back to this young woman and help her. But I would never go back. That young woman would drive me crazy. I shake my head – to think I believed I had it all figured out and that the problems were with him. Sigh.

During that time, sleep meant the opportunity to escape the pain of my life. I would shut my eyes, and for a minute, or ten, or, if I was lucky, maybe for a whole night, I would leave the sadness behind.

October 11

Could not get out of bed this morning. Just could not. I felt so comfortable and safe in my bed.

I don't have anything really to do today or reason to leave my apartment, which is a bad thing in itself. Maybe I will go for a walk later, or something like that. Maybe there is a reason to go out.

I knew I should not even consider getting involved with anyone in the next little while. But I will easily get involved with L when and if he wants to.

Seriously?! I question if I was listening to myself – where in the world was my self-respect? Why was it okay to drop everything just because L was ready? What about me? Was I ready?

Please get better soon, L. I am here for you. You know that. You know my heart is yours. You know I love you. I know, though, love is not enough. You must love yourself and deal with all your issues.

That hurts. "You have to love yourself." I was clearly so focused on L's need to love himself that I completely disregarded the need to love myself. I just kept on blaming him and promising him (at least in my writing) that everything would be perfect if he would just get help.

Still October 11

I am so scared of being alone without L. I love him so much and it hurts terribly that we cannot see each other. I really hope this turns out how I want it to. Otherwise, I am being cheated out of a wonderful friendship with someone very dear to me.

It all came down to my fear of being alone. I was terrified I would never meet anyone or that no one would ever love me, and I would be alone. These extreme thoughts forced me to settle for a man who did not love me in the way I clearly believed I deserved to be loved.

I must keep busy. My goal is to get through each hour.

I don't want to drive anywhere because I am always narrowly avoiding a car accident because of slowing down to check out cars to see if L is driving. I am a wreck. My friends never know how to speak to me and think I am still depressed. But I know I am not. I am just sad. And why can't I be sad? I am grieving the end of a strong loving relationship. I deserve to be sad.

Unfortunately, I was NOT grieving the end of a strong, loving relationship. I was grieving the end of a really messed-up relationship predicated on an overwhelming fear of being alone. There was nothing strong about that.

I am still so sad. It feels like the only thing I can do is sit here and write. And cry. It just feels like this feeling will never go away. And I know it will. I just must accept this new reality.

I don't know what else to do right now. I don't want to appreciate the beauty of the world around me right now. I am sad. I am lonely. I am close to being depressed.

Still the same October 11 day

During this time, I was trying to sell the dining room set that I had bought with J and the sofa that had meant so much to me. I was moving into a much smaller place and could not bring the furniture with me.

I think it is strange the way things go in my mind. Sometimes it seems completely bleak, and nothing is ever going to be better. But then sometimes I feel like I know where things are going, and I should be happy things are going to end up in a good way. Because I know that they will end up the way they should end up. I understand the concept of seizing your destiny, but I guess that sometimes you must accept that what is happening is your destiny.

I am confident L and I are going to be together by the end of the year. I just know it.

Yes, you can seize your own destiny, but you can also bulldoze your way right through someone else's reality. I was very good at doing that and it is what I continued to do. With each lament and melancholy "I love L" I was completely ignoring and neglecting his feelings. I was simply superimposing my thoughts and wishes on him. I truly had no idea what he was thinking, but in my head, he *must* have been feeling and thinking the way I believed.

October 12 – Just about the two-week mark

I guess it is getting easier, although it really does not feel that way. They say time heals all wounds. But I know the truth – you cannot just say those words and not do any grief work. It's not that simple.

I am going to try to deal with things the best way I can. I have not exactly figured out the plan. I seem to go through different phases, which I suppose is normal and natural. At times I think the world is completely over because I am not with L anymore. But then I think that there is a better relationship waiting for me right around the corner. But then, I think, is that person L?

I need to know how to go about getting through life and becoming ready to move on. How can I drive without scanning the road for his car? How can I stop thinking about him and the good times we had together? Should I just dwell on the negative stuff? Should I just give up and know he is not coming back to me? Because if he could tell me that definitively, I would deal with it much better than how I am doing now.

It is difficult holding on when you are not sure if you should just give up entirely. Something tells me to keep holding on because I know being with L is the relationship for me. I know it is right. If there was something (ANYTHING) wrong with it apart from his issues, it would be a lot easier to let it go. But how can I let go of something that is so right?

How about the fact I could not just accept what had happened or who he was at the time? How about the fact I was obsessing over him and had a warped interpretation of love? How about my complete lack of self-awareness, respect, and esteem?

I just must accept that yes, I will be happy again. It feels strange to say that because I feel so desolate and sad now. But I know this too shall pass. I must accept I will be happy again. I should not make it look like a death sentence. I should be excited I can start over. I get another chance at having a loving, healthy relationship. I would love to have this relationship with L, but unfortunately, I just need to accept things are the way they are and be ready to move on. I am taking the risk that he is going to come back to me.

I remember someone told me time apart is time wasted. But the thing is that for me, absence makes the heart grow fonder. For four years, L and I have been part of each other's lives almost every day.

I know everyone says just move on. But how can I move on from someone who is my true soul mate? I love him. I would make him dinner, I would massage his feet, I would clean his kitchen, I would do his laundry. I would do everything for him.

I wrote about these things like they are badges of honour. Massage his feet? Clean his kitchen? Did I really believe I was not good enough unless I had the love of this man? That I had to sacrifice my time, energy, and self-respect to get it?

I love him so much. And I always will. I told him that I am not waiting for him, but I think he knows the truth. The truth is I am waiting for him to figure things out. I would not have put this much effort into the relationship if I did not think it would be worth it.

Still October 12

Had a delicious dinner at a friend's place. My hair looked awesome, and I felt quite attractive in my jeans, boots, and my sexy shirt. I felt good.

Went to the concert at Barrymore's where we got a seat to the side in the front. I had to go to the bathroom. I did not know where the ladies' room was, so I just followed the stairs up until the men's room. A man looked at me and told me, "That is not the ladies' room," and I just kind of laughed and said, "You say that like I should know where it is!" He took my hand and held it all the way to the ladies' room. I smiled and said, "I have never been escorted to the ladies' room before, thank you." It was a simple, harmless exchange, but it felt so nice and made me feel attractive.

I never saw the guy again, but it still meant something to me. I think I have figured out what I want. I want someone in my life who wants me the same amount in his life. It would be lovely if that could be L. But if it is not with him, I will wait for someone else to come along.

Tomorrow I am going to the new apartment. It feels like something is going to happen. Not exactly sure what, but something.

October 13 – exactly two weeks after we broke up

I have decided that I must find a normal, 9-5 job again. I will find that job. I don't want to let life just pass me by. I know how precious it is.

I cannot believe that it has come to this. I mean, why would two people who are perfect for each other not *be together? Because one of them is so messed up. I just wish counselling could take him to the point where he realizes that he wants me in his life. But I do wish that I was not fighting this so hard.*

I must surrender to the world around me.

Yes, I needed to surrender, and years later, I would read Byron Katie's *Loving What Is*, which speaks about the importance of surrendering and not arguing with reality.

Yet another example of feeling conflicts in myself because I was not living in congruence with my values.

October 15 – 2 weeks and a day

Yesterday, I drove to the bookstore in the market. I was standing at an intersection in the market and saw L's car. He was driving alone. I saw him and yelled out for him. I even ran down the street. I sat down on a bench and tried to catch my breath. It was a visceral experience. He did not see me. He was probably just changing lanes.

I was relieved to see that he is okay and driving around the market. It was something we enjoy doing together. It means that he is facing his sadness and dealing with it.

Tonight, when I got home, I checked my messages. L had called. Yes. That's right. L. I could not believe it. He left a message at 7:30 pm and I called him back at 9:30 pm. It was the typical L and Tonya conversation. He was calling about coming over and returning my vacuum cleaner.

We talked on the phone for a few minutes, and then he came over. When he got off the elevator, I had that same feeling as when you are meeting someone at the airport who you have not seen for years. It was crazy. I had butterflies in my stomach.

When he came over, we hugged. It felt wonderful, like home.

I showed him my TV in the bedroom, and we had some cookies and milk. We talked. We really missed each other. We kissed and made out and stuff. But I made sure this was not sex-with-your-ex because I know it is not over. He is working hard at reading the book about starting out on your own again. And he is listening and learning. I am so proud of him. I think we both feel that we want to get on with things, but he has got to figure things out.

He said that "when the phone doesn't ring, it's me." I love that Jimmy Buffet reference. Maybe I can listen to some Jimmy now. I couldn't even handle that before.

We told each other we never want to go through that again. I think I am right. We are going to be back together within the next three months. If he continues with his therapy and reading and feeling, he should be okay. And there was a big moment last night when he admitted that he wished he had started getting better earlier. Because he knows what a great thing we have together.

I am not waiting for him. If someone comes along and wants to take me out to dinner, I am not going to say no. I want to date and meet different people. When L figures things out enough to start up a healthy positive relationship with me, we'll cross that bridge then.

I was so determined that everything was because of L and mistakenly believed the success of the relationship was dependent on L and his counselling experience. I completely ignored my own obsessive personality and serious lack of self-respect.

October 16 – Tuesday

I got through the day without writing about L.

I really love L, but there are going to be some changes if we start a relationship together. Like keeping my picture up in his apartment when his mother visits.

We had been together for almost two years, and he had not yet introduced me to his mother as his girlfriend and before her visits, he removed all photographic evidence of me. I felt so small and insignificant, but I still accepted his unacceptable behaviour.

October 19

Perspective is a powerful gift. I just saw an Oprah segment about Matty and his mother. They live together alone in a basement apartment. They both use wheelchairs and he has written a book called Heartsongs. *I don't think I can ever feel sorry for myself again like I have been doing for the past two weeks. I simply cannot.*

I was beginning to realize I needed to stop feeling sorry for myself and start thinking about others.

October 21

We ended things three weeks ago today. I still cry at times, like yesterday. It was such a beautiful day, I just wanted to spend it with him.

I tried calling L. Yes, a huge moment of weakness. I called him but kept hanging up before he could see I called. I even called him on his cell phone. I just wanted to spend some time with him.

I must find a job. I must find something in my life. As Viktor Frankl says, "We can choose our attitudes." We cannot choose our situations, but we can certainly choose our attitudes in these situations.

Instead of feeling like I am hopeless and a loser for not doing anything today, I am going to reframe it as a time for me to really get better.

I finished reading The Road Less Travelled. *I learned some more valuable lessons, one of which is, if I truly love L, then I honestly want the best for him. Regardless of whether it is me or not, if I love him, then I need to accept whatever he does or however long it takes him to decide.*

It is difficult realizing I don't have any control over what is going on.

I am not going to make a guy the centre of my life again. I know I did it all the time with him. Because I thought if I was not available to him, he may decide to find someone else who was and that he does not want to be with me anymore.

And that is crap. If I don't want to go out with him for some reason or another, I don't have to. Just because two people are in a relationship together, it does not mean they have to do everything together or be together all the time. I have learned that when you start developing a healthy attitude towards being in a relationship, you realize that by spending time apart, you can have a better time when you are together.

I have learned my relationship with L (if it does start over) needs to have some basic guidelines. More importantly, I must follow them. I can't make him the centre of my universe. I want to have a healthy relationship. I am even considering counselling as a proactive measure. I have been reading a lot in the past month and want to make some changes in the relationship — if it works out that way.

I spent so much time and energy focused on the idea of closure, and what L wanted. I had no self-esteem. I never thought about myself and what I wanted. I never thought about boundaries.

October 23

It has been a day. I spent it feeling sorry for myself. I threw myself down on the ground and cried like a baby. I wailed and sobbed. I felt terrible, but I know crying is an important and healthy part of healing.

Writing and talking to people and reading have totally saved me. They have been my complete salvation. I know this for sure. I need to respect and honour my feelings. Allow myself to feel this way, which hopefully will make things a little bit better.

I remember what they said (I think in The Sound of Music*), "When God closes a door, He always opens a window." I need to recognize and use that window wisely.*

I know that in a year, this will all be over. I know I will have moved on – in some way. I have no idea where I will be in one year, or even if I will be around. I have no clue. But for now, my heart is hurting more than I thought possible. I think this may be what a broken heart feels like. Before, I thought it hurt after I left The Architect, but then I had a dream and knew from that point on I had done the right thing. And after I ended things with J, I was able to get on with my life because I was in love with L, and I was finally going out with the right guy for me.

This hurts so much. There are times where I can see myself with someone else, in a completely different relationship. I really do have those times. But not today. I just wanted to talk to him. I miss him being part of my life. Even if that part was just a few days a week, he played a huge role in my life. I mean, L is the only person I can call just to tell him how much I love baby orangutans. I must accept that, for now, this is the way it is.

When I look back at the warning signs, I am sad. I wonder how different my life would have turned out had I paid attention to them much earlier.

October 24

Today my counsellor asked if I wanted to be married. I am quite scared of it possibly not working out and getting a divorce. I have seen what that looks like, and I have seen L going through the whole thing, and I would not want either of us to have to go through that. Marriage? I think I would be a great wife. I would be supportive and loving and kind.

It's funny. When my counsellor asked if I wanted to get married, it came down to what L wanted. That was such a red flag for my personal messed-upped ness, and one that I either blatantly ignored or simply did not recognize.

If she asks me if I want children, I am going to have to say no. But I am kind of sitting on the fence. When a person is sitting on the fence about something that significant, it just makes sense to either take more time if needed, or to just accept this is the way it is. Why should a child have to pay for my lack of commitment? I don't think that is right. I don't begrudge anyone for having a child, but I don't believe I want one for myself. I know that Mom always says it is different when they are your own. But as I don't want any of my own in the first place, that whole argument holds no water for me.

But marriage? I am not averse to the idea. I would have to make sure all the levels of commitment are met before I even talk about marriage. How would that be? You just get back together and immediately start talking about marriage?

Is L the right person for me? Am I the right person for him? Only time will tell. But I think that to make that kind of decision, we need to spend some time together seriously. After he is well and healthy.

HE is well and healthy? How healthy could anyone be if they just went from one intense relationship to another? Especially with another person who was equally screwed up? Why could I never acknowledge I was not well or healthy? Why was it always about him?

October 25

I have decided that yes, I do want to get married. I mean, I want to share my life with someone, so why not marriage? It is not the whole purpose of being with L, but I am scared of divorce. Or being a widow for that matter. But I guess when a relationship ends, it ultimately feels the same way. But divorce gets legal and very messy.

And so, it started – the seeds of my wedding obsession were planted. Over the years those seeds created the most insipid weed that wrapped around my future, squeezing it so tightly it almost crushed me.

Still October 25

I spent the most amazing afternoon at the bookstore. I discovered some things about myself that I simply cannot deny – even though they are not the nicest things to acknowledge about oneself.

I learned that I love too much. And the reason that I love too much is that I am fearful of being rejected and abandoned. I give way too much of myself to my partner and I don't give enough to myself.

What a destructive pattern I have been living. It's all about self-esteem – or rather, the lack of it. It is hard to believe that pretty much everything in life comes down to that. Amazing the amount of power that has over someone's life.

I am going to enrich my life in a lot of different ways. I want to explore life and continue learning. I want to make sure I am not going to sabotage my next relationship with all the destructive patterns I have been living.

I also read a book about second marriages. How to Make Your Second Marriage a First-Class Success. *Yes, I do want to get married. Yes, I do want that commitment, but only with the right person. If L is not the right person, that is all there is to it. The right person is out there somewhere.*

Really? If L is not the right person – clearly, I was obsessed with L being my future. Why else would I be reading that book about second marriages?

I have not been the victim in this situation. When it comes to reacting and behaving in certain inappropriate ways, I have been by-the-book. I am learning I loved him far too much, and when it comes down to it, it was not really love. It was just fear. And now I am living what I was so fearful of in the first place, and why I was not able to talk about the stuff that was disturbing me.

I never knew where I was in his life or what he was thinking. This is extremely important. If you love me, you must let me know. If you are feeling confused or hurt or angry about something, you must let me know this too. I am not a mind reader.

I usually feel good around him. The one thing that really upset me was the whole Mother thing. I don't like the idea of her hating me. She must know her son chose to start opening up to me and chose to leave his marriage on his own. I was the one telling him he needed to talk to his wife.

I want her to understand he just was not happy in his marriage, and yes, there were some things that he should have done differently.

It took me a while to figure it out, but I learned it was himself that he was not happy with. Sadly, his marriage was the collateral damage.

I am not averse to getting back together with him, while he gets therapy. But there would have to be some type of commitment made to the relationship.

This commitment would also take some will power and self-respect on my part. Before, I never wanted to leave him because I never knew if he would still be there for me. But now, after he finishes up with his recovery work, he will be making that commitment. We will be together or we won't.

I just cannot get over what I learned. Another way that I loved him too much is by smothering him. I never did anything with my friends without feeling guilty for not being with him. Because remember, if I am not with him, how do I know he is going to be there when I get back? And if I can go off and do something, he can too, and what if he does not come back at all? Those were my two issues.

Those same issues have plagued my whole life.

Next time, it is going to be different. I am not going to devote my time to him. We are not going to spend hours on the phone. We will talk for a few minutes, but if he wants to talk, he can make the effort to see me, which means he comes over to my *house, and I will* not *give him the keys to my place.*

It helped we were neighbours at this time. We did not have to drive anywhere to see each other. We just walked from one apartment building to the other.

And when I am at his place, I will not do the dishes for him anymore. I will not go out of my way to do his laundry for him. I will not do anything like that.

It seemed like I had to physically convince myself to *not* do these types of things for him, which felt kind of counter intuitive for someone in a relationship. Correction – a healthy relationship. In a healthy relationship a person will do things for their partner because they want to and because they know they would appreciate it. It is not a healthy reason to do things for your partner so they feel they need you and won't leave you.

October 26

I have spent the evening reading that Living Together for Dummies *book. I believe I can commit to wanting to marry someone. At this point in my life, all things being equal, it would be ideal for it to be L.*

I was also thinking about what I want in a relationship – whether it is with L or someone else:

1) *I want support – when I open up to you and tell you something that is upsetting me in my life, I want you to support me. That means listening and if I ask for your advice, please give it to me. It also means picking me up if I need a lift or driving me somewhere if I need to go. I will reciprocate. If you need something, I will do my best to help you. I will not necessarily compromise my personal happiness or expectations or anything like that. But I will make sure I support you.*

2) *I want companionship. I want to be able to know that on most nights, we will be able to snuggle on the couch and watch TV or just hang out together and know that we are both content with the situation. That neither of us is sitting there wishing they were somewhere else with someone else.*

3) *I want friendship. I want to be your friend, and I want you to be mine. We don't have to be best friends. But we should be very close.*

4) *I want effort. Being in a relationship does not come easy. But it is mature and respectful to show the other person that you honestly do love them and that you want to be with them.*

5) *I have been with other people. I have experienced other relationships. I know why they ended, and I don't want to go down that path again. I want to make a commitment to this relationship and to you. And I want the same thing from you. If you are not ready to make this commitment or if you feel you will never be ready to make it with me then fine. Let's be honest with each other and move on.*

6) *I would like to receive flowers and cards occasionally. I want you to be aware of how special the relationship is. You can be*

assured that you will receive things from me — to show you I care, and because I simply cannot pass over something that I think you would like. But I am not going to go overboard again. No more Beatles videos that you never watch, no more microwave ovens, and no more (or at least fewer) bags of licorice.

I was always with the lists! When I read this, I feel squeamish. Clearly, I had (and still have) a control issue. I say still because when I read this writing, I recognize I still have trouble letting go of control in my life.

October 28

I go through ups and downs. Thankfully, a lot more ups than downs of late. But still, every once in a while, it catches up to me and I get sad.

I don't know what to do or think or say. I just need to listen to my gut feeling that L and I are going to be together. That ultimately has not changed.

October 29

It has been one month since we had The Talk. I have decided the only time I am allowing myself to think about L is during my shower. I heard about that idea before, but now I think I am at the point where I am okay to do it.

October 30

I am kind of mixed up. L called me last night.

We decided that, yes, we would both like to be with each other. Right now, he is not able to be with me. I told him there is a difference between wanting to be with someone and being able to be with that person.

I told him when we do start being together again, it will be different. We agree that when we are both completely into the relationship, it is very good between us.

But the fact is that I am still very open to dating. And maybe right now, I am more open than I thought about possibly finding someone new. The conversation was great, until we started discussing my feelings. I wanted to know if he feels the same way I do.

Because I am serious, I don't want to waste my time with someone who thinks I am the wrong person for him. When I asked if he wanted to be with me, he told me he doesn't want to be a loner leading a solitary life. That response did not fill me with confidence.

November 1

I made it to November. Good for me. And I am much better than I have been for the past month.

I found another Barbara De Angelis book; Secrets About Men Every Women Should Know. *At first, I thought, how would she know? She is not a man.*

Somehow, she knows.

I read it and could not believe how much I mothered L. It was awful. She talks about how one partner always does everything for the other, and she calls that "filling in the blanks." I completely filled in all *the blanks. I want to get to the point where both of us can be in the relationship, not just me.*

We have not ended things; we are taking a break from each other. Not sure if we will be able to get back together, but for now, we are taking a break from the relationship. I think it is great.

I would love him to call this weekend, but I need to just sit back and try to get over the relationship and most importantly, find a job.

I am going to find a job that gives me an annual salary of $40,000 and benefits. People say I should be in sales, that I would be great at it. But I guess I need to find the right fit, not to mention someone willing to take a chance on me.

I thought I had it all figured out. I had a timeline, a schedule, for goodness' sake. Did I really believe we were taking a break? No, I knew we were most definitely not taking a break. It was absolutely a breakup. In typical Tonya-fashion I did not even let that happen – I simply bulldozed my way through his feelings and reality.

I wish I could have recognized the very high level of insecurity I was clearly demonstrating. I wonder if it would have ultimately made a difference. Would I have been able to fix myself?

It is doubtful. With my stubborn streak and addictive personality traits, I would have mostly likely continued the self-sabotaging thoughts and behaviours. Those were my specialties. I remembered Rick, my boss, who had told me that I had an addictive personality. Perhaps I should have listened to him.

November 4

I have no idea of what is happening. All I know is L loves me and wants to be with me.

We talked on the phone for an hour, and he invited me for dinner. We talked and laughed and told each other how much we missed each other. I told him that forty percent of the problems in the relationship were because of me and my behaviour and attitudes and beliefs and the things that I did wrong.

Wow. How generous. I took some responsibility for the problems in our relationship, but where in the world did that figure come from?

That was the first time since September that I have been over to his place. The picture of me is still up on the windowsill, and so is the card I gave him for Rosh Hashanah. That is nice. It means he has not forgotten about me entirely. I like this. Of course, if you look around my place, you will see no pictures of him because I needed to remove all evidence of him to make it through the past month without crying all the time.

When I said goodbye to him tonight, I just said, "I'll see you." He said, "Yes." And that was it.

So, unfortunately, again, I must leave it up to him. I don't know how long it will take for things to get fixed. I have never in my life been as attracted to ANYONE as I am to him. I like to entertain the idea that maybe one day I will be, but seriously, we have some intense chemistry. Today was lovely. We just lay together, talking. Then he was just holding me. It was beautiful. I am going to remember that feeling for a long time.

He loves me, and I was very proud of myself because I made one hundred percent sure that I did not mother him, either in word or action. I was careful to make sure I did not do anything for him. I thanked him for dinner and I did not pour the juice for him. I did not do the dishes for him. And last night, I just brought the ice cream dishes back to the kitchen. I did not even run them under water. You go, girl!

Really? Apparently, I could not be considerate and thoughtful because it meant that I was mothering him. What kind of reasoning was that?

I am looking forward to this week because I am focusing my job search on finding something in the sales world. I am sure I can do it!

I was hell bent on getting a job in sales but was not in any way cut out for sales. I am not and have never been competitive or interested in reaching sales quotas.

The BEAR called!!!!!!!!!!!!!!!!!!

Yep, that's right. The radio station, The Bear, called me, the completely non-competitive person with no real sales experience for an interview. (I may not have had the sales experience, but I knew how to create a resume that highlighted my strengths and showed off the value I would add to the sales team.)

November 6

I called L and we went shopping together so I could find something to wear to the interview. Ugh. Honestly, what a pathetic excuse. I felt so desperate for any excuse or reason to see him. Besides, I had lost some weight after we broke up and needed a new interview outfit.

Just off the phone with L. He says he cannot afford the money to get counselling. It meant a lot that he was getting counselling and now it feels hopeless. He has not read the books. I just don't get it. Last time I was speaking to him, it was okay. Now I feel so nauseous. I just want to be held. I just want to have someone who loves me put their arms around me. I feel like I have been kicked in the stomach. Everyone knows that going for counseling is exactly what he needs right now. I need to make sure he keeps going. I don't know what it is going to take, but I must make sure that he gets better. Even for his own sake. This is so important. I will pay for him if I need to.

ACK!!!!!!!!!! Years later I would learn about the different stages of change. I realized in retrospect that L was not in the right place to make changes in his life. Forcing him to do it because I needed him to change was not an effective, intelligent, or even compassionate thing to do. I completely disregarded what was right for him because I was so focused on my messed-up feelings.

My interview with The BEAR was successful. I met the team and afterwards, sent out thank-you cards. They called for a second interview.

I was excited and spent time thinking about my transferable skills, strengths, and weaknesses.

November 12

It looks like it is decidedly ON with L. I am not sure what exactly is going on but suffice to say that he loves me, and I love him. But I am still learning.

Yesterday I went down to the War Memorial to commemorate Remembrance Day, and it was freezing. After the service had wrapped up, there was a parade of veterans. During the parade I was clapping, along with the rest of the crowd. I secured eye contact with one of the vets and mouthed the words "thank you." He smiled and we both had tears in our eyes. It was a very special moment for me. I think I will remember it for the rest of my life. It was wonderful.

L called and left a message saying that he was going to be getting some pizza for dinner, and did I want to join him?

I called him back and we talked. I told him about the second interview coming up on Wednesday. He is very proud of me and wants me to do well. I don't imagine he will call and wish me luck. But that is okay, because I have that feeling within myself. I don't need it from him.

We are getting together for a date on Saturday night. I have discovered things are fine if I stop analyzing everything and just spend time enjoying things. While I was saying goodbye, he brought up the date next Saturday. He said maybe we could rent a movie. And then he officially invited me to spend the night. You see, if I don't do everything for him, he will suggest things to do as well. For instance, I said, "Let's get together next Saturday." He said, "Where would you like to go?" I said, "It is up to you." I like that.

It seems that I WAS getting it. I was learning to let go of control. Or so I thought – or really wanted to believe.

In December of 2001, L and I got back together. I also got a new job – not the Bear sales job. Instead, I got an opportunity to work as a recruitment officer/information officer with a local youth program.

It was a federally-funded program and I got to meet some amazing people (teachers and students from all over the country and even the world). I did some interesting things, like traveling to different parts of the province, working on the website, and creating newsletters.

It also gave me the chance to practice my French because the majority of my colleagues were francophone and the meetings were mostly held in French.

But I had a very difficult time witnessing the flagrant abuse of Canadian taxpayers' money. The program took place in a renovated school, with dorms and a cafeteria. The executive director lived in a house right beside the school and had the program chef prepare her meals. She would take time off in the middle of the day to get her hair done, and after she got a teacup Yorkshire terrier, she would bring her to work with her. When the dog needed to be walked or toileted, she would ask members of staff to do this task. When the dog went to the bathroom in each of the offices, we had to have the carpets cleaned by a professional cleaning company.

When the staff was told the program was in danger of closing, we were tasked to come up with ways to reduce expenses. I immediately suggested selling the house and having the chef stop delivering dinners to the ED and her relatives. Not surprisingly, these suggestions were not met with much support from the higher-ups.

Unbeknownst to me, my values conflicted with what was happening at work. After working there for more than two years, I was put on probation, which was completely unacceptable. I was getting loads of positive feedback from everyone I dealt with – people appreciated my efficiency, honesty, and professionalism; everyone, that is, except for senior management.

One day, I was getting ready for work, when the entire left side of my body just shut down. It went numb. Somehow, I found my way to the doctor, who determined it was not a stroke, but rather my body's reaction to the stress I was feeling from work. The doctor wrote me a note, and for the third time in just a few years, I was leaving work because of stress.

The first time I had to take stress leave I was working at the tech firm, and I was young (only 24) and did not know how to trust myself and my intuition. I should have listened. I felt bullied, and my relationship with my boss was extremely detrimental to my self-esteem.

Then, one day in December 1996 I got a doctor's note and took some time off because of stress.

During my stress leave, I took the time to regroup and tried to rebuild my confidence. Our parents were in Arizona at the time and my sisters were concerned about my employment status, I would just tell them "The universe will provide," which was not the response they wanted to hear. It made no sense to them. But I just felt that something would work out – and it did.

I know I have said this before, but I have to say it again – I am so blessed. I have everything – my incredible husband, my wonderful dog, my loving family and dearest friends... the list could go on and on...you know me, I have to share!

Chapter 32

The Moving Years

"Brilliant Disguise"

I worked at the youth program until 2004. During that time, I moved in and out of a triplex apartment. Although I loved the unit, my downstairs neighbour was a smoker, and the smoke infiltrated my apartment. My clothes smelled of smoke, and I was always sick to my stomach. Sadly, it was not a good fit. Solution? I left the smoky triplex and moved in with L. We started living together in a new place – a one-bedroom, ground-floor apartment.

We decided to share expenses so he could leave the graphics company and return to school. He was taking a one-year cabinet-making course at the local college.

Although there were some not-so-great times, it was mostly fun. We were in love and, most importantly, committed to the relationship.

But the ground floor posed some major problems, including sharing the bedroom wall with the garbage and recycling room. Once a week, we were brutally awoken by the waste removal guys – not a calm way to start the day.

I managed to get the landlord to find another tenant, so we could break our lease and move to a reasonably-priced two-bedroom, one-and-a-half-bathroom apartment on the top floor of a nearby building.

I had even started swimming in the apartment pool five times a week. I felt fantastic about that – mainly because it was the first time I was committed to exercising.

However, low self-esteem continued to fuel my unhealthy relationship with L and directed my focus to the idea of a wedding. I believed (and again obsessed about) that if L loved me, that I was good enough, he would want to marry me. This thought process was very destructive.

Hmm – after much thought, well, way too much thought, I have finally figured things out regarding the whole L wedding situation.

I am asking him to make this huge decision, and I am basically motivated by my selfish desires. When I think about marriage, my honest answer is to focus on the wedding, which is NOT a reason to get married. And I don't think the right motivation to get married is that someone has proposed to you. I mean, look at J. That was a seriously romantic proposal. He thought about it for a while and wanted to do it. He was thinking how much he would like to have the whole deal. The girlfriend/wife, the dog, the nice apartment. And if I had not stopped him, we would probably be doing that just now. But it would not be real.

And that is the one thing I can say about this relationship with L. It is real. Sometimes too real, like when he does not say the ideal thing I want to hear. But I must remind myself that honesty is much more important than the instant gratification kick of hearing, "Will you marry me?"

I think a part of what I feel is the pressure from other people. I am not strong enough to say, "Wait a minute, it is entirely okay to be living with someone." I mean, it is not like it is new to me. I lived with The Architect, and I lived with J. I am a serial monogamist, going from one long-term relationship to another. But now I have settled down. I don't want anyone else, but nothing is perfect. I want L to do more around the house – do the dishes more often and put up the pictures leaning against the wall that drive me crazy. Seriously, though, if this is the worst thing to complain about, I think I am pretty lucky.

L has often said he wants to spend his life with me but does not want to get married. I want to understand what he means when he says he does not believe in marriage. I mean, it exists. Whether or not you had a satisfying or successful one, how can you blame the whole institution of marriage? You can't. You know that some marriages last, and the partners are happy. My parents have been married for over 50 years and would both do it again.

I think that L has certainly learned things from how his first marriage ended. I hate how I feel so good inside when I hear him accidentally say, "first marriage." I resent the way society makes you feel like a second-class citizen if you are not married. And don't even get me started on the single status in our world. Ugh. Everyone wants to be with someone so badly they will settle for just about anyone. And then people can get into a situation that could end badly for them (for example, young women or men getting involved with abusive partners), and they may not be able to stand up for themselves.

I am always overly focused on what other people think of me as if they would view me as more acceptable if I had a husband. That is ridiculous. I am happy being me, which would not change if I was married. I would still look in the mirror and think that I am not the best-looking woman in the world.

That was a hard piece for me to read so many years later. I was embarrassed by my thoughts, and my lack of self-esteem made me bulldoze my way through the relationship. I knew it was wrong to insist on getting married, but I would not accept L's maritally-adjacent commitment. Everything had to be my way – even though, clearly, I knew my way was not the healthy way.

I think this really is as good as it gets – an incredible marriage that is worth every ounce of heartache I have experienced in my life, a loving and supportive family, a wonderful canine companion, a warm and cozy home, fulfilling work with lovely colleagues, exceptionally fantastic friendships, all built on a foundation of everyone's good health. I cannot imagine anything better.

Chapter 33

The Obsessing Years

"Two for the Road"

In 2003 after much research and reflection, I went back to school. I took the online Career Development Practitioner (CDP) program at Conestoga College. During my course, I met a schoolmate living in Waterloo, a city about an eight-hour drive from Ottawa. She suggested I move down to that area to work at the recruiting company where she had completed her work placement.

I could not figure out my next step in Ottawa. I felt lost and terrified of the future. I had tried to find a job but didn't know what I wanted to do or even what I could do. I networked with my school colleagues. I was desperate. Moving to Waterloo would mean leaving our friends and family, and most significantly, L would have to leave his job of about three years at the furniture company and find a job in a new city. I was scared to leave Ottawa, especially because I loved our new apartment. But I was also afraid to stay. I felt moving was my only option, and of course, in typical Tonya-fashion, I bulldozed.

We spent six months in Kitchener (we did not even live in the swankier area of Waterloo). We would always describe that time as six months of our lives we would never get back, with the only positive being close to our friends S and P. They and their family made the experience much better for us.

From the moment we moved there, we both wanted to go home. L was the one who was truly vocal about it. I just kept my feelings bottled up and tried to keep looking at the positive – we were close to our friends, and we had found a gorgeous apartment.

L found a few jobs while we were there. His organizational skills and determination were inspiring and an excellent example of how to look for a job effectively.

While he was determined to find a job, I was determined to find a wedding dress. Like so many times in my life, I became obsessed. I was so miserable at work that I would spend my lunchtimes wedding dress shopping.

We were not engaged.

We were not even really talking about a wedding. Rather, we had talked ad nauseam about *marriage*. Because even though L had no intention of getting married again, I was thinking about it all the time. Dreaming about a wedding gave me something positive to focus on during a tough time in my professional life. Finally, near the end of our Kitchener stint, I found a beautiful white dress. Strapless with buttons down the back, it was very simple and everything I wanted. (My first wedding dress was a princess style, the second was a sheath style, and now this strapless number.) One thing was for sure – I have great taste in wedding dresses.

I was embarrassed to admit I hated Kitchener and wanted to go back to Ottawa – I felt like a failure; like I could not handle it. Thankfully, L had stayed in contact with his past employer, and they welcomed him back to the team.

My work experience in Kitchener was not particularly positive – certainly not in the beginning. It was a very poor fit at the recruiting agency, and the day I told them I was leaving was the same day the boss told me, "It was just not working out." It was a brutal, but necessary, day.

Necessary because although we had made plans to move back home, we still needed to get through one more month in the Kitchener-Waterloo area. My leaving would be considered a lay-off and meant that I would be eligible to collect Employment Insurance.

After grieving the loss of my job (which I hated, but also hated the feeling of being told that I was not good enough), I immediately got in touch with the CDP program administration at Conestoga College. They needed to fill a maternity leave in Career Development Services. When they hired me, and I began my job there, I felt at home at work for the first time.

I worked with a professional and compassionate team and finally reached my goal "to be treated with dignity, respect, and integrity" at work, which created a new feeling: for the first time in my life, I felt that nothing was wrong with me. I was in my element – for a month.

We left Kitchener in November and gratefully accepted my sister's invitation to move in with her. She lived in a house in a quiet little area about an hour south of Ottawa, and it was just the place we needed. We were close to family and friends again.

I thought I would take a proactive approach to the whole unemployment experience, so I went to the nearest town to start the process. Everything was going well until I realized we needed to be living in Ottawa. The days were getting shorter, and I did not welcome the prospect of driving in the dark for an hour each way.

Something had to give. We searched for an apartment in Ottawa and found the cheapest one available. We called it the "shitty apartment," and it was made much worse by the loud and annoying guy living in the apartment right above us. L would go off to work and I would try to find a job. Or rather, I would try to avoid going out in the middle of winter. The internet made the latter possible.

It also made it possible for me to waste time not looking for a job and focus instead on getting married, even though we were still not engaged.

It hurts me beyond words how much L does not want to marry me. Why is he unable to take our relationship to the next level? It's like he believes we are already at the highest level, but, for me, marriage (and marrying someone, rather than being engaged or living with them) is taking the relationship to another wonderful level. It is a place two people want to travel to and explore together.

I feel like this complete loser just because I want to marry my boyfriend. Society tells me to get married. When you grow up, you get married – it's how it works.

So, I don't know what to do. Do we continue to get counselling together? Do I get counselling alone to overcome this want, desire, need? Is it me? Is it my fault – my problem? Am I the loser? What's wrong with me? I don't want a huge wedding, a knockout ring, or anything like that. I want pleasant and simple and loving. That's all.

But of course, I am not getting what I want. And I think I may be able to deal with all of this better if only I could understand L's point of view.

But I can't, and I cry because he doesn't understand how much it hurts me. Why is it so important not to marry me?

Sigh. I am getting the "this relationship is ending" vibe. L knows how important it is to me to get married. But I know how important it is for him not to be married. I don't believe there is a middle ground in between.

I don't think I can attribute this feeling to my PMS. Instead, I believe that the look of boredom in L's eyes makes me feel this way.

I am on the verge of tears right now. I don't know what to do. If we broke up, I would have nothing. My heart hurts just thinking about it. I don't know. I must prepare to live by myself again. But absolutely everything reminds me of us. Everything.

He just doesn't get it. We just talked about it and he said, "Pick a date." But he doesn't understand how important it is to me that he wants to marry me as much as I want to marry him.

Yet only a day after I wrote that, I texted him, telling him I love him and didn't want to lose what we have. He replied, saying he loves me too, but I should accept his feelings towards marriage when we do it.

On Wednesday evening, we had another talk. This time it was positive and pleasant. There was no eye rolling or tortured looks.

After a day of reflecting and thinking, I realized he was right. The relationship will not change. I will be as crazy and neurotic as always. It is just a piece of paper.

We talked yet again and we agreed. We would be getting married.

The ceremony and ritual are important to me. So, I am going to look after the ceremony and L will take care of the reception part.

Later that month, on January 23, 2005, L and I took a day trip to Old Montreal. It was a brutally cold Sunday, and we held hands as we walked briskly down rue St. Paul. We ducked into the Hotel Nelligan to get out of the cold. We found a private booth and ordered some warm beverages. He put his arm around me and said, "You know what would be nice? If we could stay the night." "Oh yes," I agreed wholeheartedly. But I had a career development conference the next day, so I needed to be home. He continued, "You know what would be nice? If we could come back one day and stay at the hotel." Once again, I agreed with that idea. Montreal was one of our favourite places, and the Hotel Nelligan is gorgeous. Finally, he said, "You know what would be nice? If you would be my wife." He reached into his pocket and pulled out a burgundy velvet ring box.

I wanted L to want to marry me so badly. He did not have to give me a ring – he could have MacGyvered a ring out of an old twist tie, and it wouldn't have mattered. It may have meant more – that he truly wanted to marry me.

It wasn't supposed to happen this way. Over the years, I have seen many friends get engaged and married. But it was never a struggle for them. It was natural and organic, and both people were excited to get married and spend their lives together. Why was everything a struggle for me?

Looking back, I realize L needed to do things his way and in his time frame. But I did not let that happen. Instead, I just insisted and would never accept his wishes or choices.

My lack of security trumped everything.

Our wedding planning was stressful and filled with arguments and disagreements, which happens when one person doesn't want to get married, and the other feels she is not good enough until she *is* married.

There was no dearth of things to argue about from what type of wedding to the guest list, photographer, food, music, cake – we argued about pretty much everything.

That should have been a big clue. But of course, in my Tonya way, I completely ignored everything and focused instead on the *idea* of the wedding. The wedding would make me just as good as everyone else. The wedding, in my mind, meant I would finally be good enough.

L and I were married on June 5, 2005, and if we had to do it all over again, I would do it completely differently.

I am such a different woman from that time. I had NO self-esteem or self-confidence. All I wanted more than anything in the world was to be married to L. It did not matter if it was not what he wanted. I did. Typically, I got my way.

From the moment he proposed, I was focused (or rather, obsessed) on the wedding planning. Finally, we agreed on a dessert reception as we could not afford a typical sit-down dinner. That was my idea as I LOVE dessert.

One would think that someone so obsessed with a wedding would have written more about the whole event. But I was busy bulldozing my way through our whole relationship, not just the wedding thing; I did not have time to write.

We both hated living in that apartment. Again, in typical Tonya fashion, I was very vocal about it. I wanted to find a house and move out. But even then, house prices were high, and we didn't have a lot of money. Luckily, one of my co-workers was selling her house. She insisted we check it out, and because it was something we could afford, it just made sense to make an offer on it.

In 2003, we had put an offer on The Death House in a tiny town south of Ottawa. It was full of asbestos, and fortunately, finances fell through. We didn't get the house. Of course, at the time, it was devastating. In my head, a place meant that a wedding would be next, which meant I would finally be enough.

Two years after The Death House, we bought my co-worker's house and moved in less than a month after we got married.

I love our house.
I love imagining how it is going to look when
we finish it – all our design ideas and everything. For now,
I enjoy the love that makes this house such a happy home.

Chapter 34

The Puppy Years

"We Take Care of Our Own"

2005 was a busy year. We got married, celebrated our birthdays, and bought and moved into our house – all within six weeks. Then, a few months later, in September, we found our canine soul mate who would eventually complete our little family.

It probably sounds strange to say the worst environmental and governmental disaster in American history (up to that point) affected my life in Canada in the most positive way.

Apart from watching the horror unfold on CNN, donating to the Red Cross and being absolutely sickened by George W. Bush and his cronies, I remained relatively unaffected by Hurricane Katrina.

My calm changed after I saw how the hurricane and governmental policies devastated and destroyed pets and animals. I could not sit back and watch pets lose their owners and end up in animal shelters. I wanted to do something; I wanted to help the Cajun Canines. But how could one woman in Ottawa help a dog in New Orleans?

I was right. I could do nothing, but, as a dog lover, I knew there were puppies right here in Ottawa who needed help. I left synagogue Saturday afternoon, the 17th of September, and headed to the local animal shelter. When I got back into my car, I felt depressed at the pathetic condition of the building and the entire situation. I tried calling my friends, but no one was around. I tried calling L at work but his voice mail picked up.

I arrived back home determined to visit BARK (Bytown Association of Rescued Kanines), one of my favourite websites. Immediately, I saw they had rescued four puppies and their mother from the side of a highway in Québec. Over the next hour, I had a phone interview with the BARK lady, called the foster family, and arranged to go over and meet Puppy #2. It was a bit gray and misty outside, but I was excited. What was I going to see?

When I walked into the house, a black and white and brown creature greeted me with a wagging tail and deep brown eyes. At the time, I did not know this little being would change my life forever.

The timeline went like this. I met and fell in love with him. I came home, told my husband all about him and showed him some pictures. My husband declared this beautiful pup had a "freakishly large cartoon head" but agreed to go and meet him the next day, which we did. After another few days of discussing the pros and cons, we decided to get him.

Or rather, I decided to get him. As with almost every other decision in my life, it came down to money. Long story short – I had forgotten I owed my parents some money from the wedding. They suggested I should not be getting a dog if I could not even pay them back. This remark upset me tremendously, and I resented that I was not making enough money to get this dog.

I wrestled with the idea over the next two days. As usual, I obsessed – should we get the dog? *Could* we get him? Is this a good idea? All my husband had said to me was that if I could get up in the morning and take the dog for a walk, I could get him. *Well*, I thought, *I can do this.*

I paid my parents back and determined money would not stop me. I phoned Puppy #2's foster mother and arranged to pick him up on the following Wednesday night. Beforehand, I stopped at a friend's place to get the extra-large crate she offered me. Without her gift, I doubt whether I would have been able to afford to get one, so it meant a lot to me. Her black German Shephard had been a big boy, so I was sure my little guy would fit.

Wednesday, September 21, I picked him up. They had named him Popper, but I knew that had to change. There he was – long and lanky, with black lab ears, a collie snout, the colours of a border collie, and eventually, the frame of a greyhound. What a delicious mix!

A good-natured puppy, he had no problem getting into the car for the drive home with me. We arrived home, and when I brought him inside, we discovered that he did not know how to climb up and down stairs. He would just whine when we called him to come down. Within 20 minutes of us demonstrating on our bellies how to climb up and down, he had mastered the stairs. He was nervous and had an accident in the house. I had stocked up on cleaning supplies on the way to pick him up, so I cleaned up and immediately put him outside in the yard.

Minutes later, when I went out to watch him, I gasped in horror as I quickly realized he could escape under the unfenced bottom of the deck. I ran after him, calling him by his new name "Lloyd." Nothing. He ran faster than me (and with his greyhound legs I am amazed I even caught him), and thankfully, he darted through a neighbour's open gate into their fully-fenced yard. We knew Lloyd could not be outside alone until we secured the yard. I was in no shape to chase after him again.

The next night, Lloyd had an accident in the same place as the first night, as it was the spot he had marked. L and I learned to identify the timing – between 9:30 pm and 10:00 pm, he would go to the dining room and pee. Thankfully, we figured out that if we could take him outside between those times, he would not pee in the house. Things were just fine until I was away Friday night, and L did not get up and take him out. So around 10:00 pm, Lloyd peed in the same place.

I arrived home to find an irritated husband, angry at having had to clean up after the puppy. But I also arrived home to a wonderful and loving little creature. Not a bad deal for me!

The first month was challenging on many levels. L and I had decided that because we were crating Lloyd during the day while we were at work, we wanted him to sleep in our room at night. I did not sleep that first night. Anxious thoughts overwhelmed me – was this a mistake? Am I ever going to sleep again? Is this the end of my marriage? What is going to happen? Thoughts were racing around my head. It was terrible.

It was impossible to sleep for the rest of the month. I was unwittingly experiencing what I perceive new parents go through when they bring their newborn home from the hospital. I would get up in the middle of the night to take Lloyd out to pee. I would then watch him as he ran around at 2:00 in the morning, jumping and playing, which was cute, though hard to deal with as I had to get up early for work.

One day, Lloyd ate several bristles from the barbeque brush hanging from the BBQ. He vomited six times. I called the vet for guidance, and they suggested I should monitor him and bring him in if he got worse. I cried in L's arms. "If something happens to this little fella," I said, "I will never ever get another pet." We had only had him for a few weeks, but I was already more attached to him than I thought possible.

After we adopted Lloyd, I realized some things don't matter. I remember taking a shower and not being bothered by my body for the first time in a couple of years. Usually, I would look down and see the extra pounds resulting from too many carbohydrates. Now I had a puppy that looked to me for guidance, discipline, food, toileting, and mostly, love. For the first time in my life, I was a real dog mom and found myself caring for another living creature.

The night after the day of vomiting, Lloyd demanded I get up in the very early morning hours. I was tired and wanted to sleep. It was a Saturday, and I was so angry with him, I yelled at him and felt like shaking him. I wanted nothing more to do with him. I had thoughts of taking him back to BARK and saying, "Sorry, this just isn't working out." I was worried about my marriage of only three months. We felt the stress and frustration of not sleeping. L was resentful, and I was sad and angry. It was a very unpleasant combination.

L went to work that day, not sure if there was going to be a puppy to come home to at the end of the day. I thought about everything that morning. I did not want to be one of those people who returns a dog because he did not match our lifestyle. I was determined to change my relationship with Lloyd. So, in a pivotal moment, I went to the library and borrowed all the books about dog training. I came back that day with toys for Lloyd and, best of all, a new attitude. I was already learning. I immersed myself in those books for the next few weeks and paid attention to what the authors were saying.

It was interesting timing. A month after he joined our family – a month of very little sleep and raised tempers – he decided for us. One night at bedtime, he crawled into his crate. From then on, that's where he slept, and we were able to sleep in our bed too.

The first year with Lloyd was a challenge. We took him to the dog park, but he did not listen to us after he ran off. Our mutual lack of confidence in each other made us decide not to take him back to the park. Instead, we would take him for walks around the block, regardless of the weather or anything else. Both L and I had fallen madly in love with Lloyd.

Had a delicious dinner... fun... Lloyd... music...
family... life... Bruce Springsteen's birthday...
love... health... happiness.
Joy.
Contentedness.
Everything.

Chapter 35

The Troubled Years

"Two Faces"

2005 was also filled with many disagreements that kept rearing their ugly heads. We were constantly arguing about the same things – money, taking out the garbage, my insecurity, the black cloud that seemed to follow L wherever he went. We were seeing a counsellor, but it was not an effective solution. Our problems ran much deeper, and they all began and ended with my lack of self-esteem. Yet again, I could see myself in so many songs on Springsteen's *Tunnel of Love* album.

In October of 2005 I bought a car but quickly realized that I needed a better-paying job to afford it – especially after the car dealership and the sales representative were dishonest and lied on the application regarding my finances. Ultimately, the car cost me just over $34,000 and was the source of much agitation and anger.

I found a new job recruiting healthcare professionals to work on military bases across Canada. At that job, I met a lot of nice people, a few who are still in my world so many years later.

In May of 2007, I had to attend a work conference. I didn't want to go. I wanted to stay with L and Lloyd. But I had to go, so I decided to take a positive attitude towards the whole thing. I chose to change my perspective from one of negativity to one of positivity, looking forward with excitement, not dread.

The conference gave me the opportunity to meet an interesting and attractive man. He asked me out for dinner. I called L to tell him I would be going for dinner with this guy. L was fine with it.

A red flag – my husband did not seem to care that I was going out with another man.

There was chemistry between this man and me; he made me feel great. We flirted in person and over email. He had an apartment in Ottawa. I called him Random Guy because occasionally, completely randomly, he would reach out to me, and when I got an email from him, I felt wonderful – sexy and wanted.

I felt none of these things with my husband.

Random Guy was fun, sexy, and nice. He would ask to get together, and I would always ask L if I could meet him. L always said, "Sure." RG and I would meet for dinner sometimes; other times, he would ask me out for coffee, and L would always say, "Yes."

Another red flag – things are not going right when you prefer to spend more time with another man than your own husband.

L and I went out for dinner to celebrate our second wedding anniversary. It was a lovely restaurant on the water, but our inability to enjoy one another's company ruined the dinner. To get through the evening, we had to role-play (not sexy role-playing). We had to pretend to be other people because we could not get along.

Early in 2007, I suggested we visit Halifax and the Cabot Trail in Nova Scotia. A friend of mine lived there, and we also had close friends who stayed in a cottage in a small Nova Scotia town and invited us to stay there.

At first, L's response was no because we had no money. Then, later that same week, I received my tax refund. Suddenly we had the money and could afford the trip. But it turned out that L did not want to take time off work. He had vacation time but refused to spend it on taking a vacation. He preferred to bank the time off just in case he needed it.

So, after much arguing, I gave in. I planned my own vacation, and in the middle of July, I was at the airport waiting for my evening flight to Halifax. I looked around and saw someone I had not seen in years. It was J with his wife and their daughter.

On the flight, I sat right in front of him. It was a bumpy ride, filled with turbulence, but somehow, I felt safe.

I spent the week actively getting out of my comfort zone. I stayed alone at my friend's place (they would be returning a few days later); I rented a car, drove around the Cabot Trail, and went whale-watching in a Zodiac (one of those fast-moving inflatable boats). I even started eating tomatoes – for the first time in 37 years. It was a life-changing week.

During my vacation, L stayed home and built a shed in the backyard. Each night I would call, and he would give me an update on his progress. I loved that. It gave him an opportunity to design and build something that would make a difference in our lives.

I returned home, and within the week, we were on our way to Québec City for a week. Earlier that summer, L had met a client at work who had a condo for rent in Old Québec. As luck would have it, the rental was vacant. A close friend of mine came to our house to take care of Lloyd, and off we went.

The condo was gorgeous and in an excellent location. We had a wonderful time, laughing a lot and enjoying some delicious food. We really connected on that trip – at least the beginning. An angry fight revolving around a friend's birthday – a lack of communication – marred the end. L refused to listen to my thoughts about the birthday (about when to leave so we could get there in time), and I refused to listen to him. We both dug our heels in – just like every other time.

A few months later, at work, we were given performance bonuses; I was singled out by NOT getting one, as my boss did not like me. Fortunately, that gave me the impetus to do something about the situation. I called my friends and got the word out – I missed working with young people and wanted to return to that world.

My friend CA heaved a sigh of relief. "It's about time – you need to be working with kids again." She was a member of a networking group and immediately sent me a job posting for an Employment Consultant at a local youth employment centre.

I had initially applied for a job with the centre the year before. But, at that time, there was nothing available.

Timing is everything. I got the job this time and started working with young people again.

Finally, I was working at my dream job – and yet was still desperately unhappy.

I sought help from Dr. Phil's *Relationship Rescue* book. I answered the questions and took a hard look at what was happening in our marriage.

- My worst trait is judging. When I feel that L is being inconsiderate, I get mean
- I like independence, but at the same time, I am afraid of losing love

- I can't forgive unfaithfulness, yet I am scared of being unfaithful
- Fear motivates me. I am motivated in life by a fear of loss. Fear of losing love
- I would give anything if my partner showed some initiative. I would be more lovable if I were nicer. Sometimes at night, I cry. It hurts me when my partner says means things to me. I feel most lonely when I am with L
- I dream of having a love where we see eye to eye
- If only I had not married L. I regret getting married. If only we could talk
- I am quick to blame and slow to forgive. I need to forgive myself for getting married to L. Our relationship did not start in a good way
- I feel that my partner doesn't listen to me
- I feel picked on and put down – not respected
- I have a hard time sharing my feelings and communicating
- I feel out of control in life
- I feel criticized by my partner
- I imagine/dream/fantasize about not being in this relationship
- He takes, I give
- I am angry at L and want him to feel the same hurt that I do
- I feel trapped
- It feels like there is no desire between us
- He doesn't let me be myself
- Our marriage is messed up
- He doesn't let me into his heart
- I am feeling neglected and judged by my partner
- It feels like I will never feel secure with my partner
- I chose my partner based on a lack of self-esteem
- All my friends have healthier relationships than me
- I am not hopeful about our future. I don't feel appreciated. I don't feel like L would be there for me. I feel misunderstood
- I am not treated with respect and dignity

- We don't have fun together
- I don't feel loved
- My partner doesn't enjoy spending time with me
- We don't enjoy spending time with each other
- I believe my partner will eventually leave me
- I feel I can't be honest with my partner
- I get emotional support from other people
- My partner doesn't care when I am upset or sad
- Our relationship is not important enough to L
- L does not want to hear my stories
- I don't look forward to being with my partner
- I don't feel protected or needed by L

I was able to dig inside myself. When I wrote down my emotional needs, I could see my husband was not meeting them. I knew I needed to:

- be able to share my innermost thoughts
- know that my partner shares my world emotionally
- be loved
- be told I am the one for him
- know he wants to be married to me
- know he loves me
- be supported emotionally
- be told I am attractive and loved
- be heard and listened to
- feel respected and appreciated
- be able to identify and reach goals together
- know the relationship will not be over if there are arguments or conflicts
- be able to discuss our finances
- be hugged and cuddled
- be touched, to share kisses

I was able to figure out my fears: loss, being rejected, not being good enough, being abandoned.

In November of 2007, I was in pain, so I did the only thing I could do; I wrote.

I feel incredibly alone right now. I just want and need someone to hold me tight and tell me everything is going to be fine. I want that person to be L, but he is not here.

He is downstairs in the living room, and even though he hears me crying, he still chooses to stay there.

I don't want to keep living like this, alone with someone. I want to live with a husband who is optimistic about life and does not measure everything by money. I have never had money, but I always got by. Never truly wanted for anything. Sure, there have been lots of things I would like to have in my life, but I don't have the money for them. And that is okay with me.

And I am the one who, on a salary of $26,000, took my $6,000 debt to nothing. So, I know I can do it in a way that I can still live —because we can and need to have a life.

I feel lost right now. I have this marriage I am part of, yet somehow, I feel like a lost soul. My heart hurts, and I am in so much pain.

He believes I have changed. Have I? Probably, because I am not in that same messed-up state of mind. I attract positive and happy people in my life. I must decide what I want to do and then commit to it.

But back to being lost — and alone.

Being married was the hardest thing I had ever done and if I could do it again, I would not get married. Or at least not when and how we did.

I was finally able to figure out the problem with our marriage. I felt stupid because it was that way for ages, and it took me so long to figure it out; there was a lack of emotional intimacy.

Thinking back on it, I recognized I was able to have that with Random Guy. He was in touch with his feelings, and we could talk about anything and everything, and I never felt judged. Or stupid. Or bad. We could talk about things on an intellectual and emotional level – something I could never do with L.

L and I agreed we would continue counselling for six more months. I hoped our marriage would not end. I wanted to share both emotional *and* physical intimacies with L. I told him I would not be seeing Random Guy anymore. When I told him I needed and craved intimacy from him, he said he did not know if he could give it to me.

I finally figured out what we needed to address, but we still needed to figure out how to do it.

We tried to fix things. We communicated and laughed and spent a wonderful Valentine's Day together. I even emailed him about how important our time together was to me.

Dear L,

A few weeks ago, I said that Random Guy was the first man that I had met who I was attracted to, was attracted to me, who I liked, and who liked me as a person.

I was wrong.

That man is not Random Guy. That man is you.

Last night was incredible. I was surprised and delighted and happy to see those beautiful roses. They are so very special. I knew that you would have a reason for giving me three. I knew that you would have thought about things.

I loved how you said that one just looked too lonely. And that you wanted to have the three roses to represent our little family. They are simply stunning, and I truly loved the wine glasses filled with Hershey kisses — and how thoughtful you are to choose the ones with almonds because you know I like them. That meant and means so much to me.

The calmness and peace of our evening together touched me as we shared our thoughts and ideas.

I like how we took things easy, and I did not get worked up about everything being perfect. I loved the fire — so cozy and wonderful. I loved snuggling up on the sofa and watching LOST with my favourite fella and my favourite canine. That is the kind of moment that I would like to last forever.

I loved how everything gelled last night. It made me realize we can have that on a regular basis. And the cards, oh, L, the cards, I love them. I love what you feel, and I feel the same way.

Being held by you (like last night in the living room) is the safest place in the world for me. We fit. You are the sexiest man — I love those lips, the softness and sensitivity in your eyes, your hands, and your fingers, the way they hold mine, and when you hug me.

Another part of last night that I loved was brief yet meaningful. It was our discussion of the words we would use to describe ourselves. I have been thinking of yours — yearning. I like it because it means you are looking to improve your life, so I hope that one day you reach a state of contentedness and are no longer yearning.

And when I think of you as a person, I love that person — a helpful, supportive, thoughtful, caring, friendly, silly, loving, passionate, logical, detail-oriented, careful, precise, and wonderful person. You have all of these qualities and so much more.

So, thank you, L. Thank you for being that man for me.

Love,
Tonya

Unfortunately, this emotional intimacy did not remain between us. I recognized that it was essential, and sadly, it was not there.

At least not with L.

In early 2008, I met a man and felt an instant connection with him. I could experience with him everything I was missing with L. At the time, I had no idea how he felt towards me, but I knew I felt good each time we were together. I was physically attracted to him, but much more importantly, I was emotionally attracted to him.

He had a positive attitude, and it was a pleasure being around him. He demonstrated initiative and was helpful and kind to everyone he met, including me.

That summer, L and I spent a month renovating our house. We were able to fix up the house, but by that point, the marriage was a completely different story. We were in deep trouble. A crisis was looming.

"Adult life is dealing with an enormous amount of questions that don't have answers"
~ Bruce Springsteen

Chapter 36

The Reckoning Years

"Thunder Road"

In 2008, I finally felt enough. Just like Mary in "Thunder Road," I was not a beauty, but I was okay. Of course, I was – I was married.

When I was much younger, desperately lonely and feeling so hideously ugly, those lyrics made all the difference to me. Springsteen writes about Mary, who is clearly not a beauty, but that is okay with him. That's all I wanted.

I dreamed of finding a guy who thought the same thing about me. My earliest memories of myself are having a big nose, crooked teeth, and glasses. Add to that a diagnosis of mild scoliosis, bad skin, and very fine, shapeless hair. As if all that was not bad enough, throw into the mix a pair of huge glasses popular in the '80s.

Friends were the one thing I had. Maybe it was my self-deprecating sense of humour, my attitude towards treating people nicely, or just that I am a sensitive person. I was never one of the "cool" kids – but we all knew those people. I was someone who could drift in and out of a bunch of different cliques. Not good-looking enough to be a threat to other girls, but nice enough to be treated with respect. At least by most people – but not by T.

T was my bully. She made my life hell when I was 12 years old. She threatened and harassed me, making it difficult for me to go to school without being terrified. She was physically bigger than me and seemed to enjoy picking on people who were nice, kind, and sensitive. Maybe she thought we were easy targets because we did not have strong self-esteem. We would not stand up to her, so she could easily continue to push us around.

I don't remember when, why, or how it stopped, but it finally did. Sadly, the damage was done, and the effects were long-lasting. In 2012, one of T's other victims wrote a FB post about being bullied. T responded by apologizing to her. I took the opportunity to send her a private message myself:

Hi T, It's Tonya. The last time we saw each other was at Zellers on Sparks Street. You were shopping, and I was working there while going to university.

I just wanted to thank you so much for your post on D's wall in the discussion of bullying. I have painful memories of being bullied by you; like D, it changed me. I was intimidated and scared to go to school.

The difference between bullying in our time and what is happening now is that now bullying is all-encompassing. Growing up, we did not have the technology and the social media the kids do today. I think it must be unbelievably horrible to be scared all the time, to feel ugly and abused – and never to be able to escape. When I read your post, I started to cry. It really means so much to me. And you know what? No one is immune from bullying on some level or another. Everyone bullied a small group of our classmates.

In retrospect, you probably picked on me to bully because I was sensitive and emotional, and had no self-confidence or self-esteem.

But T, my entire life has led me to become the person I am – someone motivated to help young people develop self-esteem. In my job, I see many people, and every young person I meet and work with is affected by who I am today. I am the person I am today because of who I was.

I know what it felt like to feel like a complete loser, helpless and hopeless. So, I thank you again, T. Your reply to D was courageous, and I support you wholeheartedly. I really appreciate it – more than I can tell you.

Take care, Tonya

Her response was unbelievable to me:

Hi Tonya, the only thing that comes to mind after reading your email is WOW! I really didn't realize how many people I bullied, and it pains me to find out how many people were affected by my stupidity. I must admit that it has also affected me throughout my life. I cannot believe that I had that in me, and I still reflect on the pain (mental and physical) that I inflicted on so many. Tonya, your email means so much to me; thank you for finding it in your heart to forgive me.

She had no idea that she even bullied me. I carried this terrifying experience through my entire life, and the person responsible for the effects of her actions did not even have a clue of what she did to me.

The bullying did not end with T. I learned that teachers can be bullies too.

There was one assignment I had to write in Grade 9. I wrote about the Benetton Bunch (a group of kids who I thought seemed to believe they were better than everyone else). I don't remember the point of the assignment, but I distinctly remember the feeling I had when I was hauled into Ms. R's office and reamed out. "Toe-nya (she consistently mispronounced my name – a huge sign of disrespect in my eyes). I don't remember her words, but I felt the shame, palpable for many years afterwards.

I never fit in with those attractive people. My two classmates, C and B, were cute with blond hair and blue eyes. I liked them both – they were sweet. C bought me a Springsteen book as a goodbye gift. However, they should have been my nemesis as I had a HUGE crush on D, who had no interest in me and adored my blonde classmates.

The best times in my adolescence were the opportunities to feel somewhat attractive. A drama geek, I was in the role of Stage Manager for one class production. For some reason, that role called for me to be somewhat scantily clad. I relished the chance to feel attractive.

Another time, a group presentation involved me wearing a sexy black dress my mom had worn in her younger days. Again, it felt great to be attractive. I was tall but never stood up straight. My mom and I had plenty of discussions (a polite way of putting it – she nagged me) about my posture. My mom and two sisters are shorter than I am, and I always considered them cute and petite. I described myself as an Amazon – when actually I was just taller than the rest of my family members.

So, to hear Bruce Springsteen write about a girl who wasn't a beauty – well, that was me. And somehow, she could find happiness because someone thought she was good enough for him.

It took me many years and a tremendous amount of heartbreak to feel good enough. For a man, and for me.

Sometimes I feel deliciously non-cookie-cutter-like.

Chapter 37

The Hold Me Tight Years

"Tunnel of Love"

L and I continued to get counselling throughout our entire married life to that point. We would go to our sessions, then come home and fight. And fight. And argue. And yell. And treat each other badly. And then I would cry. It was just like the song "Tunnel of Love"; when the lights went out at night, it was not just the two of us. My low self-esteem was ever-present.

I would drive to work dreaming about starting my life over. I wanted to be single and able to date that special guy I had become friends with recently. My commutes were filled with tears and feelings of desperation. I was a wreck.

I knew I had to do something. On Thursday, September 11, I went to the counsellor alone. She suggested I take my time and not jump into anything. Right. Like that would ever happen.

L came home after work and was sorting his clothes for laundry. I had written down my thoughts. I summoned up all my courage and told him that this relationship was not working for me, and I needed to get out of it.

He reacted with disbelief and then extreme anger. He demanded to know if there was another man. "No," I said, "There isn't."

There was.

This new man loved spending time with me, and I finally felt like someone cared. Back in 2008, I believed I finally had the self-confidence that had eluded me until then. Once again, I was wrong.

When I was in my 20s and pretty much 30s, I never had the self-esteem and positive attitude that I do now. And it seems to attract people —my new friend and I are developing a deep friendship. He is a special kind of person and just the kind of man I WISH I had met while in my 20s. Perhaps I would have spent less money on therapy had I met him instead of the schmucks I encountered on a regular basis.

The 20s are just the right decade for exploring — life, work, people, yourself. I had the opportunity to do just those things during that time. Looking back, the "dates" and the relationships were all worth it. From the Gut Guy to the Horny TV Producer Guy and everyone in between. If not for them, I would have fewer funny stories to share, and perhaps I would not have learned that this type of behaviour is unacceptable.

Maybe I would have kept on accepting this behaviour and just chalking it up to boys being boys. Maybe I would never have learned you can both love and trust men. My husband has taught me that not all men are jerks, and that sometimes I can be a jerk myself.

In retrospect, I cannot believe some of the things I wrote. Clearly, I was completely uninhibited, and I just told it like I saw it. Or felt it. Or wanted it to be.

I wish I could look back and not have any regrets. But I guess regrets are a natural part of growing up. Maturing has taken a long time, and some would arguably suggest I am not always there. Maturing means delaying instant gratification – a constant struggle for me. Patience and tenacity are not my strengths, but I am getting there.

I hope you realize you are not alone; everyone goes through those times of doubt, complete isolation, and feeling like you will be alone forever. Those times are scary and horrible, and you just want someone to say everything will be all right. More than that, you want someone to tell you HOW it is going to be all right, and when, exactly. But the longer I live, the more I learn that life is not like that.

Life is about growth, change, development, surprises, mystery, and challenges. The decade of the 20s is the ideal time to experience these things. But the joy of life is that it just keeps getting better and better. More mysteries, more challenges, more sadness, and more joy.

I had no idea what kind of sadness I was about to experience. I wrote:

Well, the roller coaster ride that is my life seems to have either slowed down or completely stopped. I am hoping for the latter.

After nine years of internal struggle and conflict, I could deal with it no longer. I told L that I wanted to end the relationship and I was leaving.

My announcement in turn caused him immense suffering and sadness. Our friends were completely there for him, and he spent a lot of time with them just kind of asking "why?" and telling them that he did not know how badly I had been feeling.

I did not leave our marriage to be with the other man, but on the night that I left, he was a safe place to land.

The next morning, I went to work (somehow, I was able to get through the day), and that night, I stayed with our good friends – also a safe place for me. They were as non-judgmental as possible, which was difficult when they did not understand what was going on and did not know what we had been experiencing throughout the marriage.

L was naturally devastated and felt completely ambushed by my decision. But to me, it had been years and years of lacking an emotional connection. I felt I had given everything I had to the marriage. I was exhausted and needed to leave.

I stayed with our friends for the weekend to get some breathing room.

On Sunday, three weeks later, I came back to the house. L and I talked pretty much all day in a HUGE conversation – full of crying, honesty, and talking – about what I had been missing in our relationship for so long.

I realized that, yes, I wanted to stay, and that I had some major things to fix about myself to be a better partner in the relationship.

Even though we had been seeing a counsellor since before we were married and the whole time during the marriage, I agreed to marriage counselling with a different one.

But I knew my heart was not in it.

I tried to figure out a way to tell L definitively I was still leaving so he would stop holding out hope we would get back together.

I suggested we try a "healing separation." I would move out for a designated period, and we would both heal during that time apart.

The new counsellor we met with insisted the intervention would be ineffective if one of the partners was seeing someone else. I knew I wasn't living my truth. I was still seeing that wonderful man. We were spending time together and it felt special. I did not want to give that up.

When the counsellor asked L how he felt about me, he said that he loved me. Then he asked L, "How you would feel if she left?" and he said, "Pissed off." When the counsellor said, "Pissed off is not a primary feeling; what would your primary feeling be?" L said, "Anger." The counsellor said that L clearly could not access his feelings. I had told L the same thing back in 2002 when I told him that he has repressed his feelings so deeply that he cannot access them. I wished I would have listened to myself.

Once again, I knew I was not in the right frame of mind. I still had such desperately low self-esteem – I used to ask him how he could love me if he didn't love himself. I knew later I should have been asking myself the same thing.

I signed a lease for my own apartment. Located just five minutes from my office, I would be able to go home at lunch to take the dog for a walk. I would continue to pay half the house's operational expenses so L could stay in the house. I checked with a mortgage broker to ask about options for him.

When we first talked about separating, L's reaction was to worry about losing the house. He did not want to be 44 years old and living in an apartment. For the first time in a very long time, I was finally being honest with myself; or so I wanted to believe.

When I left L in September, I was determined to start my life over. But it didn't happen that way. I stayed at home still sleeping in the same bed because L needed me; one night he woke up in the middle of the night with an anxiety attack at the idea that soon I wouldn't be there and would not be coming back.

As I had done throughout my life, I poured out my feelings on paper.

I am so very confused. I spent all my younger years wanting to be part of a couple. I wanted to do couple things, to have someone in my life, to have a companion.

Now I have all those things, but I feel like something is missing. Does this mean something is missing in me? Where should I go to find what is missing? All I know is that I cannot have a lover and a husband. It will not work.

The idea of hurting my husband is overpowering. I don't want to hurt him, ever. But at the same time, I don't want to hurt myself, either.

Does staying with my husband and living the life that I have built mean that I will never be truly happy?

Where does happiness come from? Does it come from another person, or within oneself?

How does true happiness manifest itself?

I don't want to be a cliché and fool myself into thinking that the time I spend together with my lover is wonderful and hot. It's not.

It is just refreshing and lovely to have such emotional intimacy with another human being, someone who I happen to be completely attracted to on so many levels.

But this brings me back to the whole point – I don't want to hurt my husband.

I am so confused. I am married but don't want to be. Or do I want to be married but still have the right or freedom to do what I want? Do I deem it appropriate to have an affair, to be cheating on my partner?

Or do I think I really am a serial monogamist and I believe in the concept of polyamory, of having more than one significant partner at a time in my life?

I would like to take hours and hours and sit by the water and just let the thoughts and feelings come pouring out of me. I wonder how many women would want to leave their husbands but stay married because of the financial repercussions, or maybe because they could be worried about destroying their husband's life?

I want to share passionate kisses with my lover. Ideally, it would be nice to have these kisses and emotional intimacy with my partner. Have I given up trying to create that reality so now I am finding it completely with someone else?

I am not a serial monogamist. I am someone who was in a relationship for nine years, three and a half of which we were married. I made those vows in front of God and our family and friends. I broke them.

If I was asked why I had this affair, I would say I felt an emotional connection with a man who is warm, generous, and thoughtful. Everything came naturally for him. He never pretended anything and was always open with his feelings and his passion.

I feel horrible because I am a steadfastly good person. How can I justify cheating on my partner?

I cannot.

My counsellor told me to bury this information. I am going to do that.

I am trying to do so with writing.

What has this experience taught me?

1) *The need to delay gratification and mature.*
2) *The need to make changes within myself instead of attributing everything to my husband.*
3) *That I want to make this relationship, this marriage, work with my husband. I have no interest in anyone else.*
4) *I embarked on this affair when I thought our marriage was over. Then, even after I came back to my husband, I knew*

I was just trying to convince myself I was happy with this decision. The truth was that I was not happy. And for the past nine years I have been living a lie, always trying to convince myself of my happiness and contentedness with my husband. The truth is that oftentimes I have not liked my husband very much, let alone loved him. It was hard for me to love someone who acted as he did towards me. It was hard that whenever I suggested doing or buying something, I was met with, "We don't have the money." All his negative behaviour and thinking made the last almost ten years of my life quite unbearable.

5) *I am never going to tell him. There is nothing to be gained except for the selfish motivation of potentially erasing some of my guilt. But that is a terrible reason for telling someone something that has the potential to devastate him.*

6) *I have learned that I love my husband. I love that he is being attentive. I still need to know that he made an appointment to see a counsellor. Then I will believe that I will never ever go through this lack of connection again.*

7) *That I don't know myself. That you think you know yourself, but you never know how you are going to behave or react to something until you are in the situation. And that you could feel such shame for your behaviour.*

8) *That up until this moment I could not trust myself at all.*

9) *I know there is so much grey in the world. Just because someone is married does not mean they are happily married. Before, I was going to stay and be unhappy. Now I have figured out how to alter my outward manifestation of happiness so I can be happy while still being married to L.*

10) *I never knew I could shower so much and still just not feel clean. I feel sick and dirty and disgusting. I just have to deal with these feelings of shame – ugh.*

L went away for the weekend. I tried to make myself believe I was happy with him. I even broke my lease on the apartment I had rented. I wanted to believe I could move back into the house, and we would be happy.

But I needed L to be with me emotionally. I felt we had never been able to connect on an emotional level. When L returned, we had another conversation, with him asking if we were on track. We talked and I told him I could not continue that way.

I knew it was very hard for him to understand but I had to go with my feelings and my emotions.

I did not want to rush into or out of anything. In September, L had been in such pain it was horrible to see. So, I said that I would stay. But I knew I could not get the happiness I deserved or wanted from him.

I knew L was a wonderful man – he is – just unable to give me what I needed from a relationship. I had to understand I was leaving everything behind. I had no guarantees I would find another partner in life.

But I had to take the risk. Otherwise, I knew I would remain unhappy. The resentment would continue to build, and I may once again want to find solace in the arms of a man who I connected with on an emotional level, which would be disrespectful to everyone.

I rented a room in a home in the city about half an hour from our house and went back to the original rental company and signed yet another lease to start in December.

I felt like I had lied to everyone. I *had* lied to everyone. At Thanksgiving, my family had been so happy to hear we would be staying together. But the last time we were there, everyone noticed I was not myself; I said I was just tired.

That was kind of true. I was tired of struggling for so long. I desperately wanted a relationship that was not full of drama and sadness.

At the end of October in 2008, I needed to take time for myself. I needed to get away from my life and my problems. I took the train to Montreal and stayed the weekend at the Queen Elizabeth Hotel. I was looking forward to having high tea and enjoying the swimming pool and hot tub. Mostly, I was looking forward to leaving behind both the New Guy and my husband.

The weekend did not turn out as I had planned. The hotel staff was on strike, which meant the high tea and the swimming pool would not happen like I had planned – just like our marriage.

I sat in my room and wrote.

This fancy schmancy hotel – had I known that the pool and whirlpool were closed and their room service is on strike – I would not have booked this hotel.

I am trying to decide what to do. Do I even deserve an emotional connection? What is an emotional connection? Feeling at peace with another person, putting their needs above your own, connecting on a spiritual level. Is L in love with the idea of being married, or being married to me?

It feels like he can't reach that part of his soul – and emotions are needed to answer these questions. I remember the time in December of 2007, we went to dinner at a friend's place, and when we got home, we spent the night cuddling and talking. That was an emotional connection. He has proven that he can access anger, but what about all the other emotions? Random Guy – he listened to me and showed me he was listening. It felt like our souls connected. With L, it feels like our souls may never have connected. Do our souls have to connect? Are there relationships where the souls are not connected? Why does it matter to me?

Of course, we have had fun and good times, but because of the lack of emotional connection there has always been an undercurrent of sadness and pain. That is why I always feel so alone.

I didn't realize that I was so starved.

During this time of introspection, I am thinking a lot.

There are so many things I would do differently. Am I – are L and I – destined to not have anything materially? Are we going to struggle through the rest of our lives? Are we really struggling? We would like to have all sorts of things, but the bottom line is that we already do.

I was still confused when I returned home.

I knew I needed to fully leave the relationship and the house to gain clarity. My moving date was December 15.

Halloween came and went. I realized nothing was changing with L. He was still destroyed I had left and he knew I would leave again. Still, he found some resources online about how to create intimacy in a marriage. Nothing changed. I did not know if he read them or just found them. Either way, I was going to return to my life alone.

I went to a friend's house one evening and when I came home, L and I talked yet again. This time, I noticed something different about him. He was not moping around anymore. He told me he knew I was leaving and so he had decided to enjoy the time we had left together instead of being sad. He also said he needed to be able to move on and eventually have a relationship with someone else.

That hurt. I was impressed he had changed his outlook but knowing he would be with someone else was hard for me to take.

We both knew I would be leaving. In November, we celebrated a family birthday. Our hearts were broken at the idea of it being the last family birthday we would celebrate together. L was not just losing me; he was losing my entire family.

I was staying at my rented room, and no one knew or cared if I would be coming home. I could stay out all night. On November 12, I did. New Guy and I were looking forward to that night because we could finally be together without any concerns. I was finally out of our house.

That night was the complete antithesis of anything romantic or sexy, and changed the course of my marriage with L. *The Daily Show* was on in the background and as the opening credits rolled, I realized in that moment I wanted to be with L. I wanted to watch *The Daily Show* with him every night. I did not want to be with anyone else.

But I knew that if I wanted to be with L, I needed him to know what had happened during those months. I felt I needed to put all the cards on the table so he could make an informed decision. I was terrified of the conversation, and with good reason. He was furious I had been with someone else. We were standing in the kitchen during the conversation; he grabbed the overhang of the laminated countertop and yanked it off. He was understandably livid.

I drove to my new counsellor's office, and he gave me the names and contact information for various marriage counsellors. One was available within the week.

Thankfully, L was open to seeing her. We had been talking over the past couple of weeks about how I wanted to be with him. Telling him about the other man was necessary, but I had no idea how he would react, at the time or afterwards. I was so grateful when he said he was open to us meeting with the new marriage counsellor.

We met at her office. It was awkward, but at the same time, it felt right. Expert marriage counselling saved our marriage. After many years of insecurity and power struggles, we found an amazing therapist. Within ten minutes of that first appointment, she had figured us out. She recommended we read two books – *After the Affair* by Janis Spring and *Hold Me Tight* by Sue Johnson.

L bought the *Hold Me Tight* book and brought it home. We read it out loud together, which, combined with marriage counselling, helped us get through that horrible time. L's openness and graciousness meant the world to me.

Our relationship was reborn, and we both wanted to do something meaningful for our future. I wrote an email to our rabbi explaining the situation:

"Hi there, Rabbi,

We wanted to give you a better understanding of what has happened in our marriage in the past few months.

Suffice to say, we reached a crisis point when I told L I had had enough and could not continue in the marriage.

After I had made up my mind to leave and move on, I became involved with someone who (I mistakenly believed) could provide me with all the things I believed I was missing in my marriage. So, instead of dealing with things in a respectful manner, I chose to behave in a disrespectful and disappointing way.

When L indicated that after everything that had happened, he was still willing to work on the relationship, I knew I had to disclose my actions so he could make a well-informed decision for his future and the future of our relationship. (I also knew I simply could not live with myself any longer.)

Talking about this situation was difficult and horrible, and my intention was to give L all the time and space he needed to deal with it. However, I was able to make an appointment with a highly regarded marital therapist and he was in favour of the opportunity.

Since that appointment, we have both committed ourselves to our relationship, our marriage, and each other. We both understand the importance of trust, honesty, and love.

It feels like a whole new relationship; that we are forging a new track together. I was in such pain for so long, and I have finally been able to see who L is as a man. He has been the model of dignity, grace, and respect throughout this entire period. Also, during this time, I have seen the kind of woman I want to become. I have learned I spent the last nine years in this relationship not understanding what true love, commitment, and marriage are about.

I believe both L and I are totally committed to nurturing each other's spirits and souls, and gently holding each other's hearts in our hands. We love each other tremendously, and it is at this point that we have both learned how to love each other. We are seeing our marriage therapist and working our way through the book Hold Me Tight.

We wanted to meet with you to symbolize making a fresh start to our relationship and we are both looking forward to seeing you on Friday."

We arranged to meet in the Rabbi's office on December 19.

On December 12, L's mother passed away in Florida. Her death was sudden and tragic and drew us together – we were united in grief. I looked after him, helped with all the administrative details, and we got through the terrible time together.

In February of 2009, we visited a friend in Jamaica. We stayed in a small cottage by the water and were able to regroup and warm up while escaping the doldrums of the Ottawa winter.

In May, I bought a new notebook and started journaling most nights before I went to sleep. The nightly exercise gave me the opportunity to express my innermost feelings. I was able to recap what happened that day or night and for what I was most grateful.

I did not write very often about the "affair." I put affair in quotes because at that time I truly believed I was leaving our marriage. I did not feel any hope the marriage was possibly going to continue. I thought it was over.

Writing was therapeutic after The Troubles. I found myself battling through immense feelings of guilt. Although everything was finally healthy between L and me, I still felt guilty for everything I had done – especially how my actions had caused him pain.

Those same feelings of guilt and shame reminded me of how I felt when L and I first got together.

I realized I did not want to take another moment with L for granted. I believed every moment was a gift. Finally, between L and Lloyd, I had everything I had ever wanted in life.

Now, I still deal with anxiety attacks at times. Like when I am taking our dog for a nice morning walk and I think about what it would be like to be a single dog parent if something happened to L.

One weekend the three of us were going for a lovely family walk in a local park. My mind started racing. Suddenly I was possessed by anxious thoughts. I looked at L's face and worried one day I would be living without him.

I remembered an article I read online: Things to do when you are having a panic attack:

https://www.letserasethestigma.com/emergency-action-for-panic-attacks

Look around you. Find 5 things you can see, 4 things you can touch, 3 things you can hear, 2 things you can smell, and one thing you can taste.

I looked around. I could see leaves, trees, grass, cars, people. I could touch the dog, L, my shirt, the grass. I could hear the cars, the people around us, and the sound of barking. I could smell the grass and the smoke coming from the Syrian community's barbeque. I could still taste the toothpaste in my mouth.

I calmed down.

When I was in my 20s, I saw a counsellor. It helped me to stop sleeping with men to find my self-esteem. That was a good thing.

I value counselling and I appreciate the interventions I received. I worked with counsellors for years. It got me through the toughest times. Including when our beautiful Lloyd died in April of 2018.

In March of 2018 I had a breakdown – and I shared it with my friends on Facebook.

I have been thinking about doing this for a long time, but people successfully convinced me that it would not be a good idea to share this writing, and so I didn't.

Until now.

Because today we woke up to the sad news that another wildly successful celebrity had taken their own life.

So today, regardless of judgment or anything else, I am sharing these thoughts. Because maybe, just maybe there may be one person who is feeling the same thing and may find solace in my words.

On March 13, I felt like I was losing it. I was exhausted, I was scared, and everything felt out of control. I was having massive anxiety and I could not stop the anxious thoughts running through my head. I felt desperately alone. And I know that I am not alone. I am never alone. I have a strong support system in my life. But during those moments, I felt so scared and so alone.

I thought about those people who may not have such support in their lives. Or those who know something is happening, but they can't really put their finger on it.

I reached out to a good friend who works in the mental health field. She was there for me. She gave me some resources to check into, but inside I felt a sense of urgency. My heart was beating so quickly. My anxious thoughts were racing, showing no signs of slowing down – I was so scared.

In her text to me she asked me if I wanted to talk. Here's where I was having a problem. I knew I needed to talk. I needed to get this out, but who could I talk to? I did not want to burden my family or worry them. I wanted to be strong. But I did not feel very strong at that time. I felt incredibly weak.

Thankfully, I said yes, please, can we talk. She immediately picked me up and we sat in her car, and I cried. And cried. And cried. And she sat and listened to me – without judgment or making me feel self-conscious.

We talked for a while afterwards and we focused on the benefit of saying no and looking after ourselves by not stretching ourselves too thin. I felt better. I know reaching out is not a sign of weakness. On the contrary, it is a strong person who can reach out for help.

And so, I wanted to share this experience with people. Because mental illness is the same as physical illness. If I had a bad headache or the stomach flu, I would be able to talk about it. I wouldn't worry about someone judging me.

So why can't we do the same about mental illness? Why is it that I never felt comfortable taking a sick day for mental health, but I could easily call and say I had a headache or a stomach bug without worrying one bit? And I have worked in the social services field where we are helping people. What about the people who work in fields which are less "caring" (for lack of a better word). What about people who don't have anyone to talk to or don't know what is happening or who are really scared and alone? I am thinking that the people who die by suicide largely die alone — and that is a sad thought.

We all have stuff going in our lives. No one is perfect, and no one has everything altogether. We need to talk about what is happening, we need to have resources, and we need to be able to truly listen to people when they reach out.

Anxiety, depression, and other mental health conditions are exactly that — health. I learned last week that another friend was going through those same feelings on the very same day. Everyone has a story, and we need to listen and treat people with compassion. And treat ourselves with compassion as well.

I don't suffer from depression, but I know depression and suicide have plagued some of my friends. It is real, and society needs to address it. Like physical health, mental illness does not discriminate. It does not matter if you are the richest celebrity; it is a destructive force in many people's lives.

Going through that morning made me so grateful for my life, and for the resources available to me. It also allowed me to see hope and know that this would pass, and I would be okay. It happens to everyone. It does not matter if people seem happy or okay or whatever — there can be a lot going on under the surface. Being able to find help is essential. And I mean finding help before you reach the point of desperation — people need help along the way. More mental health resources are essential.

Whew. There. I know this post was long; I just wanted to share and let people know they are not alone. And that there is help available.

I struggled with posting that on my FB, but I was gratified to see many of my friends read it and maybe some of them could see they were not alone.

Mental health is so significant, yet it is often ignored or mocked. How many times have we heard the phrase, "You're crazy" or the familiar refrain, "It's my OCD."?

As you have seen, I don't use a lot of statistics or research – which must be infuriating for some readers. I don't write from my head (or anyone else's) – I write from my heart.

Mental health needs to be addressed. I know too many people who have chosen to die by suicide. I have tried to understand what goes through their minds, and how lonely they must be feeling when they make the ultimate decision to end their suffering by taking their lives.

We need to live in a world where people understand that everyone goes through struggles even though they may not share them with others.

A few months ago, a friend of mine suggested that I may have a mild form of OCD.

At first, I was puzzled by his observation, so I questioned him. "I am not compulsive," I protested.

He went on to explain about the O in OCD.

Obsessive.

Like when you obsess about death or being killed or things like that.

That got me thinking.

When I was much younger and living in Singapore, I told my parents that if I had an aneurysm in the middle of the night, I would turn up my music loud as a sign for them. I did not realize at the time that I would likely be dead before I could signal to my parents something was wrong.

I thought about how many years I have spent worrying about death. I have expended a lot of time and energy worrying about my eventual demise.

These thoughts and worries were ever-present in my mind, but I just tried to get past them. Maybe they caused the anxiety, maybe the anxiety causes them. I don't know.

All I know is I walk around the world filled with these thoughts and concerns. I am just one person; I can only imagine how other people may be struggling.

No one wants to get sick. People who have cancer or heart disease don't want to get sick. In the same vein, people with mental health disorders or mental illness don't want to be sick either.

Don't kid yourself. Whether it is mental or physical, it is still an illness. For some reason, people don't want to talk about mental health. Maybe it is because as a society we fear it ourselves. It is almost like if we can't see it, we have a hard time understanding how it can exist.

Regardless of why we choose not to talk about it, we simply *must* talk about it. We have a habit in our society of not talking about difficult subjects. Racism, sexism, ageism – all of the "isms." It is easier for us to sweep them under the rug and hope nobody notices.

The latest (what a sick way to describe this) mass shooting has us again tripping over the enormous lump under the rug. Gun control, mental health, a culture of violence, video games, reality TV – all bandied about as causes of these attacks. Soon after our society grieved for the victims of the Buffalo mass shooting, we were mourning the tragedy at Robb Elementary in Uvalde, Texas.

But the tragedy did not start there. This horrible (and completely senseless) massacre has its roots firmly in our societal fabric. We don't know what could have caused a young man to commit this most heinous of crimes.

What we do know is that something snapped within him. Do we know if he was seeing a psychiatrist? Does it matter? Does it really matter what was happening with him? One part of me says yes, it does matter, because he was a human being and I don't believe that any sane person would want to have those feelings and thoughts. But the other part of me says that to move forward we need to change things.

Firstly, instead of saying someone who is suffering from a mental health disorder is nuts or psycho or crazy, can we just say that they have a mental illness? People are realizing words are hurtful. Members of our community are taking back the power of words and how they stigmatize ourselves and one another. We are not stuck in the '80s when someone did something stupid, they were described as the r word. Let's do the same thing for mental health. If you have ever felt depressed or anxious in your life, you have experienced a mental illness of some sort. The statistics are staggering –

http://www.cmha.ca/media/fast-facts-about-mental-illness/#. UM5Dum_LSSo

We know that mental illness is so prevalent, yet we do little to help people. Policy makers seem to want to cut out any type of program that could effect change. I challenge school administrators to focus on emotional and social intelligence, not just on who can pass the Grade 10 literacy test.

I have learned that mental health is crucial for a healthy life, but it's not in a vacuum.

Speaking of a healthy life, I am still working on my physical health. But I am not getting anywhere. I have joined countless gyms over the years, and pointlessly paid thousands of dollars on gym memberships.

The truth is that I have always hated exercising.

Right before my 39th birthday I saw a commercial for Curves – an all-female, intimate health and fitness solution. In just 30 minutes on a circuit, you could get fit. I joined – and surprisingly I loved it. Until I didn't. When we went to Europe in 2014, we walked miles and miles each day. It was awesome!

We returned to Ottawa and I learned the management had changed, the level of customer service had declined dramatically, and the machines had been replaced by hard plastic equipment. None of those changes appealed to me, so I cancelled my membership.

Since then, I have tried a couple of different gyms. I was a member of two gyms in a row and stopped going. I hate gyms and I hate working out. I like the "after" feeling, but the whole process of getting to the gym, changing into my inside shoes, waiting for the right machine to be free, and then actually doing the exercising – is exhausting.

At work, they offered us $100.00 to take some type of fitness course. I signed up for my first Aquafit class. After the classes, I enjoyed the hot tub and some sauna time. The class was fun, and I was looking forward to the next one until the pandemic hit in the spring of 2020.

*When I look into those deep brown eyes of my canine
soulmate, I feel such love. I never once in my life
believed that I would be able to experience such bliss,
such immense love in our happy little family.
I am truly blessed. Was just thinking – I share this
love because it has been such a struggle.
I am not perfect – but instead of focusing on the not-
so-great things, I now look at the positive.
Rather than being sad that I have such poor vision,
I am grateful for what does work and the beauty
that I see in the world. Instead of despairing (as I
spent many years doing) at the size of my nose,
I am grateful for my sense of smell.
I can't imagine waking up and looking into the
mirror and seeing someone typically gorgeous.
I would love to be in better shape, and eliminate the back
fat (and, let's not kid ourselves, the front fat too). I am so
grateful for everything that I have – the health of my loved
ones, the marriage that I fought so hard for, and my job
and my passion. The lumps and bumps simply don't mean
that much to me anymore. It is the love, the peace, and the
beauty in the world and in my life that make me so happy.*

Chapter 38

The Pandemic Years

"Letter to You"

I thought I had it all figured out. By it, I mean the book I had been writing for decades. I started working with an editor. I was figuring out how to take the many lessons I had learned throughout my life and add structure and support to the reader.

For years, I vacillated about how to structure the book effectively, and even now, as I write, I wonder how best to present it to you, the reader. Just as Springsteen wrote about his good and hard times and dug deep in his soul in his song "Letter to You," this book is my letter, sharing the sunshine and rain.

Because it's all about you. You are reading this, and I need to give you this information in a way that makes sense and doesn't make you wonder what the hell I am talking about.

I was working away on the book, adding more structure and removing irrelevant information. The world was struggling through COVID-19, then, on June 29, exactly one month after my 51st birthday, this happened:

"The CT scan found a mass on your ovary."

239

I woke up that Tuesday morning and experienced shooting pain while going to the bathroom. The pain was so intense my sister had to drive me to a local emergency department where I was lucky enough to see a doctor who gave me pain meds and ordered a CT scan.

The emergency doctor asked, "How forward do you want me to be?"

"As forward as you can be," I told him.

The mask hid the bottom of his face, but it could not disguise the sadness in his eyes.

My sister, parents, and my husband were waiting for me outside the hospital.

I immediately burst into tears, but quickly regrouped.

I was shocked but not surprised.

Through my tears I told him everything.

"For over five years I have been telling my family doctor about different symptoms bothering me."

I had told her about the bloating, the constantly going to the bathroom. She knew I experienced pain having sex and she knew back in 2012 there was a cyst on my right ovary. Thankfully it had resolved itself after three months.

As I sat in the blue recliner listening to what the doctor told me next, I realized this was serious.

"The gynecological oncology department is going to receive the referral today and they will be calling you by Friday." He gave me the number I had to call if I had not heard from them in a couple of days.

This was Tuesday, June 29, 2021, and the Canada Day long weekend was right around the corner.

Before we wrapped up, he wrote me a prescription for Hydromorphone. It was the same medication they had been pumping into my arm. He warned me against taking it unless I was in the kind of severe pain that had brought me to the emergency department that morning. It was a seriously addictive painkiller, and I should stick with Extra-Strength Tylenol if possible. Without missing a beat, he prescribed a laxative to accompany the medication.

I knew right then I was not going to be consuming these meds unless the pain was unbearable.

Finally, as we sat across from each other, looking into each other's eyes, the doctor asked if I had any other questions. As he had already told me, I would need to talk with the gynecological oncologist (two words no one ever wants to hear) for more answers; I knew there was no point in asking him a medical question.

The career counsellor in me piped up. "Why did you want to be a doctor?"

He was completely blindsided by the question, and I was equally taken aback by his thoughtful response.

"I have ADHD, I like helping people, I enjoy working with my hands. I needed to be an emergency room doctor."

"I see." It made perfect sense to me.

He wished me well and I bet he would have given me a hug if he could.

I was alone in the room for about a minute before Bailey, the triage nurse, came in to unhook me. I thanked her for doing what she did, and I told her I was worried about my husband. That when he had to come to see me in the room (which he was not actually allowed to do), he had tears in his eyes.

"Yes," she said, "I know. I was the one who gave him permission to see you for a few minutes."

I thanked her profusely and she asked if I wanted her to walk out with me.

"Yes, please," I said.

We walked through the sliding doors together and I saw my worried family waiting for me. Everyone was there except my husband, who had gone to gas up, and had been assured he was not going to miss anything.

I blurted out the news. "I have a mass on my ovary!"

Bailey calmly told them, "We do not have any more information yet, but Tonya will soon be hearing from the gynecological oncologist."

My husband drove into the parking lot and parked between my car (which my sister had driven) and my parents' car.

I was walking in between my dad and my sister. As we all walked quietly to the cars, I turned back and saw my husband collapse in my mom's arms. She reassured him everything was going to be okay, and that whatever happened we could handle it. At least I am guessing that is what she said. She put her arm around him, and they walked together to the cars.

My husband drove us home; holding hands, we quietly talked about what had just happened and what would be happening to me.

The word oncologist had thrown me for a loop. A big one. Oncologists mean cancer. *Was this mass, this squatter, this invader – was it cancer? Was I going to die?*

I took Wednesday off work. I knew I was not in a mental state to work, even if it was working from home.

My family was getting together on July 1st to celebrate our belated 2020 Thanksgiving, and my husband and I had taken the Friday off to make it an extra long and special weekend.

I remembered what the emerg doc told me to do. If I had not heard back from the clinic by Friday, I should call.

So, I did. Only to discover that the doctor was not there, and everyone was gone for the long weekend.

The receptionist told me they had received the referral from the hospital and that the clinic would be calling me the next week to schedule the next steps.

What should have been a fantastic long weekend together turned into a very stressful time. I was thinking *I am going to die and I have no idea what is going on inside me. I do not want to die! I just turned 51! I have a long way to go!*

I called the clinic first thing on Monday morning. They told me the mass was 12 cm and described it as a medium size. Really? Medium-sized? That sounded pretty big to me! They also told me I would be receiving a phone call to schedule my ultrasound and meeting with a gynecological oncologist. There was that double-designation again.

Not even five minutes after I hung up the phone, I received the promised call. My ultrasound would be on July 9 at 10:15 am and my meeting would be July 15 at 8:45 am.

This was July 5 and things were going fast. I was scared.

I spent the next few days panicking and freaking out. I tried hard to live in the moment, but I could not help but think that maybe I wouldn't have too many moments left.

This could not be happening to me. Each morning I woke up and worried about having more pain and worse, cancer. I could not shake that feeling no matter how much I tried.

I found myself being nicer and more caring with strangers, even more than usual.

I was terrified and spent many hours just flat out worrying about my future, about my husband's future. I had always worried about being left behind. Was I going to be leaving him behind?

I noticed I had lost about 10 pounds over the previous couple of weeks. Although as a perimenopausal woman I had wanted to lose weight, this was not what I was talking about. I googled what is happening when you have cancer and are losing weight. Apparently, it is the cancerous cells taking all the good, healthy nutrition.

It was that day I decided to have a little conversation with the squatter. I told him (because I knew it was male) he was not welcome and that we would be evicting him. I told him that I knew it was a loving and wonderful body and that is why he wanted to be there, but that respectfully, he was on his way out.

I continued to have these daily conversations with this unwelcome visitor.

Finally, it was Friday July 9. I was using my overtime hours, so I was confident I had stockpiled enough time not to worry about taking time off work.

My husband drove me to my appointment on the 7th floor of the Riverside Hospital. The Women's Clinic. We sat in the car, and I held his hand and cried. I watched as a moth landed on the windshield directly in front of me. He stayed there for a few minutes and quickly flew away. I appreciated his presence and wondered what a moth meant. He was a spiritual guide, and somehow, I did not feel alone anymore.

As we were still in the global pandemic, I had to go to my appointment alone. My husband would drive home and pick me up when I called him.

I walked into the hospital and answered the COVID questions. I was handed a blue disposable mask and instructed on how to get to the Women's Clinic.

I felt small, alone, and scared.

I took the elevator to the 7th floor and checked myself in.

Following directions, I went over to the area labeled Ultrasound. I found a single chair that looked the comfiest and sat down. I did not have my purse with me, choosing to simply carry my cell phone with my health card and my reading glasses.

Thankfully, I have a subscription to Scribd, so I had reading material. I decided to start a book called *The Gift*, written by a highly accomplished psychologist who survived the Nazi death camps during the Holocaust. When I was much younger, I would always put my bad days into perspective by saying even my worst days were never as bad as the best days for people in the camps.

I was quickly summoned, and the appointment began.

As she was doing her thing, I asked the technician, "Why did you choose this career?"

She explained. "Years ago, while I was in high school—" (I suddenly felt old) "—I saw the expo called Bodies and I was fascinated by it. I decided to be an x-ray technician, but during my placement, I was injured on the job, which meant Plan B. I learned about the possibility of becoming an ultrasound technician, and I have never looked back. I've been working here for eight years, and I love my job."

Trust me, when you are feeling small, scared, and vulnerable, knowing your technician loves her job makes everything a little bit better. Not a lot, but much better than had she been bitter and cranky.

She instructed me to go to the bathroom and when I was finished, to stand up, and then sit down to pee again. I needed to make sure I was getting all the urine out.

I did as I was told and upon going the second time, saw more than urine; there was blood in the toilet and on the toilet paper. Being perimenopausal, and even though I knew my period was completely erratic, this surprised and annoyed me.

I knew the second part of the appointment was the transvaginal ultrasound. I returned to the room feeling embarrassed. I explained what was happening, and she was so kind. She said it was not the first time for that to happen. I had to lie on the bed with my legs open and she inserted the condom-covered wand into my body. It felt weird, but not uncomfortable. It just wasn't the normal condom-covered instrument to which I was accustomed. ☺

After she completed the pelvic ultrasound, the technician advised me the results would likely be available that day.

With the ultrasound over, I needed to get my bloodwork done. CA 125 – if you have an elevated level, it could mean that you have ovarian cancer. But, on the other hand, just because it is elevated DOESN'T mean you DON'T have ovarian cancer. Basically, if I had a low level, it was a good thing, but it was not a guarantee.

I stood in line outside the room, looking at everyone else in line. What they were in for? I wondered if they were wondering the same thing about all the other people. Was I just weird?

Finally, after about ten minutes, I was in the room. I presented myself at the desk and was given the number eight. They were at zero, so I figured it was not too bad.

I found a chair on its own and sat down, again with my phone and reading glasses. They are so annoying, but such a blessing because they allow me to read things and see properly. In the middle of texting my husband, I heard a curt "Number 8, room 1." I reacted quickly, trying to put things away and respond to the summons. I was not fast enough, as I heard an even more brusque and rude "NUMBER 8! ROOM 1!"

I rushed over to the middle-aged phlebotomist who looked like she was from the Middle East. "Oh, I didn't think you were here," was her greeting.

"Well," I said, "I am."

Then the conversation began. I learned I was right. She was originally from Iraq and had raised her sons as a single mom. She was planning to move to Turkey because it is too expensive to live in Ottawa on her own.

"I hear you," I said. "I work at an immigrant serving organization, and I love working with and helping people from all over the world. I know people from Turkey. Would you like to reach out to me on LinkedIn? I would be happy to introduce you to those people."

"Oh, yes," she said, and took down my name. I was not sure if she would reach out, but I was ready to make those connections if she did.

I called my husband, and ten minutes later he was in front of the hospital, picking me up. I ran to the car with excitement, thinking to myself I could not possibly be sick like the other people around me. I was too full of vigour and life.

We got home and I started to work. The whole experience had taken about two hours. I did the calculation, and was relieved that I could use my overtime for the morning appointment.

Suddenly, I got an email message from the hospital. There was a new test result on MyChart, the secure online healthcare system. I stopped working and clicked to check the result.

I had been doing some research about ovarian cancer, so I knew what was good and what was not so good. The first page did not say too much; the second page was brutal.

Words like "irregular" and the largest diameter of 13 cm led my eye to the bottom of the page in black, bold letters: the likelihood of ratio of malignancy of this mass is 88.6%. I cried, wailed, burst into tears. My husband and my sister came running.

"What's wrong?" they asked in a panic.

I could not say anything except, "I have cancer and I am going to die."

I pointed to the screen. They read the page in horror. We sat there for a few long minutes taking everything in.

My husband rubbed my back and held my hand. Looking into my eyes, he said stoically, "We are going to get through this together."

We made the phone call to my parents that no one ever wants to make. My husband dialed and when Mom answered he asked if Dad was around. Mom called him to get to the phone. There was no laughter or silliness. My husband's tone said it all.

He told them the news. "Tonya received the results of the ultrasound, and they are not what we were hoping for or expecting." He gave them the information and we all sat there, silent at both ends of the line.

My dad, always the logical one, said, "This is something you need to talk to the oncologist about and maybe it's not as bad as we think."

After we said goodbye, I had to call my closest colleague, work husband, and partner in crime, S. With her science background, she was the person who had told me to go to the emergency department on June 29.

In tears, I told her the test results. Unable to hold back her tears, we just sat there wordlessly, trying to process this unwelcome information. Finally, she told me to take the day off, and I said I would call our manager to let her know what was happening. She knew about the scheduled ultrasound, and I wanted her to know the results – and that I would take the rest of the day off. Like the rest of us, she was gobsmacked. She, too, held back tears and wished me only the best and that she would be thinking of me.

The next few days were filled with fear, worry, and pure dread. As much as I tried to not think about it, I could not help seeing that black, bold writing – 88.6%.

But, the good news (anything helps) was that the blood test results were back, and I was in the normal range for everything for which I had been tested. I sighed with relief.

Finally, after days of tears and fear, it was time to meet the oncologist. Thankfully, the appointment was first thing in the morning; I can't imagine the level of my anxiety if it would have been later in the day. Still following COVID protocol, no one was allowed in the hospital with me. Once again, I would be alone.

Being my second time, I knew where I was going. I completed the initial COVID questioning and took the disposable mask they handed me. I heard the lady behind me ask the clerk how to get to the 7th floor. Ah ha, I thought. She is new. So, I slowed down, introduced myself and told her that I was going to the 7th floor myself, and maybe we could be each other's buddies in the hospital. We laughed and took the elevator to the Women's Clinic.

This time, I was given a long questionnaire to fill out. I tried to write clearly and legibly, but I was nervous, and my responses were a mess. I watched the clock as the minutes ticked by. My 8:45 am appointment was becoming 9:00 am. I texted my family in the group chat to let them know what was going on.

My husband and my sister had dropped me off and were parked in front of our old apartment beside the hospital. They were going to be on the conference call during my appointment with the oncologist.

A nurse came out and said "Tonya."

We walked down the hall together. She was middle-aged, with voluminous hair, and she was wearing a short skirt. She looked like she would have been at home playing shuffleboard on a cruise ship. She was nice and took time to explain everything that would be happening during the meeting with the GO. She was patient with my questions and told me that Dr. L would be examining me, both vaginally and rectally, as this was the best way to feel the mass in or on the ovary. Who knew? Certainly not this gal. She said it would take ten seconds. For the record, it did not feel like ten seconds. ☹

She told me to disrobe and lay down on the bed-like furniture and cover myself with the sheet. I did just that and spent a few minutes waiting for the GO and the nurse to appear. After what seemed like forever, they returned. It was my first meeting with Dr. L, and there I was, with my legs open, covered by a sheet. Lovely.

He performed the examination, and of course while he was doing the rectal exam, all I could think was *Dear God, please don't find anything wrong THERE too!* Thankfully, there was nothing untoward in that region, and we continued to the ovarian issues.

My sister and my husband waited for my phone call; I was waiting for the go-ahead from the GO. Meanwhile, following the exam, the nurse told me to get dressed and wait for the healthcare duo to return.

Finally, it was time for the conversation and THE PHONE CALL. All of us had written down questions. I had taken a boring little blue notebook and Tonya-fied it with a plethora of happy stickers. I figured just because I am going through a terrible experience, it does not mean my book can't be happy. 😊

I had written down 33 questions, and between his talk and the questions from my family members, he pretty much answered all of them.

He started by telling us he had indeed felt the mass, and it was something that a woman my age should not be having. *So far, so good.*

Then, he said that, in his opinion, there was a 20% to 30% chance this mass was malignant. My sister asked pointedly, "How long have you been doing this?" He replied, "Twenty years." We were all satisfied by his response. I asked him why the discrepancy between his opinion and the original report indicating an 88.6% chance it was malignant. He shrugged his shoulders and chalked it up to simply a different perspective.

At this point, he shared his suggestion about how to move forward – a full hysterectomy. We were on the same page. I wanted the invader out of my body, and since I never had any use for my lady parts when I was younger, I most definitely did not need them hanging around at my age.

My family and I sighed in communal relief. It would have been much more difficult if the oncologist and I had been on two entirely different planes.

He told me that I am not a number. I am a person. That was comforting for all of us to hear.

He explained that it would be about six weeks before the surgery. Once again, my family jumped in – is there no way he could expedite it?

Dr. L patiently explained that everyone in the Women's Clinic has or is suspected of having cancer, so no one is more important than anyone else. Once again, we were satisfied with his assessment.

I asked him about the possibility of seeing Springsteen on Broadway at the end of August. I had bought a ticket for August 28; until this news at the end of June, the biggest issue had been making sure I was double-dosed in time to attend the event.

Also, my husband and I had the opportunity for the trip of a lifetime: a free five-night cruise around the Greek Islands. Yes, free. It was going to be tight. The cruise was from August 22 to August 27, and then I would have had to quickly travel to NYC from Greece.

The doctor did not think it would be a good idea to travel, for a couple of reasons. Firstly, just in case something was to happen (like it did on June 29), international travel would be a challenge. Point taken.

He also noted if I came back from travelling and I had been in contact with someone with COVID, the surgery would be postponed.

Again, this made sense to all of us. I heard my husband's voice on the line, lovingly assuring me there would be other opportunities for a cruise; my health was the most important thing right now.

I was not completely crestfallen. I had been lucky enough to see Springsteen on Broadway in March of 2018. I just needed to find someone to buy my ticket so they could have the same opportunity.

Dr. L suggested surgery would be sometime in late August. So, instead of cruising the Greek islands for free or seeing Bruce Springsteen up close and personal on Broadway, I would be either getting operated on or recovering. Either way, it was a tough pill to swallow.

An even more difficult pill was the discussion about what happens during the surgery. Dr. L explained that during the surgery they would be assessing the mass. If it is benign, that is the best news! But, either way, they would remove the mass and remove all my lady parts. From my uterus to the ovaries, the fallopian tubes, and even my cervix, they were all out of there.

If it was malignant, they would check if there were any cancerous cells, and if there were, they would be "debulked." Then we would wait for three to four weeks for the pathology report. More waiting. ☹

Then, we would start chemotherapy.

Dr. L wrapped up his part of the meeting, and the friendly nurse continued the call with my family and me. Again, she explained everything in detail. After we ended the call, she handed me three documents, including a user manual for getting a hysterectomy. It was the first time I ever heard the words bilateral salpingo oophorectomy, and how I learned what to expect when being thrown into surgical menopause.

Then I took the elevator down to the main floor (I was becoming an old hand at this) and waited for them to pick me up.

They arrived soon after I called, and my husband got out of the car and held me tightly in his arms. At that moment, I felt I could handle everything with his support and love. Likewise, I felt the love and support of my sister with us – my other sister had to work that day – and my parents, who would meet us at our house.

It was wonderful to be able to share this positive news with my parents. After the meeting with the GO, we had a plan.

For the first time since July 9, I stopped worrying about dying. The plan meant I could start living again.

Things started ramping up quickly after that. I devoured the information they had given me, and I started watching YouTube videos from other women detailing their hysterectomy experiences. I wanted to see what they learned and what advice they gave other women, "HysterSisters."

I soon become a quasi-expert on hysterectomy.

I realized how much I had missed travelling when I found myself getting excited by being able to make a list of what to pack for my three-night hospital stay. ☺

Throughout all this insanity, I never felt alone. From the beginning, I was posting my experience on FB. I am a sharer and needed to share my thoughts and worries and fear with my beautiful FB family.

I learned I had a global army of positive warriors on my team. And, as the nurse told me, this journey would be long and slow – challenging for a somewhat neurotic control freak like me to embrace.

After I learned of the plan, the nasty one-way conversations filled with liberal uses of the F word and my personal favourite – M-F – with The Invader stopped. I had a plan and knew we would soon evict this horrible m-f.

At the end of July, I learned the eviction date. The surgery was scheduled for Monday, September 13, at the Ottawa General Hospital, time to be determined. Yet again, things got real during that conversation. I learned Dr. L would not be the surgeon. It was going to be Dr. W.

Oh, no! I was mentally preparing for Dr. L to be my surgeon; I mean, he gave me the odds of 70% to 80% that it would be benign. What if Dr. W was not as qualified or experienced?

Once again, Google to the rescue. It turns out that Dr. W is just as qualified, competent, and knowledgeable about gynecological oncology as Dr. L. *Whew!*

Things became even more real during the last week of July when I got another call from another nurse scheduling my pre-op discussion with Dr. W; Thursday, September 9 at 9:00 am at the Riverside Hospital. I was becoming a veteran at that place. The conversation would last about an hour, and L would be with me.

My sister and I went shopping to buy recovery clothing. Four long, flowy dresses with nothing touching my incision and still enough space for my swelly belly. I know a lot of women talk about their swollen bellies, and I am thinking it is kind of what happens to women after they give birth. They leave the hospital with their newborn, but still sort of looking a little bit pregnant. Whenever I tried to forget or not think about The Invader, the incessant need to go to the bathroom and the consistent bloating I was contending with reminded of his presence.

I also bought five nightdresses. Four of them were $10.00, and one was $14.00. You can't go wrong at those prices! Even after the recovery, I would be able to wear both the dresses and the pjs. So, yay for me!

I decided I would wear the black dress home because it is super flowy and, dare I say, slimming. ☺

I was full of gratitude and love and appreciation. Each time I felt scared, I thought about the good things I had going for me: 1) None of this type of cancer is in my immediate family, and 2) I didn't have an elevated level of CA 125.

I would get freaked out when I thought and worried about the future. All my fellow global positive warriors told me I was strong, but I felt so scared inside. More than anything I have ever wanted in my life; I wanted this nasty invader to be benign.

It's funny. I recognize the importance of good health, both physical and mental, but this condition was out of my control. What *is* in my control is my attitude, my humour, and how I react to whatever comes my way. This realization is truly life-changing after a long struggle with a severe lack of self-esteem.

I sought support from a local counselling clinic on September 1 and shared my gratitude list on FB:

Had an amazing counselling session yesterday focusing on somatic, body-centered therapy.

It was really helpful.

Some reflections:

1) **My nervous system is basically on fire right now.**
2) **Just received my booklets from the hospital about pain management and planning for my surgery.**
3) **I don't have bad days – only good and better.** ☺
4) **Gratitude is a special gift.**
5) **I am going to look at this like an adventure – I have never been a hospital patient before – this is an opportunity. I get to experience something new.**
6) **I remember on June 29 in the Winchester hospital; I had never experienced being hooked up to an IV and**

getting pain medication that way. But I did it then, and now, if I need to do it again, I know I can.

7) Sleep is another gift.

8) The health care provided at the Ottawa Hospital is world-class and truly second-to-none.

9) A year from now, this time will all be a memory.

10) I am focused on the results. Whenever they come, they will be positive. 🩶

I am reminded of this quote from *The Best Exotic Marigold Hotel:* "Everything will be all right in the end, and if it's not all right, it's not the end."

On September 9, the journey continued. I had bloodwork (thankfully all my results were again within the normal range), and met my surgeon. It still felt surreal. I really needed my global army.

That evening I wrote down everything I was grateful for:

The most incredibly supportive and loving family, having a very impressive and accomplished surgeon, finally being together as a family to celebrate my sister's birthday after too many spent apart.

We spent the days before the surgery getting organized, making loads of veggie stew, doing housework, and doing the final prepping for the operation. Then, on Friday, September 10, at 4:46 pm, I learned the surgery was scheduled for 8 am on Monday.

This early start meant I needed to be at the hospital by 6:00 am. Thankfully, I re-read the instructions, which told me to drink 500 ml of cranberry juice ahead of time. So, I was up at 4:00 am, drinking, showering, and getting L to paint my abdomen with the disinfectant solution.

The night before a good friend sent me this prayer by Alden Solovy: "Before My Surgery."

God of health and healing,

I surrender myself to the physician's hand,

The surgeon's knife,

The nurse's care,

Placing my body in the cradle of others,

Just as I place my soul in Your loving arms.

Bless my surgeon with a steady hand,

Keen vision

And a passion for healing.

Bless my caregivers with wisdom and skill,

With compassion, focus and dedication.

Bless my family with ease and comfort.

Give them energy and endurance, tranquility and peace.

Remind them to care for themselves and each other,

Even as their hearts and prayers turn to me.

Bless my body with strength,

My spirit with courage,

My thoughts with hope

And my life with renewed purpose.

Source of life,

Bless us with Your guidance,

Make us Your partner in healing

And grant a full and speedy recovery.

It meant so much to me, and I shared it with my friends who were also facing upcoming surgeries.

After my shower that morning and the requisite tummy painting, I drank the last of my required drink and off we went. It was the next step of the journey.

Without speaking, we drove to the hospital on quiet streets. As per my request, Springsteen was playing throughout the drive. We pulled into the parking lot. I wore my black dress, sports bra, underwear, and my new little slip-on sandals from Skechers. And my glasses, and, of course, my mask.

I was told not to wear my contact lenses, and to leave them at home. I was scared at the idea of not being able to see things clearly.

Suddenly I was inspired not to just listen, but to dance to Springsteen. I turned up the volume and stepped out of the car and started dancing to "Glory Days." Singing along in the brisk early autumn weather, I was getting out all sorts of anticipatory anxiety.

My husband carried my bag and we walked in silence to the administration desk on the second floor. We were surprised to have to say goodbye to each other so quickly.

He gave his name and contact information to the admitting clerk. We learned the surgery would start at 8:00 am and end at 11:20 am. Things were getting very real.

The clerk told me to say goodbye to my husband and walk through the big metal door. We looked at each other with tears in our eyes.

Over and over, we said, "I love you," and kept kissing each other until we finally said goodbye.

Then, the door opened, and after a few steps towards it, I turned to look at him. We blew each other kisses, and the big heavy door started to close behind me.

I found a seat, and before I could wipe away my tears, I heard my name. The journey had begun.

My nurse A introduced herself and took me to Bed #21. She gave me a hospital robe and instructions on how to do it up. Apparently, I needed more instruction because I could not figure out how to keep it on without things falling out.

I went to the bathroom, and after A helped me get back to my bed, she went to see my neighbour. When I heard her ask him questions, I started preparing my own responses.

My nerves were off the chart; I reached into my bag to get my phone and reread the poem.

A returned to my bedside and started asking me those same questions she had asked my neighbour. When she asked me if I had any prosthesis or anything metallic in my body, I could not resist. I replied, "No, they're real, and they're spectacular."

She cracked up laughing and told me that she had binge-watched Seinfeld during her recent mat leave and she completely got the reference to my breasts.

I continued answering her questions, and after she moved on to the next patient, I waited for P, the porter, to take me to the OR.

Breathe.

Breathe.

I put away my glasses. I had thought I would feel vulnerable in a blurry world, but I was surprised to feel a sense of calm.

P rolled me to the OR. He wished me the best and told me the surgeon would be there shortly.

Breathe.

Breathe.

Sing. Springsteen's "Dream Baby Dream."

Close my eyes.

Wait.

Need to go to the bathroom.

Wait for someone to take me there.

Meet the anesthesiologist resident. He measures my mouth (three fingers, for the record) and checks my blood pressure. He tells me he is surprised such an anxious person has such low blood pressure. He is not the only one who is surprised!

I meet Dr. G, my anesthesiologist. She is from Columbia and proposes that she gives me an anesthesia spinal block. ACK!!!

Even though the idea terrifies me, I say, "Go for it. I am in your hands."

This was my opportunity to ask if she would be able to play something by Bruce Springsteen as I go under. She says, "Absolutely, how about 'Dancing in the Dark?'" I am on board with it, and then she asks, "Would you like to hear a Columbian version of it?" I tactfully suggest a rain check for that option. She laughed.

A nurse walked me to the bathroom and waited for me.

Breathe.

She held my arm as we walked back to the gurney.

Breathe.

Breathe.

Dream baby Dream.

Breathe.

My surgeon comes by to reassure me.

A nurse asks if I can walk into the OR.

I can.

I do.

The OR is bright and shiny. I am unable to see clearly, but I can decipher some things.

They ask me to sit so Dr. G can insert the spinal block, and to relax and "be like a banana." I became a banana, and they insert the block.

The last thing I remember was hearing people discussing the Springsteen request, and then someone playing Eric Clapton's "Tears in Heaven."

NO!

I don't know if I said that out loud, or just to myself, but someone said, "Oh no, that's not Springsteen." They turned it off, and played Springsteen's "Streets of Philadelphia," a depressing song about the AIDS epidemic. It was *not* "Dancing in the Dark."

The next thing I remember, I was waking up in recovery. I was not in pain, just groggy and feeling strange.

I lay there for hours, listening to the sounds of the recovery room. Thankfully, I had watched videos about what happens in the recovery room, so I had some idea of what to expect.

The nurse kept coming back to tell me they were still trying to find a room for me. I had no idea of the time.

At 5:30 pm, the nurse came over and I asked if I could have my phone to call my husband.

I struggled to make the call and was beyond happy to hear his voice.

As we said hello, I could hear him crying with relief.

I was so out of it on pain-killers, I could not really understand everything he said.

I do remember he told me they took my appendix out as well. *What?* That threw me for a loop. He said something about the slide that was taken during the surgery sounded like good news. Hearing his voice was all I wanted at that moment. Well, that and a place to sleep that night.

At around 8:30 pm, a nurse told me they found a bed for me. *Yay!!* Unfortunately, one of my fellow patients had to sleep in the recovery room because there were not enough hospital beds.

Just as we were ready to leave the recovery room, the nurse told us there was an emergency in the ward and I could not go up there yet. Argh!! I was exhausted and all I wanted was to see my dear husband that night.

N, the porter, came over to wheel me to my room, and we decided to pass some time away by going on a tour. I still did not have my glasses on, so everything was still the same blurriness it was in the morning.

We wheeled into the pre-op room I had been in, and I told him that I had started my journey in Bed #21. The attending nurses got a kick out of the tour we were on, and we continued down to the OR hallway. Finally, after about ten minutes of wasting time, we figured they would be ready for us.

They were, and thankfully it was a private room. I breathed a heavy sigh of relief. Thank goodness for insurance and effective pain medication.

The nurse in charge gave my husband permission to visit me that night. I called him with the great news, and he was in my room within twenty minutes. I don't know if I could have been happier than when I watched him walk through the door.

He did not stay long, and after he left, my amazing nurse, M, came in to give me my pain meds and a shot in my stomach (I think to prevent blood clots). He was a fantastic nurse, and I asked him how he got into nursing. We chatted for a few minutes, and I learned more about him and his career decisions. Talking with people about why they chose their careers always makes me feel better.

I spent my night waking up several times to a nurse giving me my medication; I was finally able to get two hours of sleep before a troop of residents woke me up.

"Hi Tonya!" came the cheerful hello.

The pain meds were doing their job. I was feeling fresh and silly. They asked me how I was feeling. It was a reasonable question to which I answered, "Like a monkey," a completely unreasonable and ridiculous answer.

I couldn't help myself. I love the word monkey; it makes me smile and my husband and I refer to each other as monkeys all the time.

Of course, they were surprised by this unconventional response, and they were probably all wondering how their manuals would tell them to respond.

The primary surgical resident proceeded to tell me that everything was looking good. I had been avoiding looking at the incision, even though it was covered.

She also told me something about my bladder. I had no idea what she was saying, and I tried to keep up with her. All I knew was that she mentioned my bladder. I was already on edge, worrying about the mass, and now she was talking about my bladder.

After they left, I continued my boring day of resting, getting pain medications, trying to sleep, and trying to feel comfortable. I was so grateful a YouTube lady had recommended bringing a power bank. I had my tablet and phone constantly plugged in, ready to use.

I had brought books, but I was just not into reading them.

M came in and told me they were taking me off the IV and taking my catheter out. I panicked. How was I going to go to the bathroom? He assured me everything was fine; I had been urinating in my catheter all night. He showed me the very full bag. I was impressed by my ability to pee without knowing it.

"How are you going to remove the catheter?" I asked quizzically. "No problem," he explained, "It is like deflating a balloon, and it comes out very easily. See, it's gone." 😊

So now I needed to get up and go to the bathroom.

OMG!!! The pain was horrible. My body had been sliced open, and now I had to get up and use the toilet myself. He helped me to the bathroom and placed what he referred to as a nun's cap into the toilet. I would be urinating into that little plastic receptacle used to keep track of the amount of urination.

The first time was a challenge, but soon enough, I could go like a rock star. I was so proud of myself.

Shortly after I went to the bathroom, breakfast arrived. I was not particularly hungry for my first foray into hospital food, but I knew the importance of eating to pass gas and eventually have a bowel movement. I ate the yoghurt, and that was about it.

Brushing my teeth was another challenge; with patience, I accomplished it. My hair was still reasonably clean, and pulled back in a black hair band.

I started wearing my glasses just before my husband visited me. I found it interesting I had felt such a sense of calm while not wearing them. I figured maybe it just gave my brain a bit of a break from all the things it had to deal with at the time. But I am no scientist, so I could be completely wrong about that.

I was thankful I had bought my nightdresses at Giant Tiger and did such a great job packing my bag – watching all those hysterectomy videos paid off.

As per instructions, I started walking around the floor. I put on my fuzzy pink robe and set off on my walks three times a day. It was exhausting, but I did it. With each lap, I was grateful for my private room and my ability to walk. I did not realize it at the time, but my pain medications were incredibly effective. I also noticed a group of people wearing jackets that said Social Worker on them. *Hmm, I would benefit from speaking with a social worker.*

Tuesday night was terrible. I woke up in the middle of the night, needing to go to the bathroom. As I walked the short distance to the door, I had this awful feeling. OMG, this pain is brutal, and will never go away. I suddenly felt nauseous and started to dry heave.

I was over by the window, getting something out of my bag, and felt like my stomach was splitting open. I grabbed a pillow and walked back to my bed, clutching it. I sat on the side of the bed, heaving and clutching my pillow, and crying out in pain.

M came immediately and I told him what was going on. He injected me with a pain killer, and I was feeling better within about 15 minutes. I was able to find a relatively comfortable position with pillows all around me. (I had brought my own pillow and little fuzzy blanket; they were my lifesavers).

Another troop of residents again disturbed my sleep. The primary one from the day before asked how I was feeling. I told her that I had been thinking of the conversation from yesterday about the bladder.

"Oh," she said, "I did not say anything about your bladder. You must be getting mixed up."

"No, I am not getting mixed up. I know you mentioned my bladder, and so did the other residents." It felt like gaslighting to me.

I tried to explain. "I heard correctly. Because I am already on edge, I am paying very close attention to anything involving other potential organs. Such as my bladder being affected."

Nothing I said swayed her, so I just stopped talking.

Later, another wonderful nurse, F, came into my room, and I told her what happened. She suggested I could speak to B, the Patient Coordinator.

Several hours later, B came into my room. She listened attentively to what I told her about the conversation I had, and that I felt unheard and shut down. After years of being shut down and ignored by my doctor, I did not want it to happen again.

I explained that although this physician is clearly a talented surgeon, she needs to listen to patients. I added that I had been asking other medical professionals if they had ever been a patient in a hospital. Most of them said yes, they understand what it is like to be in a hospital bed.

During the conversation, I mentioned I needed to speak with the surgeon who operated on me. I wanted to hear whatever I could hear from the horse's mouth. The young physician spoke in an unconfident manner that did not instill a lot of confidence or reassurance in me.

A few hours later, my surgeon called. She explained the young physician had done an excellent job stitching me up and the stitches were dissolvable.

Cool, I thought, *that means I don't have to go in for a follow up in seven days.*

She also explained why they removed my appendix and that the in-surgery examination indicated a borderline tumour. Fortunately, it was not malignant, therefore, no chemotherapy would be needed.

Even though this was the best news possible, we would have to wait for the pathology results to celebrate.

Within minutes after that call, I passed gas. Victory!!

The next thing was to have a bowel movement. A pretty tough ask considering I was not eating any of the terrible hospital food.

I was, however, eating the delicious bunch of grapes that my love brought me on Wednesday evening. I was so thankful for him visiting me every day. His visits were easily the highlight of each day, and I appreciated how much he was doing, working all day, taking Frank to the dog park after work, and then coming to see me.

Wednesday evening was also Kol Nidre, the beginning of Yom Kippur. The holiest of days in the Jewish calendar saw us in my hospital room watching the service on our individual devices. Definitely not what we thought we would be doing.

Finally, Thursday morning arrived. My discharge day!

Early in the morning, after yet another sleepless night, the troop of residents came into my room. This time, I asked if I could speak to the primary one alone.

"Sure," she said, and dismissed her colleagues.

She bent down to speak with me. I told her about our previous conversation and why it had upset me so much. I explained the importance of listening to people and not talking over them. I told her how vulnerable patients already feel, and they did not need to contend with a physician who was just shutting them down and making them doubt themselves.

I told her she is already a talented surgeon, but when she listens to people, she will become a great healer. I also told her she needs to sound more confident in herself, and that she is an amazing woman.

I felt very proud of myself for telling her that; I hoped she would take my words to heart and really does start listening to people.

I called my husband to tell him I was ready to leave – both of us felt ridiculously happy! I packed my bag and waited for him to arrive with a wheelchair. No bra, dirty hair, and bent over clutching a pillow. Talk about attractive! 😊

The drive home was thankfully uneventful, and I arrived home to a beautiful Welcome Home sign and a dining room filled with colourful balloons strung up everywhere. I can't even imagine where he found the time!

Recovery was painful, intense, and challenging. I could not eat (probably as a reaction to the swill I was served at the hospital and forced to eat before I could be discharged), could not get up without incredible pain, and when I walked around, I had to clutch a pillow to my abdomen. In fact, I had to clutch a pillow ALL the time. I needed the pressure around my stomach.

My face felt disgusting, as I had not washed it since 4:00 am on the morning of my surgery. I finally asked L for a washcloth so I could clean my face. That felt amazing!

For the first time in my life, my skin was dry. Pre-surgery, I would often joke that my skin was so oily, it could rival an oil-producing nation. Not anymore. Now it was the complete opposite.

Each morning, I would carry my pillow and blanket and I would station myself on the couch. My darling would bring my box of medications, my personal little fan for any hot flashes, prunes, water, crackers, and my thermometer.

Each hour, I would make myself get up and walk to the bathroom. Each day, I would take a longer walk. Eventually, I was able to walk back and forth for a whole 30 minutes doing laps between the kitchen and the living room. The show, *Friends,* would always be on TV.

L brought me all my meals until I was strong enough to get up and get something on my own. My level of helplessness was through the roof, with not one iota of independence remaining. It was brutal.

At night, I would be in so much pain, I would be crying, and L would hold my hand. I learned I should take the Hydromorphone, so I started taking them on an as-needed basis. I kept a record of my medications that I started taking on September 16 until October 13. I know some women stop taking their pain meds right after they get home, but not me.

I started taking more meds on September 29 after being diagnosed with an infection in my incision.

The one thing that really made a consistent difference in my recovery was creating and posting my gratitude lists on FB pretty much every day.

I made my first post after surgery on September 13.

Will write more later. Love you all so very much. 💙💙

I just wanted my beautiful and caring community to know I had made it through the operation.

I did not post an update until September 17 after we returned from the hospital –

Will update soon. Love you all so much!!🖤🖤

I posted the pictures of the Welcome Home sign L had made and all the happy balloons he had strung up in the dining room.

Coming home meant getting some sleep, eating healthy food, and being surrounded by love from L and our dog.

It also meant having to manage my pain by myself. I was so terrified of having to go back to the hospital, I kept taking my temperature several times a day. I feared having a fever and having to be a patient again, and face hospital food.

I was also able to eat again, but my stomach was not ready. Maybe I was still dealing with the trauma from the food situation at the hospital.

Getting up to go to the bathroom was excruciatingly painful. I found the best little pillow to hold on my tummy and I kept it there for pretty much the next few weeks.

I did not post anything on FB for a few days as I slept on the sofa, ate, walked for a few minutes at a time, and then returned to the sofa.

I knew it was important to write my gratitude list so that I could get my mind off the pain, and I missed feeling connected with friends and family. So, the next day, I was ready to start sharing it on FB.

Time for a gratitude list!

1) **L – he is looking after me with such love**
2) **My beautiful family and friends – love you all so much!** 🖤
3) **Prunes**
4) **My happy nightdresses**
5) **Devices and battery power**

6) Pillows
7) A normal body temperature
8) Sleep...😴
9) Bruce Springsteen and the E Street Band
10) Life itself 🤍

The surgeon warned me about the constipation problem, and I was taking some Senna to help move my bowels. Nothing was happening. Prune juice was not effective, so I started eating the prunes I had bought before the surgery. A wonderful gift! A day later, I posted:

It was a painful brutally long night, with no sleep until 5 am. Took a Tylenol, and later, a more effective pill, which finally brought a couple of hours of slumber. This morning I was on the phone with Dan at Samsung in a tearful, hour-long conversation to help fix the phone situation. Thankfully he was able to walk me through everything and my phone has been fixed. Afterwards, had a breakdown on the phone with Mom. About 15 minutes later, the family showed up. The support ninjas swooped in and went to work, and then went to Walmart and bought me a big body pillow.🤍🐾 🤍 Been sleeping off and on all day – and walking for about five minutes every hour. Discovered the joy of a frozen ice pack wrapped in a towel (and the frozen Magic Bag) held against my incision. Tried not to cough several times, spoke with my dear friend in Spain, and am planning to take a pill before bed so that I can get some sleep tonight. Love you, everyone! 🤍🤍

Gratitude has always been an essential component in my life, especially during the most challenging times. My list included:

1) Receiving gorgeous flowers from Tina - I love them and you. 🤍
2) GIFS and texts from loving friends.
3) Pills...and sleep...and body pillow. 😴

4) Love 🩶
5) Talking with friends...and the nurse
6) Cakes, chocolate, cards, texts, flowers, check-ins – support from so many wonderful friends.
7) My support ninjas are awesome!!
8) Showers – even if painful.
9) Rainy days.
10) Talking with my friend in Spain. 🩶
Hugs and love to you!! 🩶

September 23 was Bruce Springsteen's birthday (yay) and I wrote my list:

Gonen Sagy and family for an apple baking extravaganza 🍎

Breanna Pizzuto for the veggie sub, cleaning my room, watching The Great Depresh with me, and helping me have a shower with much dignity, privacy, and love. 🩶

Getting 8.5 hours of sleep 😴 (in total).

Celebrating the birthdays of important people on September 23rd. 🎂

Emails and texts filled with love and support.🩶

Watching Mayim Bialik host Jeopardy.

Guided meditations.

Frank and his silliness.🩶🐾🩶

Hearing other people's wonderful news.

Love. 🩶🩶

The next day my list included the following:

1) Was able to take one pill at 9:30 pm and it kept the pain at bay until 6:00 am
2) Great catch up with Sophea Khem-Smith – so much laughter!
3) Good medical news for a loved one today – now we are both waiting...
4) Love looking at my beautiful flowers from my dear friend C.
5) Lilies – Tina Kapur – love you. 🩶
6) Wonderful catching up with my Scottish friends Dave Thomson and Jackie Mitchell – we need to connect! 🩶🩶
7) The bat and his stuffie picture.
8) Laughed with Dad on the phone today.
9) So glad I made all that veggie stew.
10) It's Friday – wishing you an amazing weekend. What are your plans? 🩶

With each day, I added a list:

1) I went outside today!! L and I spent some time on our deck. Yay!!
2) Last night I slept from 9:30 pm until 3:16 am, and then from 6 am until 8 something.
3) Gonen's amazing apple deliciousness.
4) It does not hurt as much to get up.
5) A shower this morning!!
6) Fantastic grapes.🍇
7) Spoke with my parents today.
8) Watched Temple Israel's Shabbat service – thankful for the virtual option.
9) My cozy pink robe.
10) Clean sheets.

11) My friend Steve Houk – he is so talented, smart, and compassionate. I love listening to his live music gigs!♥

Thank you for sharing your days with me! I hope you too had a wonderful day. ♥

Later that day, I asked my friends for some help:

1) Please have a dance party for me. I want to get up and shake my groove thang – but I can't. Could you please do it for me?

2) Take your dog on a dog walk or to the park and think of me. I miss our daily morning walks and the trips to the dog park. 😓

3) When you change positions or get up off the sofa or out of bed without pain, please don't take it for granted.
Thank you. That's it for now!! ♥

Each day I thought about all the things I was grateful for:

1) I took a shower – by myself!!

2) The delicious apple baking extravaganza – yummy!!!

3) L made a fantastic breakfast, and we ate together watching CBS's Sunday Morning – our routine!

4) Another gorgeous day today.

5) L's breakfast making booty shaking impromptu dance party this morning.

6) Able to get to the sofa alone while L and Frank were at the dog park today.

7) 7 hours of sleep last night – woo hoo!!

8) Grapes – the last of the best grapes ever. 🍇

9) You guys sharing your pics and stories of your weekends. 🌼

10) My work husband – Sue!!! ♥

The next day I felt the drugs kick in, and I was starting to freak out about the physical changes in my body over the past few weeks.

I also kept up my gratitude list ritual –

1) **Spoke with my nurse practitioner today. Sent her a couple of pics of the incision. She told me I was doing the right thing.**
2) **Jonny Nation – love you soooo much!! 🖤🖤**
3) **Lana Fawcett Helman and her dung beetle card. 🍁**
4) **Slept from 12:30 am until 6 am and then from 7:30 am until 9:30 am.**
5) **L and I have a system figured out to get me down to the sofa and upstairs again.**
6) **Spoke with my mom and my dear friend Margo Rosen 🖤🐾🖤**
7) **L and his Pata Pata dance – 🖤**
8) **Spoke with my nurse Helen at the Riverside Women's Clinic. She gave me a game plan to keep an eye on the incision.**
9) **No fever. 😄**
10) **Thoughtful neighbours who drop off yummy meals.**
And you...always you. 🖤

I had never experienced physical recovery before – this feeling of helplessness was overwhelming. I was deeply grateful for all the support from my husband (including visiting me every night in the hospital), my friends and family, and the surgeon and the surgical residency team who were in the OR, to all the amazing healthcare professionals – they truly are angels.

My gratitude lists always included my amazing FB community from all around the world –

1) **I walked for ten minutes in a row today! Yay!**
2) **Slept on the sofa last night – five hours in a row.**

3) Made an appointment to see my nurse practitioner tomorrow afternoon. Looking forward to touching base and making sure all is healing well.
4) Had another solo shower today. ☺
5) L brought me a yummy apple and peanut butter snack this afternoon. 🍎
6) Subway for dinner.
7) Great pre-birthday chat with one of my favourite people.
8) Absolutely gorgeous day – as appreciated from the sofa. ☼
9) So thankful to live in this beautiful city.
10) Grateful for all my moments – and that you are part of them. 🤍

Ah gratitude – the gift that keeps on giving. 🤍

1) Iryna – and yes, dogs make me very happy – and so do you!! 🤍🐾🤍
2) My big pink cozy robe.
3) L being able to join me at my appointment today.
4) It looks like there may be a complication, but so glad we don't have to pay for healthcare.
5) Things are overall looking good – great incision (according to those who have seen it), and no fever or anything else untoward. It's just the possibility of an infection, so I am starting a course of antibiotics today. Hopefully, I will be able to see my surgeon soon to get to the bottom of things.
6) Wore my contacts for the first time in two weeks and two days.
7) Sue Fitzgerald – you and Paddie are just the best!! I love the card! 🤍
8) Sharon O'Brien Moore – you inspire me so very much! Thank you for everything! 🤍

9) I painted my toenails blue before my surgery, and people tell me they like it, which makes me smile.
10) Sue and Mark – thank you for such a delicious dinner!
11) My Daily Bruce Juice from the lovely Karen Pawlowski – thank you!!

Thank you so much for your wonderful everything my dear friends! 🩶

Having friends stop by with a bag full of groceries, with dinner, flowers, gifts, or just for a chat, really meant the world to me.

My days were filled with laps around the main floor – going between the living room and the kitchen. I would position myself on the sofa and sleep when needed. I knew my body needed to heal, and it needed sleep.

For the first four weeks after my surgery, I could not stand up straight. I was in such pain; I could barely get up off the sofa.

During my appointment with my nurse practitioner on the Wednesday, a doctor prescribed antibiotics and suggested I see my surgeon about the pain.

Thankfully, I was able to get an appointment to see my surgeon the next day. L and I waited for about 30 minutes to see her. Not surprisingly, a resident was there with her. They saw how much pain I was in and ordered a CT scan. They also confirmed that antibiotics were the best course of action.

Later that day, the pain seemed to be waning, and by the following day, the pain had disappeared altogether. L and I agreed that even if I no longer had pain, it would still be a good idea to get the CT scan.

With each appointment, test, or meeting I reached out to my FB community – my global army of positive warriors. They were certainly the source of all my strength, courage, and positivity.

When I felt the worst, I would create and share a gratitude list. This practice inspired other people to keep their own gratitude lists. That was an awesome feeling!

Over the next few weeks, I would watch copious amounts of *Friends*, visit with my own friends, and express my gratitude for the wonderful people in my life with FB posts like this:

> **I feel so blessed to be able to appreciate the tiny things that make life special – the good parts about life and the more challenging ones. Because when you are surrounded by love and support and friendship and wonder, you are never alone, and you have the strength to get through that "something" that life sends your way.** 🩶

I made smart decisions, like waiting for L to return from the dog park with Frank before I had a shower – just in case something happened.

On the first of October, I was able to do the dishes – what an accomplishment!

My friends would post dog and Bruce Springsteen-related links on my FB, so I would get my daily Bruce Juice and fill of dogs (although to be fair, when do you ever really get your fill of dogs?).

Insomnia kept me awake most nights, so I would share random Tik Tok videos I had watched.

One day I decided to share my gratitude list with a twist:

Gratitude list with a twist... 🩶

These past three weeks have completely changed my life and perspective. I have done a lot of sleeping, resting, thinking, and reflecting. I am grateful for things I have, and I am also excited to be looking forward to doing a lot of things. Such as...

1) My daily morning walks with Frank
2) DOGPARK!!! 🤍🐾🤍
3) European Extravaganza Part Deux...
4) Visiting my friend in Spain.
5) Going to Montreal for the first time since December of 2019.
6) Making a nice dinner for L.
7) Being able to help with the housework.
8) I want to shimmy, shake, jiggle, wiggle, waggle, dance, boogie, shake my groove thang, and just bust a move!!!
9) Visit with friends while NOT relegated to the sofa.
10) Bottom line, I just want to get better and know everything is working how it should be working and nothing is there that shouldn't be there. ☺

I hope you had a super-duper day filled with all sorts of gratitude – and movement. ☺

I would also take the opportunity to give shout-outs to my friends experiencing health challenges of their own.

They say that when you when you are feeling the most defeated, challenged, or sad is the time you most need to create your gratitude list...so here goes...

1) Carolann Cameron, for being there for me and coming over here when I was panicking today
2) A work colleague called to check in on me this afternoon. ◌
3) L for being there for every emotional outburst and each big, huge, ugly cry of mine.

4) Breanna Pizzuto for making me smile all the time.
5) Margo Rosen for sending me some beautiful poetry.♥
6) Sharon O'Brien Moore for the yummy soup.
7) Found a great book about Friends. Love it!
8) Crave TV for airing Friends. Watching the whole series from the beginning. 😃
9) Spoke with my surgeon today and she is still wants me to get a CT scan. This will hopefully give me some reassurance.
10) No fever. 👍

Feeling weird, strange, and scared. I promised myself that I would not read the pathology report if it arrived before my follow-up meeting with Dr. L.

It showed up on MyChart this evening.

Need to summon up all my will power to not look at it.

I learned my lesson from my ultrasound report in July which caused me such angst and upsettedness.

Hope you had a happy day and happy moments. 🤍💜

Whew…a tough day. Grateful for many things –

1) Steph calling me last night and being there while I cried, and we talked about all the challenges recovering from surgery.
2) Friends. It is comfort food for my soul.
3) Had a fantastic talk with my dad today. Each time we talk I am reminded of what a good person and wonderful dad he is.
4) Finished off the Chocolate Chip Cookie Dough ice cream last night. Don't like the fact that I am losing

so much weight, but word on the street is this happens after surgery.

5) L – always. Today he brought me a delicious bowl of fruit after dinner, before he did the groceries and the recycling.

6) Everyone who called, emailed, texted – I was exhausted today but will get back to you. I thank you and love you.

7) My nurse practitioner called to check up on me. I don't think I have ever had better service from a health care provider.

8) Walked around a few times today and put dishes away in the evening.

9) Love Tik Tok and all the different pages. Lots of Indigenous people are sharing on the platform. I appreciate listening and learning.

10) Grateful my antibiotics seem to be working.

And each and every day I am deeply grateful for this community of dear friends whose words feel like a warm, giant hug. I love you!

OMG my emotions were all over the place. Even for me – it was too much. Was I losing weight from the crying and anxiety? I tried listening to some Springsteen and started crying – and I could not even get up and dance to put myself in a better mood. Argh.

A good day...

1) Love the fan that I bought from Amazon. My friend had one and it was amazing. Bought one for myself – excellent purchase.

2) L made me the best fried egg sandwich today and made me a delicious apple and peanut butter snack.

3) Amal Aramouni is just wonderful. Thank you so much for being you – Peace by Chocolate and for loving Friends – and Frank. 💚🐾💚

4) Great conversation with my awesome manager.

5) Fab text from my dear friend, colleague, and work husband, Sue Turpin

6) My goal was to get through the morning without taking a nap. Mission accomplished. 👍

7) Walked for a full 30 minutes today while watching Friends.

8) Derrick Burgess – 💚

9) Got to chat with my mom today. 😺

10) You guys. I really appreciate you reading my posts and reaching out to give me support and love.

It means everything to me, and I am so grateful for you. 💚 So many things to be grateful for, but here is the one at the top of my mind – caregivers. Partners, family, loved ones, friends – you are absolute rock stars. I think about the many friends of mine who are dealing with health issues. We all rely on you so much – for our meals, for cleaning up, taking the garbage and recycling out, for doing laundry, for taking care of house stuff, dog/animal stuff. Everything. We love, need, and appreciate you so much.

Thank you!💚

Remembering what makes someone rich. It is not money or possessions or the size of their house or what kind of car you drive. Being rich means sharing love (with a partner, your family, your friends, your pets); creating memories with those you love, a warm hug, a sweet kiss, an email that says I love you, it is really listening to your child, it is saying thank you. It is enjoying life. It is laughing. It is being so very grateful for what you have, and not lamenting what you don't. It is feeling secure in yourself. It is living in the moment – not mourning the past or worrying about the future. For me wealth is not found in the bank, but rather inside my heart. Thank you for being there, my dear friends. Xox

Whew...a very tough day. I am a sad little monkey. 🐒 Experiencing some pain, so big thanks to Hydromorphone.

Years ago, I realized that other people's celebrations and happiness bring me joy. So, my gratitude list today is about other people's happiness...

My dear friend who was just offered a new job where he will be awesome.

Another dear friend who is getting back on her feet. My friends and amazing admin colleagues Dave Thomson and James McGuire for their hard work with the Everything Bruce Springsteen group.

My OCISO colleagues and friends – I miss and love you 🖤

Good news health-wise for my friends. Talking with my friends and of course, L – always. For the pizza, the ice cream, holding my hand, wiping my tears, understanding how hard this is, loving all of me – crazy and all.

This surgery experience has given me so much appreciation for everything, and an understanding of something I had no clue about.

On Saturday, October 9, I shared the following;

> I got dressed!!! I had a shower, fixed my hair, and even put on lipstick. Woo hoo!! 😊

Love. Humour. Contentedness. Friendship. Learning. Exercise. Sleep. Healthy eating. Gratitude. Family. Joy. 🖤

Just two days later I was going for walks!

Big day for this gal! I walked twice – once, around the block and then an hour or so later, I walked to my friend's place, but she was not there, so I walked back home. Apparently, it is .6 km, so walking back and forth means I walked over 1 km today! 🖤

Sometimes I would post the memories that FB would suggest, like this one from October 2020.

October is my favourite time of year. In fact, two of my weddings were supposed to be in October, but there was only one and it was in June.

I love that it is a gentle goodbye to summer – one filled with beautiful colours, crunchy leaves, crisp air and sweater and boot wearing temperatures.

I love that some days are super warm and others are glove-worthy. There is a chill in the air, but it's far from the minus 40-degree January weather.

To me, October is like a hug, and and this year, when hugs are forbidden during the pandemic, I appreciate getting my hugs any way I can.

I love that Canadian Thanksgiving is in October, and this year in particular, I am so grateful for:

1) **the health of my family and friends**
2) **having a job I love and getting to work with the most incredible group of people changing the world in a positive way**
3) **the memories of being Lloyd's mom**
4) **being Frank's mom**

5) being L's wife (even and especially during those times that we are both driving each other crazy)

6) ice cream (even though I am eating less of it than before ☹)

7) laughter

8) my friends – from all over, from all different times of my life, in the real world and virtually

9) flannel pjs

10) water – for drinking and just being around...

The list is probably endless, but mostly I am grateful for being in Canada and living in this democracy with leaders who respect and uphold the laws.

On October 13, I was getting scared.

Sigh...things are getting real again tomorrow. I have my meeting to get the pathology results. Feeling scared and nervous but also hopeful.

The CT scan is scheduled for October 28.

Two more steps – thank you all so much for all your support, strength, and love. You have been with me through this journey, showering me with incredible love, beautiful flowers, delicious meals and groceries, fantastic pies and ice cream, donuts, desserts, my happy-dogs hoodie, prunes ☺, puzzle book and other great stuff, thoughtful cards, chocolates, posts, and encouraging comments, emails, calls, and visits.

Thank you for thinking of me and loving me. I appreciate and love you. 🩶

October 13 was a busy day for me:

I did a lot today. Connected with my awesome OCISO family, made my own lunch, did some dishes, went for a walk. Slow, purposeful, and steady, with lots of encouragement to myself, "You can do it!" "Go Tonya...keep going...you've got this" "Look at how far you've come."

I met up with a friend as I slowly passed her house, and she was doing some gardening.

We talked and laughed and commiserated about the challenges of menopause.

She offered to drive me home, but I told her I needed to continue walking. And I did.

Then the wonderful moment of turning the corner and seeing L's car in the driveway. He had a busy day and was gone when I left. I love that special feeling of coming home to him.

Then, later in the day while L and Frank were at the dog park, I fed Frank, prepared a frozen lasagna (thanks, Sue Turpin! 🩶) and made some three-ingredient banana oatmeal breakfast cookies.

I was very busy and felt so proud of myself.

Thanks for letting me share my accomplishments.🩶

It's good news!

The pathology indicated a borderline tumour.

It is a Mucinous borderline tumor, which is an atypical proliferative mucinous tumor and requires no more therapy.

Getting this news has allowed me to breathe and for the first time since June 29, know what is happening in my body – and know that I am okay.

It is possible that it had the potential to become malignant. I truly do believe that Dr. B in Winchester saved my life.

We must advocate for our own health. It is essential.

Ladies, please, please pay attention to your body. You know your body better than anyone else. I knew my body too, which is why I kept going to my doctor with many of the different symptoms of ovarian cancer.

She always told me, "It's hormones," or "It's perimenopause," or "It's what happens at this time of your life."

NO!!! It was something else, and I am so grateful for every one of you for being here along with me on this crazy rollercoaster of emotions, worry, mindfulness, sadness, hopefulness – and of course, my recovery from losing my parts. I am so grateful for absolutely everyone on my healthcare team.

I have one more step – the CT scan on October 28. I feel very positive about this – I think the pain was a result of the shifting, and maybe a muscle issue.

My gratitude list is overflowing today. I am so blessed.

Love you guys so much! ☺

When I get better, I will be focusing on doing what I can to change the hospital food situation and help raise awareness for ovarian cancer. September is Ovarian Cancer awareness month.

https://nationaltoday.com/ovarian-cancer-awareness-month/

290 | SEX, SELF-ESTEEM & SHEER STUPIDITY

This experience has changed my life forever. I thank you all so much for being there with me, thinking of me, and sending your love and support. 🤍

These past five weeks have given me a lot of time
to reflect on so many things that I am grateful for.
And by things, I really mean people.
Like my friend Patrick Doyle. We met while I was at CERC,
and I needed some counselling. I went to see him, and from
the first moment I met him, I felt a connection. He was calm,
compassionate, and accepting. I felt supported and listened to.
He shared information about meditating and
mindfulness, and most importantly, years later,
he provided me with the name of an amazing
marriage counsellor. By helping me find myself,
and learn to love and accept myself,
Patrick helped save our marriage.
After this we became friends,
and he has been such a source of support
and love over the years.
I am eternally grateful for our friendship,
and he will always have such
a big place in my heart.
Love you, my friend! 🤍

Later that day I shared some more thoughts:

Took an hour-long walk today, and just made myself a snack.
While getting Frank's dinner, I was reflecting – three years ago, I
had my guided core needle biopsy because the ultrasound found
something suspicious in my breast. Now, I am recovering from
this surgery due to suspected cancer. Twice in three years...
if anyone wonders why I feel such gratitude...
well, that is one huge reason. 🤍

October 17 was a big day for me:

**I AM WEARING PANTS!! For the first time in over a month.
The waistband is folded over a few times to protect my
incision, but still, my beloved yoga pants. What a feeling!!**

A day later, I posted:

**It is hard to believe five weeks ago at this moment I was lying in
the recovery room at the General Hospital. Today I am wearing
leggings (woo-hoo) and I did the dishes, walked all the way down
to the basement, and am not taking any medication. Yay!!!**

Before the surgery, I was so scared of three things.

   1)   **the surgery and hospital stay**
   2)   **what they would find**
   3)   **sudden menopause**

**Now, I am simply beyond grateful the first two things are in the
rear-view mirror. I am blessed with the results, and also because
my infection is going away.**

And now, I am in sudden menopause.

**During one of my sleepless nights, I discovered an incredible
resource about menopause. This woman is amazingly helpful!
https://menopausetaylor.me**

**Women are warriors, and post-menopausal women (those women
who have transitioned to menopause) are the strongest women.**

**I am learning SO much about this new part of life, and with the
help of fantastic resources like this, I am getting ready to tackle it
head-on (after recovery).**

I hope this resource also helps other women – and I hope it helps people to be able to talk about. It needs to come out of the shadows!!

Later, after seeing my friend Jonny's post, I shared:

Thank you, Jonny – we absolutely DO need to talk about menopause.

Because of the lack of hormones, women lose estrogen and progesterone (for example). Both play vitally important roles in keeping women healthy.

Many women don't know about the increased risk of osteoporosis, heart disease, Alzheimer's, and breast cancer. Essential elements for a healthy lifestyle during menopause include exercise, lifestyle, diet, understanding, humour, compassion, and self-compassion, sleep, communication and support.

Being able to make well-informed decisions is critical.

A few days went by without posting a gratitude list until October 20:

1) My family's health.
2) Chili – thank you my dear friend for dropping it off – it's delicious!
3) L continuing to do the grocery shopping
4) The beautiful cards I received this week from my incredibly supportive army of positive warriors
5) Being able to walk each day
6) Being able to do the dishes
7) The sun shining
8) All the amazing professionals I have been lucky enough to deal with through this unexpected journey
9) So grateful to be living in Canada
10) Both of my wonderful aunts

I spent a lot of time thinking about sharing my story on LinkedIn. On October 25, I shared with my FB community:

Last week I shared my journey on LinkedIn. This is what someone wrote –

"I wish you a full recovery, Tonya, & thank you on behalf of all the mothers, aunts, wives, sisters & nieces who'll continue as part of our lives because of the information you've shared."

And that was exactly WHY I shared it. 🖤

The next night I posted:

Last night as I went to sleep, I listened to Bruce Springsteen's song "Dream Baby Dream" and sang it as I did to get through my surgery day and my stay in the hospital. I used to think this song was special because it inspired me to dream big. Now, I find it inspiring because it helped me get to this point. I will forever be grateful for this man and for making my journey that much happier. To all those who are facing challenging situations – I send you love and remember to dream baby dream. 🖤

Finally, October 28 and my CT scan day arrived:

Done!!!

Less than an hour, fantastic healthcare professionals and the requisite giggling.

I was told I may feel like I peed myself – and then yep, it felt like that, so had to giggle.

Loud enough so L could hear it in the waiting area.

My meditation really helps in these situations. I closed my eyes and breathed.

I was given a wedge for my legs – something that I definitely should have used in recovery.

Then the tech told me about getting up and gave me some helpful tips to prevent a hernia.

As always, thank you guys so much!! 🩶

By this time, I had made the decision to go back to work (from home) on Monday, November 1.

Even as I was posting my gratitude lists, I was also coping with the realities of being thrown into sudden menopause.

The biggest impact on my life has been my sleeping. I used to be able to put my head down on my pillow and fall asleep until the morning.

I would often wake up in the morning and think about how lucky I was to sleep so well.

Those days are gone. I have not been able to sleep properly for weeks. Now, I must turn on my fan at least several times a night as my body temperature skyrockets.

I wake up in the middle of the night every night, and I am not sure which comes first. Is it the need to go to the bathroom that wakes me up or vice versa?

I am taking estrogen and progesterone cream; the latter because it is supposed to help me sleep – as I lay awake, I question its efficacy.

My joints are aching, my urine is leaking, my anxiety is sky high, my moods are swinging, my skin is unbelievably dry, and my pelvic floor is sagging. I am grateful for the support I am receiving and will receive from my pelvic support therapist, my menopause doctor and my new gynecologist. It really does take a village. 😊

I have ordered books about menopause and learned estrogen is the hormone that has an impact on pretty much every organ and function in my body.

Menopause is scary for me, because of all 22 (at least) annoying symptoms, and because it can greatly increase the chances of getting osteoporosis, Alzheimer's, and heart disease. I am already at increased risk of breast cancer because of my dense breasts, but thankfully because all my female reproductive organs (and my appendix) were removed, it's likely I don't have to worry about any gynecological cancers.

Over these past seven weeks, I spent a lot of time reflecting on my life and what I want to do with the rest of it.

I discovered I want to help other women, especially younger women, deal with their crazy menopausal adventures. I want to embrace my menopause and also support other women to embrace their own.

The first thing I want to do is finish this book and get it out into the world. For years I have struggled about when and how to end it.

This medical experience has given me the answer to both questions. I am going to end it now by taking you back to the beginning – by introducing you to the journey through my 20s, the men I met and the man who I would eventually marry – and the challenges that we have faced together. And the challenges we have yet to face together.

Because I know that sex, self-esteem, and likely, sheer stupidity, are going to be part of the rest of the journey.

But here is what I have learned – the hard way:

You need to start saving in your 20s. And I mean save. You need to get an RRSP (or whatever savings vehicle makes the right sense for your financial situation).

Even if you have only about $25.00 a month to save, do it. I am not going to talk about compound interest right here, but let's just say that compound interest is your friend. It means time is the most important part of that equation – so the earlier you start saving regularly, the better.

I was 26 when I first heard about the importance of compound interest. I attended a presentation about how to start investing, and very soon after that, I had a portfolio and I was transferring $50.00 per month into RRSPs.

I saved up enough money to use my RRSPs for a down payment on our house. But, now, at 51 years old, my eye is on retirement, not starting out.

The thing to know is that financial stability is entirely intertwined with the career choices we make.

The problem with these choices is that we make them without any kind of strategic thinking or well-informed decisions.

We see our parents working, and we either want to emulate their job, or we have seen them hating their jobs or being laid off (or sometimes both), and we know what we DON'T want. That can be helpful to some extent; but not entirely. We still need to figure out what we want, how we define success.

My father's definition of success was education. Mine – well, like most people, I never thought about it. Until I was into my 30s, I never even considered that concept.

When my father told me to get an education, I did. I chose to go to university; or did I? Looking back on it, the decision was made *for* me. After high school, I was going to university.

So, I did – and hated it.

I met very few people, just kind of doodled and kept a journal during most classes (especially the boring ones), and basically just kept my head afloat so I could graduate.

Thankfully, at that time, I had access to a loan and a grant, and we also had some money set aside for educational purposes. I was also glad my student loan debt was not crushing. It was affordable, and I could handle it.

Completely different from today's post-secondary situation.

The key thing is to figure out your definition of success and then work backwards from that.

Save money. Be smart with your money. Know what you want and what you value. Make your decisions based on those things.

But you must know what you value and what's really important to you.

And don't sell yourself short. Don't accept less than you are worth. Know what you are worth. I never knew this value about myself. I spent my 20s figuring that out.

In 2009, as I was writing this book, I also became a rather prolific poster on Facebook. I joined in 2007, and mostly just laid low for the first two years.

After The Troubles, I found myself in a much happier and joyful place. I shared posts about Lloyd, our beloved canine soulmate, my job, and our marriage. I was authentically happy for the first time ever, just like the Springsteen song.

I have always liked planning and having things to look forward to. In 2009, I was planning L's 46th birthday and my 40th birthday. I was also excited about a new venture in my life, going back to school.

In 2010, I heard the story about dying with the music still in you and it hit a chord. Later in the year, I received a copy of the alumni magazine from my high school in Singapore. One of my former schoolmates had written (and published) a book. I read the article describing the book; I was not jealous; rather, inspired. I cried as I realized I needed to do something

Also, that year, as someone who loves making lists, I spent a great deal of time creating lists of what kind of party I wanted. I struggled with the whole birthday thing. I did not struggle about turning 40, as I was excited to make this transition to a new decade.

It was about how I was going to mark such a milestone event. I debated between having a party with my dearest friends or something much more intimate. I shared my thoughts with L – a party, who should come to it. Finally, about a month before the date, I told him I would not plan anything; he would have to make the birthday plans.

The only stipulation for my birthday was I wanted to go to synagogue for a blessing for my special birthday.

The day arrived, and, after synagogue, L brought me home to change into some shorts – but he would not tell me anything more. The wonderful surprise was a day of kayaking! L had thought of everything – renting the kayaks, bringing the water and snacks, and ensuring I wore sunscreen and brought a hat. It was a beautiful day. The sun was shining brightly, and the water was calm, save for the boats zooming by.

Dinner was another surprise. We went to a local lakeside restaurant and enjoyed a yummy dinner. We chose to forgo dessert and instead enjoyed some delicious cupcakes at home.

May 29, 2010, was an exceptional day and a lovely way to start my 40s.

Later that year, after a lot of research, discussion, and reflection, I made the commitment to go back to school (again) to study coaching.

As a career development practitioner, I know the value of making a well-informed decision, and having an informational meeting with someone in the field.

I reached out to a handful of different coaches, and not one of them responded. Finally, I found a coach in Kingston who called me back. She told me taking the program would change my life and asked me what my heart was telling me.

My heart was telling me to go for it. My bank account, on the other hand, was busy putting the brakes on the whole thing until I could figure out a way to make it happen.

With some creative financial footwork, I was able to increase my line of credit to cover the program cost. Mission accomplished!

The Kingston coach was right. I started the program and instantly I knew it was the right choice for me. It was such an easy fit. With the program based in Australia, I had to contend with exceptionally early morning classes and those late in the evening. It was a long slog, but I got through it.

Along the way, in December of 2010, I started to feel very run down and draggy. I also experienced sharp, shooting pains in my left breast. Of course, my brain went straight to *OMG what if this is breast cancer?*

Spoiler alert – it was not. It was shingles. Until then, the most pain I had ever felt. By the time I was diagnosed, it was impossible to put on clothes. Even flannel pjs caused searing, shooting pain through my body. I couldn't even hug L, it hurt so much. It was brutal.

Thankfully, with the right antibiotics and over time, the pain diminished and eventually disappeared completely in the new year.

2011 also saw the creation of Puddle Jump Coaching, my own business helping young people figure out what – and who – they wanted to be when they got older.

I had been working at the employment centre since 2007 and I knew what I was good at and wanted to do. I learned I was incredibly empathetic, which no one had ever valued in my life. I was resourceful and able to give people a lot of information to help them make well-informed decisions.

I learned people opened up and talked with me. I did not judge them, and they felt safe. I met parents whose children had schizophrenia and were scared in their own homes. I met women who had attempted to die by suicide and others who were victims of domestic violence. I met young guys who could not talk to anyone but felt at ease with me.

I felt so profoundly grateful that I had found my place in the world. While I knew this organization was not the right place for me anymore, it had shown me my aptitude for working with young people, and I knew I wanted to help them achieve their goals.

One of the best parts about owning a business was getting to choose the name. It did not come easy, but I remembered what I had learned – take an adjective, a noun, and a verb. E.g., Black Dog Marketing or Rain Forest Crisps.

I made my lists of possible names – Green Apple Coaching, Ready Set Go Coaching, Spark, Ignite, Gemstone, Bumble Bee, Hidden

Gem, Sunshine Coaching, B2R (Born to Run) Coaching, Step Up, Colour Burst.

I was googling up a storm, and one day, I walked into the spare room and saw Lloyd on the bed. "Hello, little puddle jump!" I exclaimed.

And it stuck! ☺

Puddle Jump Coaching was born, and I continued to work at the employment centre. Finally, in October of 2014, I had enough of working for an organization that did not share my values; I did not refer to people as "service units."

After much reflection and research (but clearly not enough honest self-awareness), I decided to branch out on my own and work full-time as an entrepreneur. This decision did not end well.

It turns out that although I am a natural coach, I am NOT a natural or even a particularly good businessperson. I read all sorts of books, joined mastermind groups, and attended plenty of networking events. But it was not easy.

It was a tense time for our marriage, with L the main breadwinner for a few months. Although I was on employment insurance, it was not enough to make a difference. It was stressful, but we got through it. I found a job (that I completely hated) which I soon had to quit. A coaching classmate, Divya Parekh, and I had joined forces and co-wrote the book *Unlock Your Future: The 7 Keys to Success*. When my employer denied me time off to attend the book launch event, L and I had another conversation. With his support, I quit the job.

Immediately after leaving, I returned to Puddle Jump Coaching full-time once again. However, this time was different. I focused on marketing our book and secured an interview about it on CBC radio. Afterwards, an educational advisor at a local college contacted me.

Surprisingly, she offered me the opportunity to teach a career development class to students in a networking program. Of course, I jumped at the chance! It was an excellent fit, so I decided to increase my skills. Off I went back to Algonquin College to take the online part-time Teaching and Training Adult Learners program.

It was my third online program: I had become quite comfortable with online learning. Between my comfort in the learning platform and my natural aptitude, I excelled in the program. I graduated with an A+ average in five courses and an A in another.

Happily, I secured a couple more teaching contracts and continued to love it. I really enjoyed meeting the students from around the world and getting to teach them about career development. I loved that part but did not particularly enjoy the marking part. I wondered if other teachers feel the same way. Something tells me they do. ☺

Finally, I found a posting for my dream job to be a part-time Job Search Workshop Facilitator for OCISO, an immigrant-serving organization. It was perfect. Since 2010, I had been volunteering as a career mentor with them, and I had just graduated from my teaching adult learners' program. I was so excited!

The excitement was short-lived. After the interview, I learned I did not get the job; they gave it to an internal candidate. The bane of many job seekers.

Interestingly, they offered me the opportunity to co-facilitate a workshop for volunteer mentors. I had taken the same workshop to be a mentor, so I was comfortable with it – as much as a person with anxiety can be.

A couple of weeks later, I got a phone call from the manager who had interviewed me. She offered me the opportunity to work on a contract with the mentorship program for the Federal Internship for

Newcomers (FIN) program. I panicked. In my 20s, I tried to get into the government, but I failed the test. What did I know about the government?

Thankfully, I ignored that inner voice questioning and doubting myself. Instead, I listened to a friend, a former coaching program colleague, who helped me get past myself and allowed me to embrace the possibilities of something wonderful.

They hired me as a consultant, and I was thrilled to see a copy of the book I had co-written on her shelf.

It turns out the FIN mentorship facilitator job is the best job ever for me. I get to use my interpersonal skills, demonstrate my caring and compassion, and talk to people from all over the world. I get to live my mission – to help others achieve their goals and show them how they can contribute their unique potential to make the world a better place.

I am a natural matchmaker, and to me, this is not a job. It is my passion. The amazingly accomplished mentees are so inspiring to me, and I love being able to find just the right mentor for each of them.

The people I work with are exceptional, and I feel blessed to work there every day.

When I turned 40, I realized I needed to change my life and started to keep a journal. I made lists of the reasons I loved my partner and my dog.

101 Reasons to Love my Partner:

- If he sees a show that I may be interested in watching, he will tape it for me
- He warns me not to watch or read something on the internet if he knows it will upset me

- He practices catch and release of mice in the shed
- He loves my family (and they love him)
- He calms me down with his sense of humour
- He is funny – like stand-up comedian kind of funny
- He is a loving partner
- He mows the lawn and the backyard
- He is resourceful and creative
- He loves animals
- He is good at math
- He dusts
- He loves tennis, photography, and *The Beatles*
- He has a peanut butter and jam sandwich five to seven times a week
- He wants to give his money to animals when he dies because they don't have a voice
- He supports me in my Puddle Jump Coaching
- He loves the movie *Oliver!*
- He takes puppy to the park
- He is romantic – does the dishes and housework without being asked
- He does not love golf, but enjoys playing it with our friend, G
- He tears up when he thinks of how much he loves his family
- He cries when he sees something emotional or special on CBS *Sunday Morning*
- He supports me
- He believes in me

A 101 Reasons to Love my Dog (modelled after 101 reasons to love my partner)

- He is so soft
- The sounds he makes with his long nasal passages
- He is the biggest puppy at 10.5 years old
- He loves to cuddle and snuggle
- He keeps me warm at night

- He loves getting scritched on his bumby (dog parents and their special language)
- The way he dives head first along the side of the bed
- His long legs
- His furriness
- His floppy equilateral triangle ears
- The way he jumps off the deck
- He chases squirrels and birds in our backyard
- How he likes to sit on the deck, surveying his kingdom
- The way he makes gravy when he finishes eating and then licks the bowl four times
- How he loves getting his treats we keep in the old broken-down dishwasher
- Everyone loves him
- How he jumps over the fence at the park
- How much he loves the park
- His long tail
- His whiskers that fall out of his snout
- He is the best furry co-pilot
- He loves being under the deck
- His white ruffle around his neck
- His speckly legs and specklyness
- His squeaky toy hamburger
- His green weight toy

After The Troubles were over, I kept a journal. I wrote about what made me happy – spoiler alert, it was our dog.

From the moment we adopted him, until April 21, 2018, Lloyd always made me happy.

That day, my heart broke and my world would never be the same.

We said goodbye to our beautiful Lloyd, just one month shy of his 13th birthday.

From the moment I laid eyes on him, I was deeply in love with him. My husband took a little longer, but ultimately, felt the exact same way.

Lloyd had that effect on people. He made people smile and brought joy to those who saw him. We loved taking him for a walk and seeing people's reactions to him. We can't even count the times people would smile at him and talk to us about his beauty and uniqueness. Because he was so unique. We spent most of his life never seeing any other dog who looked like him. He was a very special hound.

Since that Saturday in April, my husband and I had been living in grief. In the first few days immediately afterwards, we could barely breathe. Each moment and each minute felt insurmountable.

Losing your best friend, your reason, your purpose, is like losing yourself. Or maybe it's worse than losing yourself. It is a feeling unlike any other feeling I had ever felt. The pain was so intense and searing, so horrible. I found myself sobbing, wailing, and at times, collapsing to the floor. And it did not matter where I was or who was with me. My grief was all-encompassing.

The day after we said goodbye, we had to pick up all his stuff. We could not handle seeing all the reminders all over the house. His bowls on the food bench my husband (and his thoughtful doggy dad) had made for him; the tennis balls, his Kong he would enjoy each night before he came upstairs to bed. How he would lay down and cross his paws and just relax. We put away his food, his treats, and his brush.

We put all his stuff away. But that night, as I was getting ready for bed, I looked around my bedroom. He was gone. All his stuff was gone. It felt like he had never existed, like that last 12.5 years had not happened.

I needed something. I need to hold something of his. Something that smelled of him. That Dorito-feety smell that I loved so much when I kissed his paws. I dug through the bags of stuff. There were the clothes I was wearing when we said goodbye. When we sat on the carpet by the sliding glass door in the living room. Where we held him and rocked him back and forth and sang to him and kissed him and held back our tears so we could be strong for him, and he could feel safe and secure. Like he always did, knowing that his mommy and daddy would always do everything to keep him safe.

Like when we had his lumps removed, his teeth cleaned, got him neutered, gave him ear drops and eye drops, cleaned up after he was sick, made sure he did not feel stupid or shame after his dementia became too much for him and he started to poop in the house. How we brushed his teeth, brushed his tri-colour fur and removed any foreign objects from where they should not have been.

As he was passing, we told him we would honour him by rescuing another doggy friend when the time was right. When the amazing vet team told us he was gone, we both broke down. The tears flowed down our cheeks. We were now members of a very sad club that no one wants to join. We had lost our baby boy.

So many things have happened since that time. We held a celebration of his life, and 12 friends came to support us. Half of them had never even met Lloyd before, but he had made an impact on their lives through our stories, my FB posts, and our mutual love affair.

He was beyond sweet. He was sensitive, and kind and loving and fun and wonderful. He is in my heart. I always feel him there.

But the one thing I want most in the world is to hold him, to feel his body, to stroke his velvety soft fur. I want to hear him breathing and want to see him staring at us during his nightly Vulcan mind meld he would do to get a Milk-Bone. "Do you want..." was all it took to get him to run to the old dishwasher that held his treats and had never been used as a dishwasher.

Our friends were there for us. The love and support they gave us was overwhelming. It was so appreciated. The vet team from Claire Place and the after-life care provided by Eternal Companions was exceptional. Both teams treated him with respect, dignity, and love.

We started going to Pet Bereavement support groups. Twice a month, we met with other pet owners who were going through the same profound sense of loss. It is not a past tense. It is an ongoing thing.

Meeting other people and sharing our stories in a safe space with no judgment, only love and support, meant so much to us. We met some truly wonderful people whose pain matched our own, and somehow, we felt less alone.

I would stop to talk to pretty much every dog I saw; especially the black ones or those who resembled Lloyd in any way. I still talked to him every day. I wake up in the morning, walk past the office where his ashes are kept, and I say good morning. At the end of the evening, on the way to my bedroom, I stop into the office, tell him how much we love him and miss him, and wish him good night. The last thing I see at night is the beautiful portrait a thoughtful friend painted of him and the pictures of him I have taped to the side of my dresser beside my bed.

As I went to sleep during those first few months, I clutched his orange plastic ball and held his puppy blanket. At times, I was able to smell those Dorito-feeties and ran to L, imploring him to smell it. As time passed, that sweet scent diminished.

Years ago, before he passed, I would think about living life without Lloyd. How would it even be possible to go on in life when he is not with us? I was scared and anxious and had to remind myself to breathe and live in the moment.

As we continued our life without him, I realized my fears were baseless. In fact, we are not living our lives without him. He is very much still here. In my heart. And in a strange way it is almost like he is closer than ever because he is living in my heart.

So, Lloyd is at the Rainbow Bridge. He is playing with countless other friends, jumping and rough-housing and having a wonderful time. He is safe, healthy, and waiting for us to cross over the bridge together. He will always be part of our lives.

For the six months after he passed, I was distracted and unable to focus and concentrate. I would make foolish mistakes because I was not paying attention to what I was doing. It was my first time to experience grief in this full-on, in-your-face, no-holds-barred kind of way.

It changed my life.

But with each cry or sob, I knew I was healing. I will never be the same, but I knew that we would get through this grief. After we lost him, we kept repeating "We are not okay now, but we will be okay in the future." It was the only way we could get through that horrible time. Knowing Lloyd was in pain and anxious made the decision inevitable.

Six months later, we adopted our big, black, squishy – Frank. Rocky Road Rescue rescued Frank from Lebanon and brought him to Ottawa. We are not sure of his background, but he teaches us that we can love him just as much as we loved – and still love – Lloyd.

Frank has taught me patience, understanding, love, trust, what it is like to be fearful and traumatized, what it is like to celebrate the tiny victories in life – like pooping on a walk, pouncing on a ball or just cuddling like there is no tomorrow 😊

Chapter 39

The Sunshine Years

"Land of Hope and Dreams"

It can still freak me out that I am married. That I have a dog. That I have a house with a washer and dryer. That I am 51. Scratch that – 52. And that, just like in Springsteen's song "Land of Hope and Dreams," I have the best companion for this next phase of my journey.

Over the past 30 years, I have evolved from an insecure, unconfident young women with no self-esteem to a secure and confident 52-year-old post-menopausal middle-aged woman with a strong level of self-esteem.

I weigh more, my hair is thinning, there are lumps and bumps that weren't there years ago, and I can't eat the same things I enjoyed in my 20s. No more eating cakes and ice cream for breakfast, now I can barely have them for dessert without pangs of guilt.

Although my own frame of reference is based on my relationships with men, I surmise that low self-esteem is just that, regardless of sexual orientation.

November 19, 2021

It has been a long, and at times, exceptionally bumpy ride. I have made some seriously stupid mistakes and errors in judgment. Truth be told, I still do stupid things all the time. I say the wrong things sometimes, I don't respond promptly to texts, I have not finished my taxes yet, and I am not the active person I would love to be.

But then I must ask myself – what is stopping me from being more active? Only myself. And I must really dig far deep inside myself to change that. Because this is it. No more false starts or joining gyms and never going.

This is my last chance. If I do not become more active, I will not grow old gracefully. It's important to retain my balance, my stamina, and my energy for as long as I can. I know only an active lifestyle combined with a healthy diet and sleep will be the only solutions to the menopausal problem.

And right now, post-hysterectomy, I don't have a lot of energy. By the end of the workday, I am exhausted. I know in time, things will get better, but now, I feel overwhelmed and defeated.

Part of cultivating a strong level of self-awareness is being able to handle my limitations. Although I am feeling this way right now, I know this feeling will also pass. And even now, with all the menopausal insanity, I am grateful.

Firstly, I am alive. I know too many people dealing with cancer and terminal diseases, and I am unbelievably grateful I am healthy.

My personal medical crisis has given me a higher level of empathy and understanding. I know what recovery feels like. I know that feeling of being helpless on the sofa and having no stamina or energy at the end of the working day.

Secondly, I have reached a point in my life where I have security in myself and my relationships (both marital and others). I don't have people in my life who bring me down. Instead, I surround myself with people who are living their authentic lives or trying to do that.

Thirdly, once again, now when I look at myself in the mirror, rather than concentrating on the dark circles under my eyes (thanks to the menopausal assault on my quality of sleep), I smile at my reflection.

Instead of being self-conscious about or ashamed of my hysterectomy scar, I am revelling in it. It is my battle scar, and it probably saved my life.

I know myself. I know I still have lots to learn – about myself, my skills, my creativity, and my place in the world.

But I know where I belong. I know where I want to be and who I want to have with me on this journey.

I know what brings me pleasure and what puts me in a state of flow.

I need to help others see the value and strength they can contribute to making the world a better place.

What about you?

What are your next steps? How are you creating your future?

I hope you found value in the time we spent together, and that you have enjoyed our journey.

I am excited for the next part of your meaningful life!

I hope I have helped you see the amazing person you are and how you can contribute your skills, aptitudes, and strengths to make this world better. And not just for some – for everyone.

Diversity, equity, and inclusion are more than trending words to me. They are what life is all about. Our society, community, and world are richer with more diversity. I can't even imagine how boring life would be if everyone was the same.

The focus of my life unexpectedly changed during the creation of this book. I am now ready to support and empower perimenopausal and post-menopausal women on their journey into mid-life. My work with OCISO energizes me and nurtures my soul. It gives me the energy to share information and knowledge and raise awareness for ovarian cancer.

With this book finally complete, I am looking forward to my magnificent mid-life beginning, and even though I can't include his lyrics, I CAN say how I feel about them. I remember listening to a particularly poignant version of his song, "Jungleland," and I had to share it with my fellow Bruce Springsteen fans in our FB group.

I listened to this magnificent version, and I was deeply overwhelmed. Everything about it touched me on a cellular level. I felt love, sadness, grief, mortality, community, innocence, sharing, togetherness, getting older, generational change, camaraderie, beauty, rawness, passion, joy,

honesty, authenticity, caring, resignation, acceptance,
beginning, family – it was absolutely overwhelming.
I had to stop and live in this awesome (in
the true sense of the word) moment.

To life! L'chaim!

Appendix

Signs and Symptoms of Ovarian Cancer | Early Signs of Ovarian Cancer

Listen to your body:

Ovarian cancer may cause several signs and symptoms. Women are more likely to have symptoms if the disease has spread, but even early-stage ovarian cancer can cause them. The most common symptoms include:

- Bloating
- Pelvic or abdominal (belly) pain
- Trouble eating or feeling full quickly
- Urinary symptoms such as urgency (always feeling like you have to go) or frequency (having to go often)

These symptoms are also commonly caused by benign (non-cancerous) diseases and by cancers of other organs. When they are caused by ovarian cancer, they tend to be persistent and a change from normal – for example, they occur more often or are more severe. These symptoms are more likely to be caused by other conditions, and most of them occur just about as often in women who don't have ovarian cancer. But if you have these symptoms more than 12 times a month, see your doctor so the problem can be found and treated if necessary.

Others symptoms of ovarian cancer can include:

- Fatigue (extreme tiredness)
- Upset stomach
- Back pain
- Pain during sex
- Constipation
- Changes in periods, such as heavier bleeding than normal or irregular bleeding
- Abdominal (belly) swelling with weight loss

Helpful Resources

The Four Agreements
https://www.thefouragreements.com/the-four-agreements/

Living Your Colors
https://www.amazon.com/Living-Your-Colors-Practical-Wisdom/
dp/0446679119

The Michael Singer Podcast
https://www.resources.soundstrue.com/michael-singer-podcast/

Charity Village Career Assessment Questionnaire
https://charityvillage.com/career-assessment-questionnaire-2/

Hold Me Tight
https://www.amazon.com/Hold-Me-Tight-Successful-Relationships/
dp/0749955481

Loving What Is
https://www.amazon.com/Loving-What-Revised-Questions-Change-
ebook/dp/B08YNMK69N

Mayim Bialik's Breakdown
https://www.iheart.com/podcast/269-mayim-bialiks-breakdown-
76170345/

The Puddle Jumping Philosophy

CONNECTION
Connect with yourself • FRIENDS • The Earth • Animals
• Nature • Music • Kindness • Family • Knowledge
• Respect • Your talent

CLARITY
Clarity of PURPOSE • Passion • A Calling • Your story • Life

CONFIDENCE
Take POSITIVE ACTION • Create & reach your goals
• Reframe, refocus & regroup when necessary

Know you are ENOUGH • Right now • Just as
you are • Not when you get your dream job,
• Or have a baby • Or two or three • Not when you get
that fantastic pair of shoes
• Or lose that baby weight • Or figure out what you want
to be when you GROW UP

Enough doesn't come with a lucrative job or that new car
smell or the number of friends you
have on FACEBOOK • Enough isn't about your
Instagram or Twitter followers

You can't find enough in your clothes, the size of your
house or the kind of CAR you drive
• If you are looking for enough, look INSIDE

Action • Growth • Outside your comfort zone • The world
• The people who LOVE you & the people who you love

Enough comes from SACRIFICE & determination
• Enough is hard work

Adventure • Change • Transition • Resiliency • Challenge
• Live by your values • BE MINDFUL • Volunteer

Authenticity • Laughter • Knowledge • Compassion

LISTEN to your journey • Discover your place in the world

Enough is expressing GRATITUDE for what you have
• It's the way you treat others
& the way you let others treat you

Enough is not what you wish you were

It's celebrating, respecting and loving who you ARE

Enough is not a skin colour • An AGE • A religion
• A nationality • A weight • A height
• A level of EDUCATION • A gender • A sexual
orientation • A physical or mental state

Enough is STRENGTH of character, not a body type

Enough is eating well, exercising & getting enough sleep
• It's not taking things personally

Enough is INSIDE you

Pay attention to the clues • DIG DEEP • Take baby steps

LOVE your life

Acknowledgments

I know the normal way of doing acknowledgments is to have a dedicated page, but the rest of this book is not normal or traditional, so why should this page be that way? It should not!

It is filled with thanks –

Bill Benoist for being my coach, friend, and the kicker of my butt to get this book going after procrastinating for so many years.

Steph Coolen, for writing the foreword, the many hours of discussion, and for always being the support and the motivation I need.

My editor, Lynn Thompson of Living on Purpose Communications, for the innumerable Zoom calls and emails, and mostly her patience in getting this book finished. There is no way I could have done this without her support, sense of humour, compassion, and understanding. She certainly knows everything there is to know about me by now. I appreciate her very much.

Loreto Cheyne at Lola Design Ottawa, for creating this magical cover to match the spirit and soul of the book.

Breanna Pizzuto for friendship, doggy babysitting, tears, helping me shower post-surgery, and delicious holiday baked goods.

Sophea Khem-Smith for being my work-husband at CERC, for fixing me up in the bathroom (not just once), and for years of friendship with many more to come.

The Jew Crew:

Lana Banana for her incredible writing talent and friendship and looking after me so well after my surgery and Gil for being a fantastic cook and host.

Christine and Garry Kessler for years of friendship, laughs, and tears, and for standing with us on the bimah on June 5, 2005.

Cantor Dave Malecki and Leon Mendlowitz (honourary members of the Jew Crew).

Margo Rosen for years of friendship and countless delicious Shabbat dinners.

Lynn Parent just for being there and for so many years of friendship and love.

Mark Kamins and Sue Potechin for years of friendship, love, and dinners (Shabbat and otherwise).

All my Singapore friends – I love you so much!!

Rabbi Garten and Patrick Doyle for being you and helping me become me.

Sandra Levine Slover for getting us through The Troubles.

Dave and Gillian Thomson (and Cara Anne and Brodie), and James McGuire and the whole Everything Bruce Springsteen family.

Gonen Sagy for his motivation, friendship, love, and yummy baked goods,

Fady Hannah, my friend and kindred spirit for his support and love.

Raseel, for rescuing Frank and so many other beautiful canine souls.

The people on FB I have never met in real life but who I love and who mean so much to me.

My CED team and OCISO family I love very much, and my dear friend Sue Turpin, my partner in crime and faithful work husband.

Family – two best aunts in the world – Auntie Carole and Auntie Dingbat for their love and for inspiring me to be the best person I can be, and my fabulous cousins, Cheryl May and Tracee Lamy and Darrell Lind.

The amazing FIN team (and the incredible team lead), and the inspiring FIN mentors and mentees.

My Temple Israel community, and David Shentow (of Blessed Memory), a beautiful man and a Holocaust survivor who shared his story so that everyone who heard it could be witnesses too.

My PR friends, my honey bunches of oats (Derrick Burgess, if I was a gay bee...). 😊

My work friends and clients over the years.

To everyone who wrote an endorsement, offered encouragement, and told me they could not wait to read the book.

The subject of my life-long one-sided love affair, Bruce Springsteen and the E Street Band.

I am so grateful for everyone, and especially my parents and sisters, our dogs, Lloyd and Frank, and of course, my husband. Thank you for being my beshert, the love of my life, the best card picker-outer ever, an excellent cook, giver of the most amazing hugs, understanding my emotions, and for sharing this journey with me. You are my favourite orange chocolate monkey and I love you.

About the Author

Tonya Pomerantz is a middle-aged, menopausal woman who survived her 20s and, in her 40s, became invisible. Now she is speaking out.

As the founder of Puddle Jump Coaching, Tonya helped many young people figure out what (and who) they wanted to be when they grew up. Now, she focuses on being heard and supporting all women to find their voices. People describe Tonya as warm, caring, and inspiring.

Along with a B.A. in Sociology-Anthropology and a diploma in Public Relations (with Honours), Tonya has certificates in career development, coaching (International Coach Academy), and recently, Teaching and Training Adult Learners.

During her coaching training, Tonya collaborated with a fellow student, Divya Parekh, to self-publish *Unlock Your Future: The 7 Keys to Success*. Tonya feels incredibly grateful for living in many locations worldwide, thanks to her dad working for the Canadian foreign service. She is a huge Bruce Springsteen fan, loves animals (especially dogs), and lives in a state of perpetual gratitude.

Operating from emotion, she strives to make the world a better place. Tonya lives with her husband, dog, and the music of Bruce Springsteen in Ottawa, Canada.

* 9 7 8 1 9 5 8 4 0 5 3 7 6 *